technical analysis 2015/2016

Formula 1

The 2015 **SEASON**

Despite Mercedes' technical and sporting domination, the 2015 season will be remembered as that of Ferrari's return to winning ways. Great merit for this result was due to the internal restructuring conducted at the behest of the new management of Sergio Marchionne and Maurizio Arrivabene and, above all, to the revolutionising of the entire project for the 2015 car under the leadership of James Allison. In practice, the project eliminated all the weaknesses of the F14T, in many ways a revolutionary car but a disappointment in terms of performance.
The most significant progress came in the form of the greater efficiency of the complex Power Unit, which was thoroughly revised. The only tie with the was past was the reten-

tion for the fourth consecutive season of the pull-rod front suspension configuration. Arrivabene's promise of two wins made on the presentation of the SF15T during the season of reconstruction was bettered thanks to a total of three wins (Malaysia, Hungary and Singapore) and a pole position, all results recorded by Sebastian Vettel in a year that was however again dominated by Mercedes.

MERCEDES DOMINION
For its part the Stuttgart firm ignored the received wisdom that a "winning car was not to be touched". The W06 in fact represented a true revolution rather than the logical evolution of 2014's W05.
The outward family look was deceptive as

under the skin everything had been redesigned, starting with an incredible rationalization of the various components of the Power Unit and its cooling system which was completely revised.
All this work translated into far superior results in terms heat dispersal efficiency and drag, but also improved internal fluid dynamics with even "cleaner" sidepods.
The exhausts were completely redesigned to privilege the power delivery of the internal combustion engine, with longer manifolds that were no longer sacrificed as on the W05 where they were enclosed in a kind of lung to the detriment of maximum power delivery.
It was no coincidence that one of the Mercedes' great advantages was that of

being able to use, when necessary, the most extreme power delivery mode, both in Q3 and the most delicate race phases.

RED BULL DISAPPOINTMENT

The 2015 season was the worst in Red Bull's recent history with the team slipping two places in the Constructors' championship and above all failing to secure a single victory for the first time in the last seven years. The principal reason for this "failure" was the Renault Power Unit, without doubt the least efficient in the field, despite the decision to install Mario Illien as a support for the development of the French six-cylinder engine. This factor led a combative Dieter Mateschitz to risk a dramatic divorce from the engine

supplier Renault. However, it should be noted that the RB11, above all at the beginning of the season, fell short of the standards of the recent cars by Adrian Newey.

The imposition of the titanium skid plates on the stepped bottom risked compromising the competitiveness of the "rake" set-up which was only recovered well into the season and above all following the introduction of the short nose version of the RB11 at the Spanish GP.

WILLIAMS CONFIRMS ITS STANDING

Williams repeated its third place in the 2014 Constructors World Championship, pulling off the miracle of finishing ahead of the "richer" Red Bull. Pat Symonds' car was at its best

on the fast circuits, while revealing its limitations on the slower tracks and in particular on wet surfaces. Williams scored points in 16 of the 19 races (failing only at Monaco, the Hungaroring and Austin).

The FW37 was also the first 2015 car to be launched to the press and the first with the short nose applied to a design that did not need to be revolutionised. A lot of work was done to cut weight and improve the centre of gravity, with the car proving to be lightest in the field.

The rear suspension was completely revised withe raising of the arms to the benefit of aerodynamics, while the gearbox was also redesigned but still fabricated in metal to contain costs.

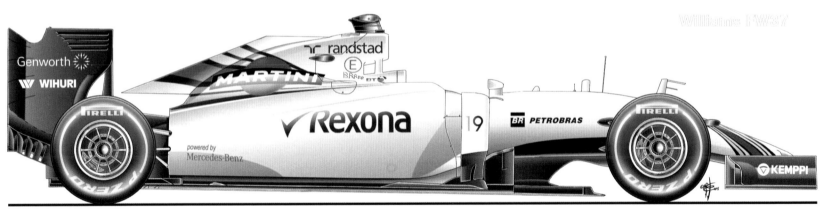

Williams FW37

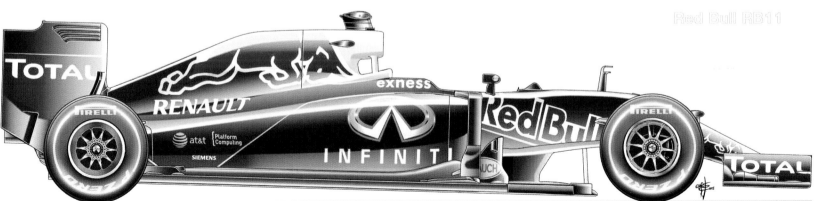

Red Bull RB11

HONDA'S FLOP

Honda's long awaited return to F1 proved to be a major flop with the excuse that the Japanese company had been away from the sport since 2008 not being enough. McLaren's experience with the Mercedes Power Unit in 2014 was of little help and the Honda version proved to be lacking in power and above all unreliable, relegating the team to penultimate place in the constructors' standings. Having focussed on the reduction of dimensions to create a "size zero" rear end was perhaps counterproductive and led in practice to the create of a scaled-down version of the 2014 car. This conditioned the definition and development of the power unit. In contrast with Mercedes which opted for a large turbo to guarantee sufficient recharging power for the hybrid system, the Honda Research Centre chose a very small turbo compressor unit that could be installed in the V of the engine, with the ambition of producing energy sufficient to guarantee the same power output as the Mercedes, but with a turbocharging system spinning at 125,000 rpm rather than the 80,000/100,000 rpm of the larger compressors. This proved to be one of the principal sources of the repeated mechanical failures that afflicted the McLarens.

THE FORCE INDIA SURPRISE

The laurels for technical innovation went to Force India with the "nostrils" introduced to the nose of its cars from the Austrian GP. It is nice that every so often a team without a huge budget distinguishes itself with a new feature, in this case confirming the solidity of the outfit led by Andy Green. The VJM08 was also the car that came closest to the values of the Red Bull "rake" set up.

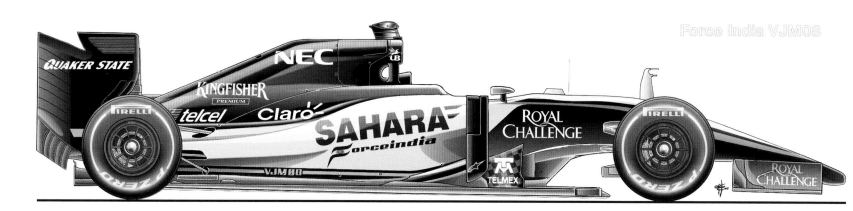

Force India VJM08

Lotus E23

Toro Rorro STR10

2017 REGULATIONS:
WIDE PIRELLI TYRES AND HALO

The 2015 season also various and successive proposals presented by the teams (Red Bull and McLaren to the fore) to define the new regulations, in view of the 2017 car that will finally have the wider tyres requested by Pirelli and an innovative aerodynamic configuration. In testing following the Austrian GP experiments were conducted to simulate the different downforce loadings guaranteed by larger extractor profiles. Another feature for the future was the "Halo" proposal designed by Mercedes to protect the drivers from objects striking the cockpit area.
In both cases the features have been analysed in the 2015 and 2016 seasons.

AN AMERICAN TEAM
IN F1 AND ARCHIVE

The 2015 season saw the confirmation of the return to F1 in 2016 of an American team, Haas, powered by Ferrari and supported in the building of the car by Dallara.
This edition of the book has been enriched with an analysis of the 2016 season through to the United States GP and saw a radical change in the author's working methods with the integration of his archive with that of Motorsport.com, a site of international standing the Italian version of which is directed by Franco Nugnes, who for this edition wrote the chapters dealing with Engines, Tyres and the 2017 Pirelli Tyres. Particular thanks go to Ing. Andrea Pellegrini (Brembo) for the data supplied for the Brakes chapter, to Kazuhito Kawai (tyres table), to Michael Schmidt (statistics) and to Francesco Pizzolante for the collation of data. Once again this edition had drawn on the contribution of 3D animations to "recount" the technical developments.

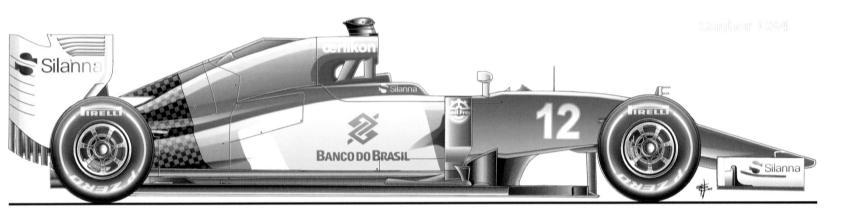

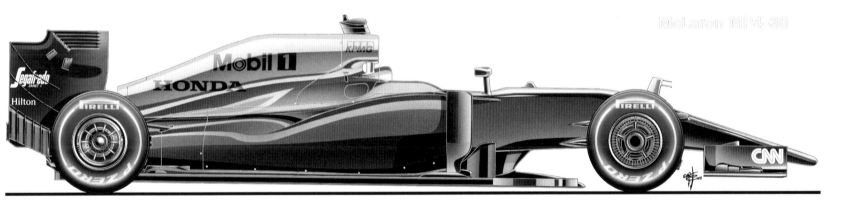

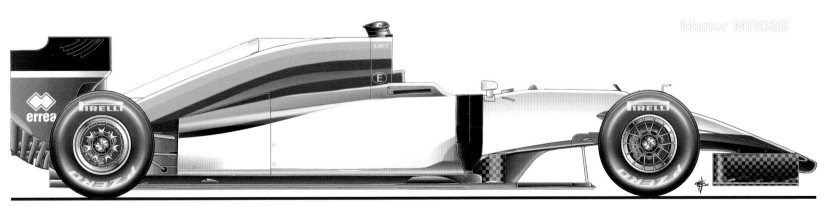

Chassis HYSTORY

With the parc fermé between qualifying and the race that came into force in 2008 and the abolition of the T-car, the number of chassis built fell significantly and in 2015 just three teams built five monocoques: Mercedes, Ferrari and Red Bull.

All the others built four, with the exception of Manor which actually built just three.

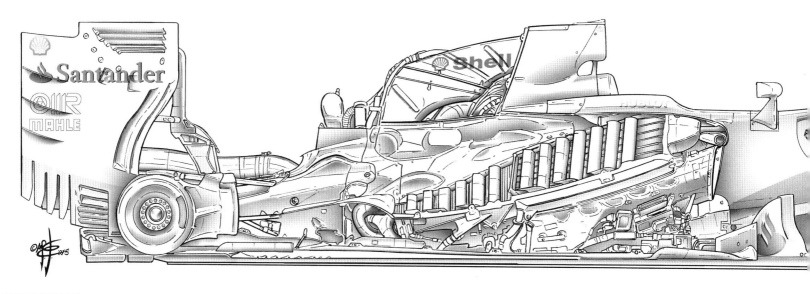

MERCEDES • *W06* • N° 44-6

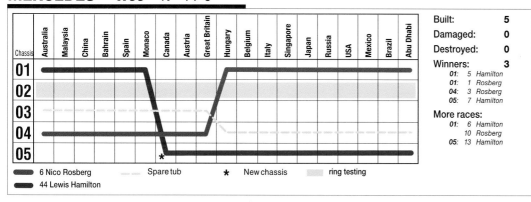

Chassis	Australia	Malaysia	China	Bahrain	Spain	Monaco	Canada	Austria	Great Britain	Hungary	Belgium	Italy	Singapore	Japan	Russia	USA	Mexico	Brazil	Abu Dhabi
01																			
02																			
03																			
04																			
05																			

— 6 Nico Rosberg – – Spare tub ★ New chassis ▨ ring testing
— 44 Lewis Hamilton

Built: 5
Damaged: 0
Destroyed: 0
Winners: 3
- 01: 5 Hamilton
- 01: 1 Rosberg
- 04: 3 Rosberg
- 05: 7 Hamilton

More races:
- 01: 6 Hamilton
- 10 Rosberg
- 05: 13 Hamilton

FERRARI • *SF15 T* • N° 5-7

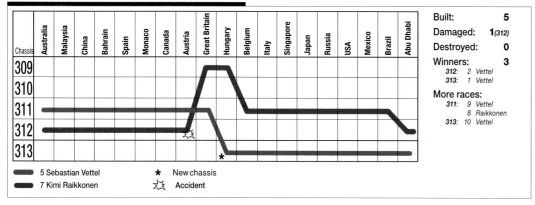

Chassis	Australia	Malaysia	China	Bahrain	Spain	Monaco	Canada	Austria	Great Britain	Hungary	Belgium	Italy	Singapore	Japan	Russia	USA	Mexico	Brazil	Abu Dhabi
309																			
310																			
311																			
312																			
313																			

— 5 Sebastian Vettel ★ New chassis
— 7 Kimi Raikkonen ✸ Accident

Built: 5
Damaged: 1 (312)
Destroyed: 0
Winners: 3
- 312: 2 Vettel
- 313: 1 Vettel

More races:
- 311: 9 Vettel
- 8 Raikkonen
- 313: 10 Vettel

SPARE CHASSIS ASSEMBLED FOR THE RACE
Only one team, Red Bull, had to assemble the spare chassis (02) for a race, when Kvyat crashed his car (03) in qualifying for the Japanese GP. Red Bull again had to repair two chassis, 03 damaged in the race by Kvyat at Austin and 04 during a crash test with the short nose.

VICTORIOUS CHASSIS
Only three drivers won races during the 2015 season: Hamilton with 11 wins (seven with chassis 05 and four with 01), followed by his teammate Rosberg with five victories (four with 04 and one with 03). Vettel took the other three races (two with 311 and one with 313).

chassis	first run	track	km test	km race
309	01/02/2015	Jerez	3627,2	1466
310	12/05/2015	Barcellona	1532,4	-
311	24/02/2015	Barcellona	2385,5	11527,4
312	13/03/2015	Merbourne	-	6033,6
313	24/07/2015	Budapest	621,7	7180,4

	laps completed	finishes	technical failures	accidents
Mercedes	2048 (98,4%)	35	**3** engine - turbo - throttle	0
Red Bull	1936 (93,0%)	31	**6** (2) engine - (2) electronics - gearbox - suspension	1
Sauber	1905 (91,5%)	32	**4** engine - gearbox - brakes - steering	2
Williams	1900 (91,3%)	32	**3** (2) dumper - gearbox	1
Ferrari	1883 (90,5%)	31	**4** MGU-K - puncture - brakes - loose wheel	3
Force India	1877 (90,2%)	31	**2** engine - turbo - brakes	4
Toro Rosso	1778 (85,4%)	26	**10** (3) engine - battery - electrics - turbo / loose wheel - injection - brakes - electronics	2
Manor	1700 (81,7%)	31	**4** oil leak - driveshaft - suspension - rear wing	0
McLaren	1482 (71,2%)	23	**13** (3) engine - (3) gearbox - (2) MGU-H - (2) exhaust / ERS - turbo - brakes	2
Lotus	1466 (70,4%)	22	**10** (3) brakes - (3) suspension - (2) gearbox / (2) handling - engine - clutch	4

The most reliable team was Mercedes, followed by Red Bull, Sauber, Williams, Ferrari and Force India, Toro Rosso, Manor, McLaren and Lotus. The unenviable record for technical problems went to McLaren and above all the Honda Power Unit, with no less than 13 failures over the course of the season.

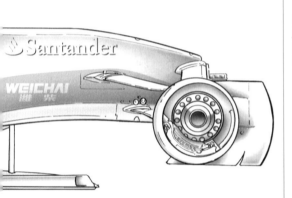

MOST RACES

The only driver in a leading team to complete the entire season with the same chassis was Felipe Massa with the Williams chassis No. 02. Perez with the Force India also used the same chassis, 02. Sainz completed 16 races with the Toro Rosso chassis No. 04.

WHEELBASES

The longest car of the 2015 season was the Renault, followed by Sauber, Toro Rosso, Ferrari, Red Bull, McLaren, Williams and Force India. Note the Mercedes, along with the Force India, was the car with the shortest wheelbase.

Lotus	3.602 mm
Sauber	3.542 mm
Toro Rosso	3.533 mm
Ferrari	3.508 mm
Ferrari	3.508 mm
Red Bull	3.459 mm
McLaren	3.491 mm
Williams	3.483 mm
Mercedes	3.411 mm
Force India	3.411 mm

WILLIAMS • FW37 • N° 19-77

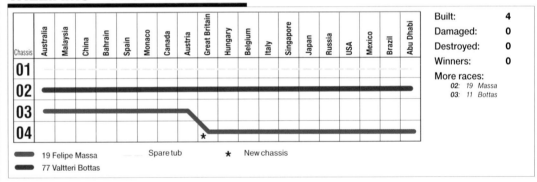

Built: 4
Damaged: 0
Destroyed: 0
Winners: 0

More races:
02: 19 Massa
03: 11 Bottas

19 Felipe Massa — 77 Valtteri Bottas — Spare tub — ★ New chassis

RED BULL • RB11 • N° 3-26

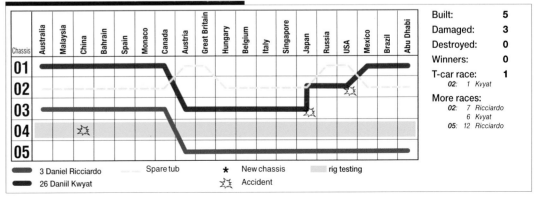

Built: 5
Damaged: 3
Destroyed: 0
Winners: 0
T-car race: 1
02: 1 Kvyat

More races:
02: 7 Ricciardo
6 Kvyat
05: 12 Ricciardo

3 Daniel Ricciardo — 26 Daniil Kvyat — Spare tub — ★ New chassis — rig testing — ✷ Accident

Car TABLE

		44-6 MERCEDES	5-7 FERRARI	19-77 WILLIAMS	3-26 RED BULL
CAR		**W06**	**SF15-T**	**FW37**	**RB11**
	Designers	Paddy Lowe Andy Cowell Aldo Costa	James Allison Mattia Binotto Simone Resta	Pat Symonds Jakob Andreasen	Adrian Newey Rob Marshall Dan Fallows
	Race engineers	Andrew Showling Tony Ross (6) Peter Bonington (44)	Riccardo Adami (5) Dave Greenwood (7)	Dave Robson (19) Jonathan Eddolls (77)	Paul Monagham Simon Rennie (3) Giampiero Lambiase (26)
	Chief mechanic	Mattew Deane	Francesco Ugozzoni	Mark Pattinson	Chris Gent Lee Stevenson
CHASSIS	Front track	1470 mm	1470 mm	1480 mm	1440 mm*
	Rear track	1405 mm*	1405 mm*	1420 mm	1410 mm*
	Front suspension	Push-rod 2+1 dampers and torsion bars	Pull-rod 2+1 dampers and torsion bars	Push-rod 2+1 dampers and torsion bars	Push-rod 2+1 dampers and torsion bars
	Rear suspension	Pull-rod 2+1 dampers and torsion bars	Pull-rod 2+1 dampers and torsion bars	Pull-rod 2+1 dampers and torsion bars	Pull-rod 2+1 dampers and torsion bars
	Dampers	Sachs	Sachs	Williams	Multimatic
	Brakes calipers	Brembo	Brembo	A+P	Brembo
	Brakes discs	Brembo Carbon Industrie	Brembo CCR Carbon Industrie	Carbon Industrie	Brembo
	Wheels	BBS	BBS	O.Z.	O.Z.
	Radiators	Secan	Secan	IMI Marston	Marston
	Oil tank	middle position inside fuel tank	middle position inside fuel tank	middle position inside fuel tank	middle position inside fuel tank
GEARBOX		Longitudinal carbon	Longitudinal carbon	Longitudinal titanium	Longitudinal carbon
	Gear selection	Semiautomatic 8 gears	Semiautomatic 8 gears	Semiautomatic 8 gears	Semiautomatic 8 gears
	Clutch	Sachs	Sachs	A+P	A+P
	Pedals	2	2	2	2
ENGINE		Mercedes PU106B	Ferrari 059/3	Mercedes PU106B	Renault Energy F12015
	Total capacity	1600 cmc	1600 cmc	1600 cmc	1600 cmc
	N° cylinders and V	6 - V90°	6 - V90°	6 - V90°	6 - V90°
	Electronics	Mercedes	Magneti Marelli	Mercedes	Magneti Marelli
	Fuel	Petronas	Shell	Total	Total
	Oil	Petronas	Shell	Total	Total
	Dashboard	Mercedes	Magneti Marelli	Williams	Red Bull

[1] non official value   *extimated value

27-11 FORCE INDIA	8-13 LOTUS	33-55 TORO ROSSO	9-12 SAUBER	14-22 McLAREN	28-98 MANOR
WJM08	E23	STR10	C34	MP4-30	MR03B
Adrew Green Akio Haga	Nick Chester Martin Tolliday	James Key	Mark Smith Eric Gandelin	Timo Goss Matt Morris Peter Prodomou	John Mc Quillam Gianluca Pisanello
Bradley Joice (27) Tim Wright (11)	Julien Simon-Chutemps (8) Mark Slade (13)	Phil Charles Xevi Pijolar (33) Marco Matassa (55)	Erik Schuivens (9) Graig Gardiner (21)	Claron Pelbeam Mark Temple (14) Tom Stallard (22)	Edward Reegan (98) Josh Peckett (28)
Andy McLaren Will Wickery	Greg Baker	Domiziano Facchinetti	Reto Camenzind	Paul James	Kieron Marchant
1480 mm	1450 mm	1440 mm	1460 mm	1470 mm*	1470 mm
1410 mm	1420 mm	1410 mm	1400 mm	1405 mm*	1405 mm*
Push-rod 2+1 dampers and torsion bars	Push-rod 2+1 dampers and torsion bars	Push-rod 2+1 dampers and torsion bars	Push-rod 2+1 dampers and torsion bars	Push-rod 2+1 dampers and torsion bars	Push-rod 2+1 dampers and torsion bars
Pull-rod 2+1 dampers and torsion bars	Pull-rod 2+1 dampers and torsion bars	Pull-rod 2+1 dampers and torsion bars	Pull-rod 2+1 dampers and torsion bars	Pull-rod 2+1 dampers and torsion bars	Pull-rod 2+1 dampers and torsion bars
Sachs	Penske	Koni	Sachs	McLaren	Sachs
A+P	A+P	Brembo	Brembo	Akebono	A+P
Hitco	Hitco	Brembo	Brembo	Carbon Industrie Brembo	Hitco
BBS	AVUS	O.Z.	O.Z.	Enkey	BBS
Secan	Marston	Marston	Calsonic	Calsonic - IMI	Secan
middle position inside fuel tank	middle position inside fuel tank	middle position inside fuel tank	in gearbox	middle position inside fuel tank	in gearbox
Longitudinal carbon	Longitudinal titanium	Longitudinal carbon	Longitudinal carbon	Longitudinal carbon	Longitudinal carbon
Semiautomatic 8 gears	Semiautomatic 8 gears	Semiautomatic 8 gears	Semiautomatic 8 gears	Semiautomatic 8 gears	Semiautomatic 8 gears
A+P	A+P	A+P	A+P	A+P	A+P
2	2	2	2	2	2
Mercedes PU106A	Mercedes PU106A	Renault Energy F1 2015	Ferrari 059/3	Honda 615H	Ferrari 059/3
1600 cmc	1600 cmc	1600 cmc	1600 cmc	1600 cmc	1600 cmc
6 - V90°	6 - V90°	6 - V90°	6 - V90°	6 - V90°	6 - V90°
Mercedes	Magneti Marelli	Magneti Marelli	Magneti Marelli	McLaren el.sys.	Magneti Marelli
Petronas	Total	Total[1]	Shell[1]	Mobil	Shell
Petronas	Total	Total[1]	Shell[1]	Mobil	Shell
P.I.	Renault F1	Toro Rosso	Magneti Marelli	McLaren	Magneti Marelli

GIORGIO PIOLA

2015 REGULATIONS

Following the revolution in the F1 regulations for 2014, the FIA decided to introduce minor changes for the 2015 season. The most conspicuous difference was the elimination of the long proboscis at the front of the cars. Two motives lay behind this decision: the first was associated with safety, the second aesthetics. Those "stingers" were truly ugly and could also be dangerous: in the case of a rear-end collision the "nose" could in fact slip under the rear diffuser of the leading car and lever its rear end, potentially putting the helmet of the driver in the following car at risk. As it had done in 2013, soon after the introduction of stepped noses, and in 2014 with the advent of low front ends, the Federation made amends by banning the ugly designs adopted by many teams.

In theory, the walrus-type nose of the Lotus and the finger or proboscis designs of Williams, McLaren, Force India, Sauber, Toro Rosso, Marussia and Caterham were outlawed. In order to obtain this result, the dimensions of the nose were modified: the length was extended from the 750 mm of 2014 to 850 mm, defining the areas involved in three different sections: the first of 60,000 mm2, a second of 20,000 mm2 located 750 mm from the front axle and a third furthest forwards of 9,000 mm2, all three with widths defined by the deformable structure: 330 mm in the central section and 140 mm at the extremity.

To improve protection in the case of side impacts against the cockpit a panel in Zylon was added and the minimum weight of the car was thus increased by 10 kg to 702 kg. During the winter break it was hard to see very long noses and instead, from the first presentation such as those of Williams and Force India, the long nose was replaced by a kind of short "stub" that effectively allowed the section to be reduced drastically and consequently to improve the flow of air in the lower section. This feature guarantees a kind of Venturi effect in the central neutral zone – the front wing has to have in the central 50 cm an absolutely neutral plane - permitting minimal downforce to be achieved in this zone too. This rather delicate zone determines the condition of the flows towards the central part of the car through to the diffuser; hence the need to develop configurations that per allow greater aerodynamic efficiency to be guaranteed.

The short "stub" feature was then adopted by Sauber, Toro Rosso, Manor and Red Bull, while Mercedes and Lotus opted for a short nose without this expedient. Ferrari and McLaren instead went for a long, low nose although, from the Austrian Grand Prix the British team adopted a particularly short nose, leaving Ferrari as the sole team to race with the long nose throughout the season. There was still the possibility of exploiting the passage of air between the upper and lower parts of the nose via the so-called S-DUCT, reintroduced by Sauber in 2012 and also adopted by Red Bull, McLaren and Force India.

The regulations still permitted an aperture in the lower part, leaving unchanged the restriction of the 150 mm from the axis of the front wheels, as prescribed by Para. 37.8 of the regulations. Lastly, in order to counter the "trick" devised in 2014 by Adrian Newey, who placed the TV camera behind the "vanity panel" so as to prevent unwelcome filming towards the central part of the car, a restriction was introduced regarding the longitudinal axis: a minimum distance between the two cameras of 150 mm.

However, the most important novelties concerned the power unit. Above all, we saw a reduction in the number of units available to each driver from five to four per season. With a calendar of 19 races, each power unit would have to cover at least five Grands Prix to avoid penalties (10 grid positions when the fifth power unit is fitted and five positions in the case of replacement of each component of the unit, CPU, battery, MG-H, MGU-K or turbocharger).

The engineers were permitted to update the units by using 32 development tokens: Mercedes spent 25 for the homologation of the PU106B at the end of February, while Ferrari used 22 and Renault just 20.

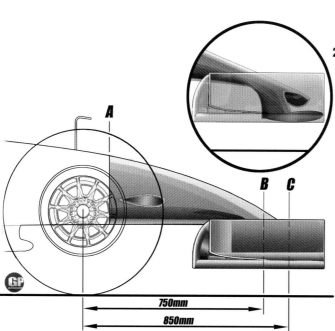

A
B C

750mm
850mm

2015 NOSE REGULATIONS
ART. 15.4.3

The "finger" of the 2014 single-seater is transformed into an entire "talon" as seen in the illustration; in the circle, a more linear interpretation of the regulations. The possibility of passing from the 330 mm of the B section to the 135 mm of the C section was exploited. In fact, Para. 15.4.3, as well as the extreme section of 9,000 mm2 with a minimum width of 135 mm located 850 mm from the front axle, introduced a further section of 20,000 mm2 located 750 mm from the same axle with a maximum width of 330 mm.

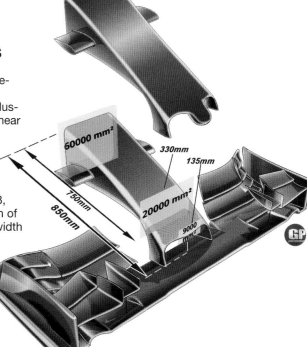

60000 mm²
330mm
135mm
750mm
850mm
20000 mm²
9000 mm²

BANNED FEATURES. ART. 15.4.3

The ugly features such as the Lotus "walrus" nose (which also proved to be rather inefficient) and the finger/proboscis-style noses adopted during the 2014 season by McLaren, Williams, Force India, Sauber, Toro Rosso, Marussia and Caterham were effectively outlawed.

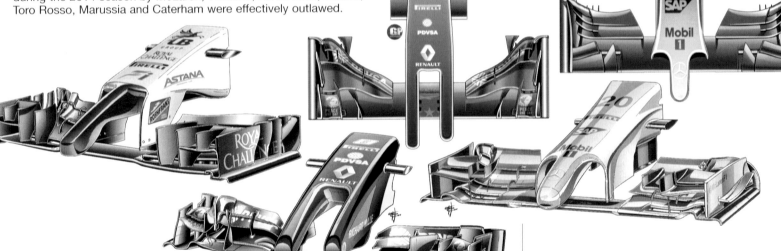

The remainder were available to be spent over the course of the season: Mercedes 7, Ferrari 10 and Renault 12. Honda, making its debut with the six-cylinder RA615 H supplied exclusively to McLaren, obtained 9 tokens that represented the average of those remaining to the other constructors.

Only Mercedes proved capable of respecting the rotation schedule (the first of the team's units was used for six race weekends and over 4,100 km, a true record for F1!), while Renault and Honda suffered serious reliability issues and Ferrari preferred to anticipate the first replacement and make recourse to a fifth unit.

Among the restrictions that came into force in 2015, mention has to be made of that concerning the gearbox which had to last six grans prix rather than five and the entire season had to be completed with a single gear train chosen at the start of the season, while in 2014 it had been possible to change at least once during the course of the season.

In the early races of the 2015 season the FIA noted that there were teams that had managed to find a way round the fuel flowmeter regulations: from the Chinese Grand Prix, the FIA decided to measure fuel flow upstream and downstream of the control system.

This provision was clearly insufficient given that from Barcelona a further clarification was added to the regulations that imposed a constant fuel flow of between 90 and 100 kg/s when the power unit was running.

The federation's technicians also introduced more severe aerodynamic regulations: from the Canadian Grand Prix the front wing flaps were not permitted to flex more than 3 mm when subjected to a static load of 60 kg.

MERCEDES AND FERRARI

The 2014 Mercedes nose instead proved to be too short at just 50 mm (has seen in the view from above) and the Stuttgart firm in fact presented a version similar in shape to that of the 2014 season but longer. The Ferrari nose could have been retained without significant modifications to its original shape, but the Maranello-based firm preferred a very long and low nose.

LOTUS

From the US Grand Prix in Austin, Lotus had already been experimenting with a preview of the 2015 nose, which featured simple, square-cut forms in place of the two-pronged walrus nose.

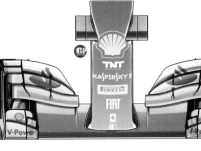

GIORGIO PIOLA

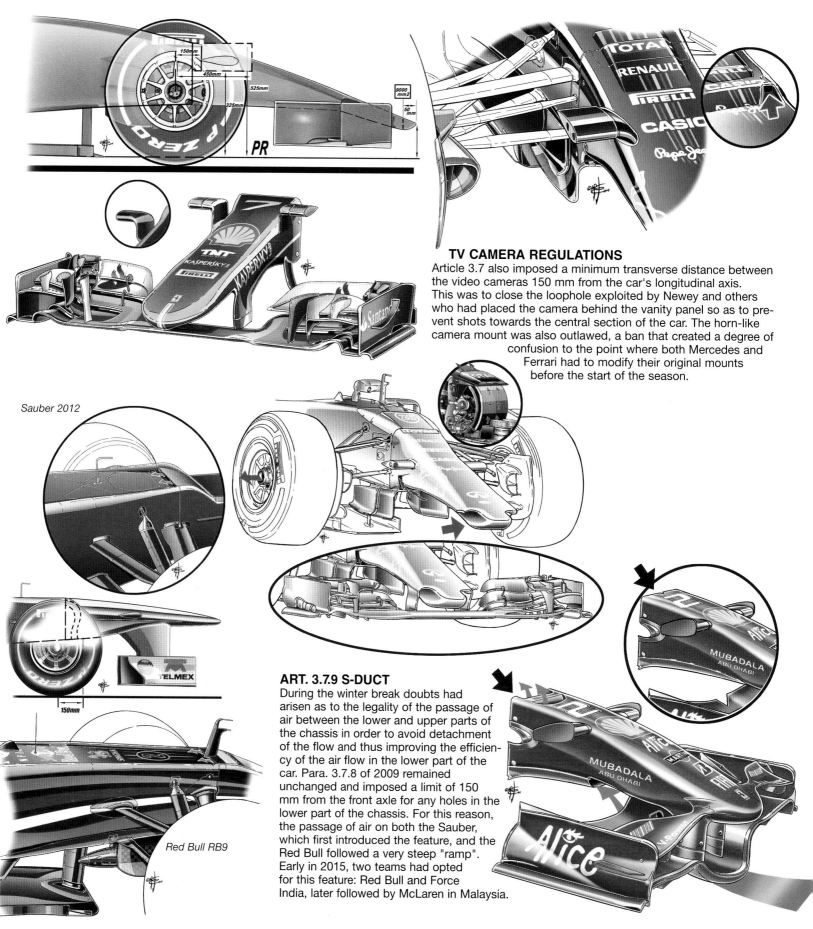

TV CAMERA REGULATIONS

Article 3.7 also imposed a minimum transverse distance between the video cameras 150 mm from the car's longitudinal axis. This was to close the loophole exploited by Newey and others who had placed the camera behind the vanity panel so as to prevent shots towards the central section of the car. The horn-like camera mount was also outlawed, a ban that created a degree of confusion to the point where both Mercedes and Ferrari had to modify their original mounts before the start of the season.

Sauber 2012

Red Bull RB9

ART. 3.7.9 S-DUCT

During the winter break doubts had arisen as to the legality of the passage of air between the lower and upper parts of the chassis in order to avoid detachment of the flow and thus improving the efficiency of the air flow in the lower part of the car. Para. 3.7.8 of 2009 remained unchanged and imposed a limit of 150 mm from the front axle for any holes in the lower part of the chassis. For this reason, the passage of air on both the Sauber, which first introduced the feature, and the Red Bull followed a very steep "ramp". Early in 2015, two teams had opted for this feature: Red Bull and Force India, later followed by McLaren in Malaysia.

The possible evolutions of the Power Units through to 2020

Power unit element	engineering details	token	2015	2016	2017	2018	2019 + 2020
crankcase	space between cylinders, engine cover, crankcase ribs	2	■	■	■	■	■
crankcase	all bore dimensions relating to the water cooling passages	3		■	■	■	■
cylinder head	everything associated with the above mentioned modifications	2					■
combustion	all elements defining combustion. Includes manifolds, pins, combustion chambers, valve geometry, valve opening and closing times, injector jets, coils, plugs. excludes: valve positions	3					■
valve axis position	includes the angle of inclination, excludes movement along the axis	2					■
valve guides	from the valve to the cam: position and geometry, exhaust inlet. includes the valve return to the cylinder head	2					■
valve guide-camshaft	From the cam to the valve gear. Geometry with the exception of the cam profile. Includes the damping system linked to the camshaft. Inlet exhaust.	1		■	■	■	■
valve guide	includes position and geometry of the valvegear and the vibration dampers	2		■	■	■	■
covers	rocker covers	1		■	■	■	■
crankshaft	main bearing diameter	2	■	■			■
crankshaft	main bearings	2		■			■
gudgeon pins	includes bearings associated with the pins	2					■
pistons	includes bearings and rollers	2					■
pneumatic valves	includes air pressure regulating device	1	■	■			■
auxiliary controls	from the controls to the power source. Includes the position of the controls as permitted	3	■	■			■
oil pressure pump	includes filter. Excludes internal parts not in contact with the pump body	1					■
oil scavenging pump	any oil scavenging system	1					■
oil scavenging	oil degasser, oil reservoir, scavenging oil reservoir	1					■
water pump	includes Power Unit water passages	1					■
injection system	fuel system components (high pressure fuel tubes, injection rails, fuel injectors, accumulators). Excludes injection jets	2					■
air intake	air box. Excludes turbocharging pressure, intake manifolds throttle valves and associated parts	1					■
air intake	intake manifolds and throttle valves and associated parts	1					■
air intake	intake manifolds and throttle valves and associated parts	1					■
turbocharging pressure	between compressor entrance and exit	2					■
turbocharging pressure	turbocharging pressure	2					■
turbocharging pressure	between exhaust flange and turbine entrance	1					
turbocharging pressure	actuators connected to the wastegate	1					■
electrical system	fixing of electrical components to the engine (cabling, sensors, alternator). Excludes actuators, plugs and coils	1					
injection	coils, control unit	1					
lubrication	all parts where oil circulates at high pressure (gear pump, passages, accessories)	1					
MGU-H	complete. Internal parts including bearings and external casing	2					■
MGU-H	position, connection to the turbine	2					■
MGU-H	power electronic controls	1					■
MGU-K	complete. Internal parts including bearings and external casing	2					■
MGU-K	position, connection to turbine	2					■
MGU-K	power electronic controls	1					■
ERS	cabling	1					
ES	battery cells	2					■
ES	BMS	2					■
ERS cooling/lubrication	cooling and lubrication systems	1					■
heat treatment of friction surfaces		1					■
rotary or movement seals		1					■

■ procedure that cannot be undertaken

POWER UNIT AND TABLE
The Federation allowed the teams to update their power units by freely using the 32 development tokens, the value of which is highlighted in the drawing and the table.

FRONT WING FLEXING TEST

In order to avoid arguments, the Federation made the front wing flexing test even more severe, passing from a tolerance of 20 mm to just 3 mm, albeit with a slightly lighter load (60 rather than 100 kg).

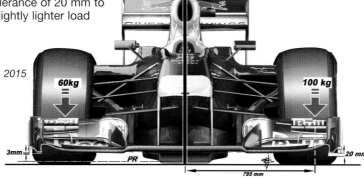

2014

2015

60kg

100 kg

3mm

PR

20 mm

795 mm

HALO: COCKPIT PROTECTION

Objective safety. From the start of the 2015 season there was much discussion around the possibility of improving the safety of the cars, above all to reduce damage in what remains the great danger for F1 cars, that of uncontrollable lift off in the case of contact between tyres and rolling in the case of collisions at roughly 90° both of which imply great risks for the driver's head.

Fresh in the minds of everyone were the dramatic images of the collision at the start of the Belgian Grand Prix triggered by Grosjean's Lotus to the detriment of above all Alonso in the Ferrari, and Liuzzi's Force India's flight at the start of the Abu Dhabi Grand Prix in 2010 which grazed the head of Michael Schumacher in the Mercedes.

In both cases, the episodes were archived as miracles, but such a word is ill-suited to a sport like F1 and for this reason the FIA sought to take remedial action by investigating various features that initially even included a modern take on of the fighter-style canopy adopted on the Protos F2 by Mike Costin for purely aerodynamic motives back in 1967. Even though this solution was almost immediately discarded, the FIA did not abandoned the idea of providing increased safety for the driver's head and officially commissioned Mercedes to develop a structure that offers greater protection for the cockpit area.

On the eve of the new season, Mercedes presented the project to the working group of technicians and it was carefully evaluated before being passed to the Federation for the approval phase. A process similar to that followed two years ago with the side-impact intrusion protection. On that occasion the Federation commissioned Red Bull to work on deformable structures either side of the chassis offering greater protection in the case of lateral impacts. This novelty was introduced to put and end to the fashion for the protections to be fitted to the steeped bottom rather than the monocoque. Result: in the 2014 season, all teams had to adopt the feature according to the regulations.

Mercedes came up with an unusual design with a structure that did not impede lateral vision above all allowed free use of the mirrors with no blind spots with respect to the track and other cars.

A horseshoe-like form was created, based on a slim but robust vertical support designed not to create visibility problems for the drivers. A structure that, among other things, guarantees greater protection in the case of overturning and that, naturally, had to pass crash tests as strict as those to which the current two anti-roll bars fitted to all cars are subjected.

In a way, the central vertical support at the front of the cockpit recalls Rolf Stommelen's March 721 Eifelland designed by the imaginative but rather inconclusive Luigi Colani who provided for an unusual rear-view mirror mounted centrally on a vertical support.

A feature that, as always is the case in these situations, aroused contrasting opinions among the drivers. It should also be remembered that when protection was introduced either side of the driver's head in the 2000 season, some protested, with David Coulthard actually having a slice of these structures cut away for the first day of practice at the Australian Grand Prix, Even though he subsequently became accustomed to having less lateral movement while driving.

The same difficulties were encountered with the introduction of the Hans collar in experimental form back in 2002 before becoming obligatory in 2003 and now universally accepted by drivers in all categories.

The incredible accident between Fernando Alonso and Kimi Räikkönen during the early laps of the Austrian GP drew attention to the Mercedes project, with the Spanish driver invoking new safety measures to provide greater protection to the cockpit area.

The 2015 season concluded with the FIA increasingly determined to move on to the production phase for this protection structure with diverse new features introduced from the US Grand Prix in Austin such as, for example, a kind of tubular protection that was less sophisticated than the Mercedes project.

MARCH 721 EIFELLAND

Luigi Colani, the well-known designer from the 1970s, created this "imaginative" aerodynamic package for the March 721 of the new Eifelland team. Curiously, only the vertical support for the central mirror and the engine air intake remained in the two successive versions of this bizarre project.

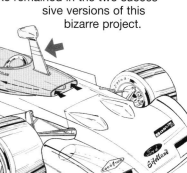

JORDAN 2001

At the 2001 Monaco Grand Prix, Jordan turned up for scrutineering with this small winglet mounted on a vertical pylon to recover downforce. The feature was judged to be dangerous and therefore not used in practice.

MERCEDES RING

These sketches illustrated the research programme conducted by Mercedes on behalf of the Federation with the aim of protecting the cockpit area in the case of intrusion by other cars or objects. A kind ring-shaped carbonfibre structure mounted on a very slim vertical pylon that had to pass the same crash test as the roll-bars. Its rising configuration either side of the driver's head, seen in the side view, means that the rear-view mirrors are not obstructed and frontal visibility should not be impaired. If it is approved by the F1 technical commission it should become obligatory for all cars in the FIA's definitive form.

2014 CAR PROTECTION STRUCTURES

For the 2014 season the FIA had asked Red Bull to design protection structures that offered greater safety in the event of lateral impacts. They had to be fixed to the chassis and not the stepped bottom and identical for all cars, inevitably conditioning to some extent the shape of their front ends.

SIDE STRUCTURES

When deformable structures either side of the driver's head were introduced in 2000, David Coulthard asked McLaren to cut away a portion to allow him more freedom of lateral movement, but he was then obliged to fall in line with his colleagues.

SAUBER 2006

At the French Grand Prix of 2006, the two conspicuous vertical fins mounted behind the upper part of the BMW nose were initially considered to be legal. This extreme feature could compromise visibility and Jacques Villeneuve himself had expressed doubts prior to the first track test, asking for them to be made in transparent plastic. Their function was to restabilize the air flow, above all when the cars were slipstreaming, improving the quality of the flow to the central and rear parts. Surprisingly, ahead of official practice, these strange appendices were banned.

HANS COLLAR

When it was introduced in 2002 in an experimental trial the Hans collar also provoked opposing reactions among the drivers but was then made obligatory the following year, becoming a crucial element in protecting the drivers.

PROTECTIONS

The technical commission and the FIA are evaluating this system for protecting the cockpit area composed of three tubular elements that link the top of the dynamic air intake (the roll-bar) and the front part of the cockpit opening. This structure features a central mount and a further two at the start of the opening itself.

Proposals 2017

The 2015 season was already being run in view of the developments provided for by the revolution in the regulations the FIA is due to introduce from 2017, with the involvement of teams that have developed designs on the basis of the requisites imposed by the Federation.

The first proposal, discussed by the working group as far back as the August of 2015, came from Red Bull.

This was a true project, commissioned early in December

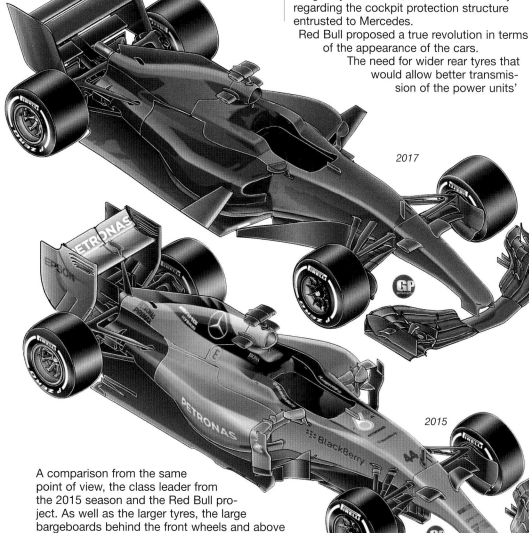

2017

2015

2014 and drawn up on the basis of the first suggestions emerging from the preceding meetings and on the basis of the desires expressed by Bernie Ecclestone himself who, for 2017 would like faster cars and a more exciting sound.

For this reason an additional wastegate exhaust was discussed, like those used back in the Eighties turbo era.

For some years the Federation has relied on the teams to help improve safety, as in the case of the deformable structures for the 2014 season, realised by Red Bull and made obligatory for all cars, and the latest study regarding the cockpit protection structure entrusted to Mercedes.

Red Bull proposed a true revolution in terms of the appearance of the cars.

The need for wider rear tyres that would allow better transmission of the power units'

horses to the track, improving the cars' mechanical grip is clear.

There is also a notable increase in maximum width (2000 mm against the current 1800 mm), bringing the cars back to dimensions in force through to 1997. The principles behind this feasibility study relating to the 2017 car provide for: increased mechanical grip, wider tyres front and rear and a wider front track, notably enhanced ground effects thanks to a wider bodywork with much larger barge-boards and, above all, a taller and longer diffuser and a lower and wider rear wing to create less drag and produce faster cars.

To this end, Williams, following the Austrian Grand Prix, conducted experiments designed to simulate the uprating of the diffuser, with sideskirts and flaps added to the area in front of the rear wheels.

Both features, totally illegal according to the current regulations, were to be mounted for on-track testing and verification. In order to simulate the lower wing, the Williams lapped with the flap fully open.

The beam wing, the low profile abolished from the next season, will also return.

A profile that is less influential in terms of slipstreaming effect but which instead provides great support in that it works in synergy with the diffuser, enhancing its effectiveness. However, the first results of the CFD simulations revealed alarming data in the form of an increase in performance such as to gain almost seven seconds per lap with no drastic reduction of the downforce deficiencies associated with the slipstreaming effect.

Also under consideration is the proposal for a much smaller front wing, although this will have negative effects on the flow, which ought to permit a reduction in the deficiencies caused by the front wheels.

The increase in width of the cars from 1400 mm to 1800 mm will permit the creation of very different shapes, but above all the bottom will inevitably have irregular forms that are not perfectly linear but with a minimum width of 1600 mm.

This is because each car will have a maximum area usable for the floor that is not compatible with a zone 1800 mm in width. This area starts at the cockpit opening and reaches the tangent of the rear wheel, varying according to the track dimensions of each car. These regulations should stimulate the imaginations of the designers and lead to the creation of car very different to one another.

At the last race of the season a number of the extravagances of the Red Bull project were abandoned, as seen in the series of drawings ahead of approval by the technical commission.

A comparison from the same point of view, the class leader from the 2015 season and the Red Bull project. As well as the larger tyres, the large bargeboards behind the front wheels and above all the arrow shape of the wide rear wing are immediately noticeable as are the halberd-shaped vertical turning vanes. The dimensions and the shape of the complex rear wing are completely different.

FRONT VIEW

(1) The maximum width of the cars is due to rise from the current 1800 mm to 2000 mm in accordance with the corresponding increase in the width of the tyres.

(2) The width of the front wing has also increased from 1650 to 1850 mm to maintain the same alignment with respect to the front tyres that are themselves wider (from 245 to 305 mm). (3) The rear wing will instead be drastically lowered from 950 mm to just 800 mm, but it will be (4) wider at 10000 mm against 800 mm.

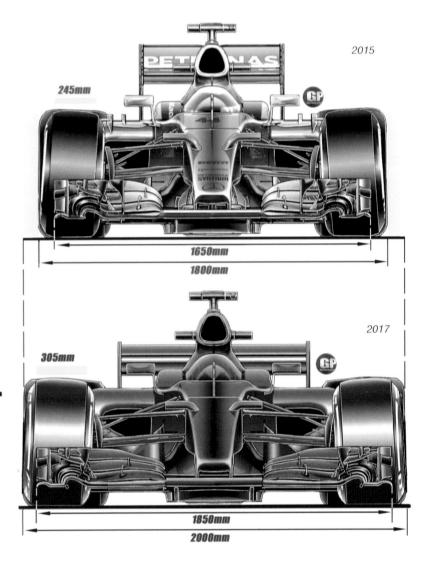

2015

245mm

1650mm
1800mm

2017

305mm

1850mm
2000mm

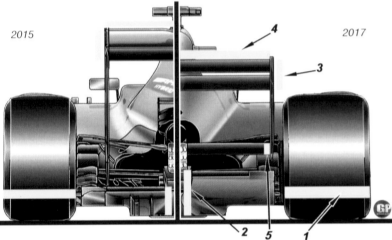

2015

4

3

2017

2

5

1

REAR VIEW

(1) The rear tyres will be wider, passing from 325 to 400 mm, but will have the same diameter. (2) In order to achieve greater ground effects, the diffuser will be much taller at 225 instead of 125 mm. (3) The rear wing will be lower: from 950 mm to just 800 mm, but the area of the profiles will still be contained within 200 mm. (4) It will however, be wider: 1000 mm instead of 800 mm. (5) The beam wing, the profile attached to the protection structure, will return and will be located between 300 and 370 mm from the reference plane.

TOP VIEW

(1) The front wing is due to increase in width from the current 1650 mm to 1850 mm and will have an arrow head shape (2), with a difference of 200 mm between the point and the extremities of the endplates, unchanged with respect to the current ones. (3) The barge-boards behind the front wheels and ahead of the sidepods are also much larger. (4) Their angle of attack will be 15°. (5) The shape of the stepped bottom (still at a height of 50 mm) is not rectangular in plan, but wider at the front and narrower to the rear. (6) The rear tyres will be wider at 405 mm against the current 305 mm. (7) The width of the rear wing will be increased from 800 mm to 1000 mm.

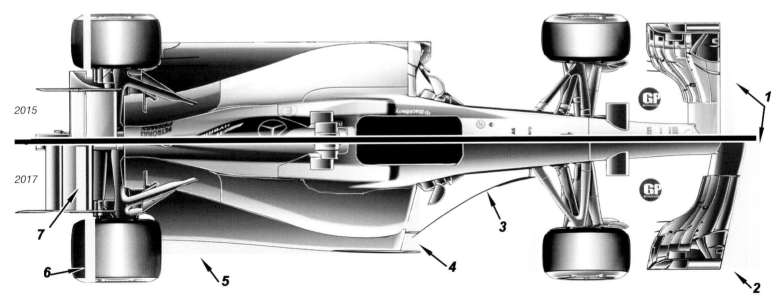

2015

2017

7

6

5

3

4

1

2

SIDE VIEW

(1) The front wing has a distinctive arrow head shape, with an obligatory difference between the point and the front of the (unchanged) endplates of 200 mm. (2) The bargeboards between the front wheels and the sidepods are much larger. (3) The imposition of a fixed angle of 30° for the leading edge and 45° for the trailing edges of the vertical turning vanes is particularly curious. (4) The diffuser is uprated in that it is both taller (225 mm), as seen in the rear view, and longer (now starting 330 mm from the rear axle. (5) The height of the rear wing drops from 950 mm to 800 mm, retaining the 200 mm containment box for the profiles. (6) The shape of the rear wing endplates is restricted once again, with a forward inclination of 30° and a 25° at the rear, a width of 525 mm and an overhang with regard to the rear axle (7) of 740 rather than 500 mm.

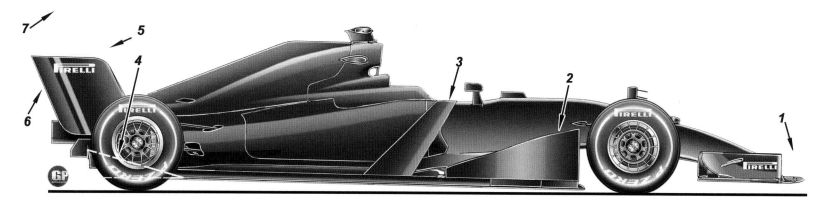

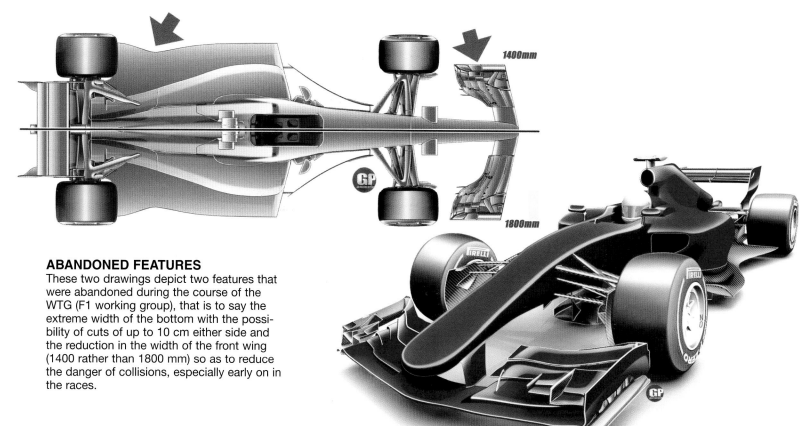

ABANDONED FEATURES

These two drawings depict two features that were abandoned during the course of the WTG (F1 working group), that is to say the extreme width of the bottom with the possibility of cuts of up to 10 cm either side and the reduction in the width of the front wing (1400 rather than 1800 mm) so as to reduce the danger of collisions, especially early on in the races.

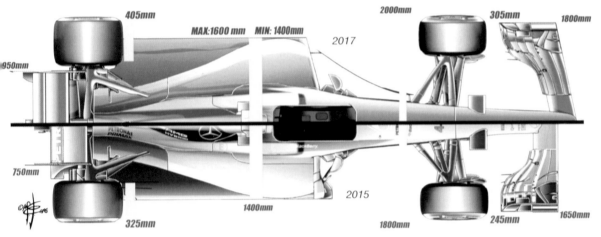

405mm
2000mm
305mm
1800mm
MAX:1600 mm   MIN:1400mm
2017
950mm
2015
750mm
1400mm
325mm
1800mm
245mm
1650mm

ABU DHABI PROPOSAL OVERHEAD VIEW

At the last race of the 2015 season a number of modifications emerged with respect to the features illustrated previously, such as the disappearance of the wide floor (1800 mm) and the possibility of very different forms. The maximum width of 2000 mm instead of 1800 mm was retained, as was the 1800 mm front wing against the 1650 mm of the current wings, but an arrow head shape was imposed (200 mm). The dimensions of the tyres were unchanged, wider both front and rear, in order to guarantee greater mechanical grip; the large barge boards behind the wheels and the different rear wing dimensions were unchanged. The width of the bodywork and the floor was changed, with a maximum of 1600 instead of 1800 m against the current 1400 mm.

FRONT VIEW

No change to the front view, both in terms of the overall width and that of the front wing and, of course, the tyres. The different position and shape of the wider but lower rear wing is clear.

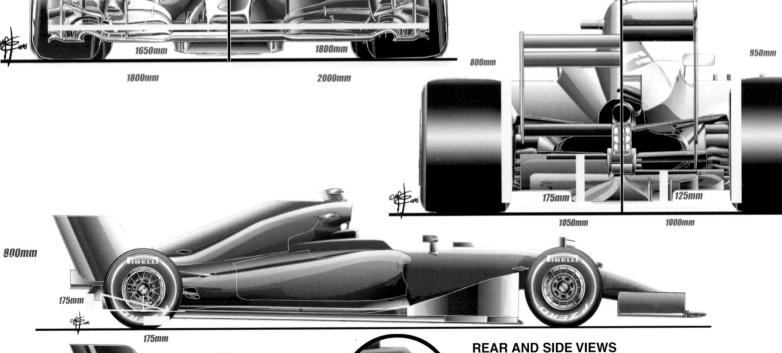

245mm
305mm
1650mm
1800mm
1800mm
2000mm

800mm
950mm
175mm
125mm
1050mm
1000mm

800mm
175mm
175mm
330mm

REAR AND SIDE VIEWS

The halberd-shaped vertical turning vanes present in the Red Bull proposal have disappeared and the diffuser has been shortened: it no longer starts 330 mm from the rear axle but from 175 mm. It is however much more powerful as the old design started from the rear axle and was lower and narrower, guaranteeing, together with the return of the beam wing, a significant increase in downforce.

GIORGIO PIOLA

New DEVELOPMENTS

Following the revolution in the regulations introduced in the 2014 season, the 2015 World Championship was again dominated by Mercedes both on track and in technical terms, albeit with Ferrari returning to the centre of attention thanks to greater competitiveness with respect to the revolutionary but unsuccessful F14T from 2014.

The 2015 season opened with developments in the field of aerodynamics, first and foremost the length of the cars' nosecones, the only part that was subject to a change in the rules, as detailed in the Regulations chapter. From the debut of the cars, in fact, the most important novelties were to be found in the aerodynamics sector, along with new features such as the Lotus engine air intakes, the dual intakes on the Toro Rosso and the wing support that passed inside the large exhaust and the unusual brake duct shields on the McLaren. This last continued to work on the rear suspension with aerodynamic functions, despite abandoning the unique "shutters" introduced in 2014.

With the return of the oil reservoir to its classic location between

engine and monocoque rather than between engine and gearbox, Ferrari adopted a new exhaust layout passing inside the gearbox casing, as had already been done by the Mercedes-powered teams in 2014.

In place of the oil tank there was now the passage of the exhaust with two lateral rings in the carbonfibre structure and central hole in the upper part. A hole documented in the drawing of the Sauber but which was actually present in the gearboxes of all the 2015 cars.

It should also be noted that the gearboxes became taller with the differential raised; a trend also seen on other cars such as the Mercedes, Red Bulls and, in more extreme form, the McLarens.

The feature that

undoubtedly aroused the most curiosity came from a second division team, Force India, which in testing following the Austrian Grand Prix introduced a nose with new apertures that in practice combined the advantages of the two nose designs (short or long) while respecting fully but cleverly the technical reg-

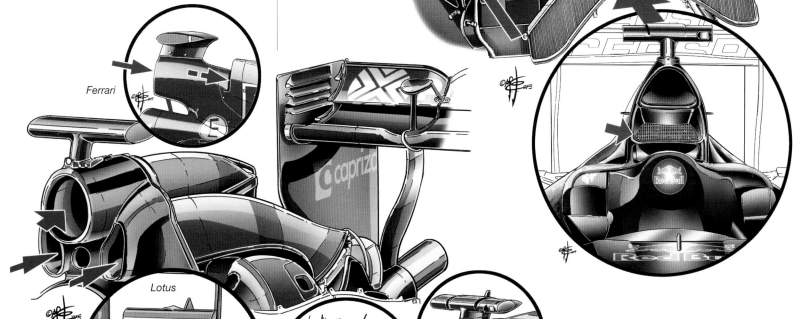

TORO ROSSO
Toro Rosso retained the dual engine air intake on the STR10 to cool a new inverted-V radiator that was for the first time as wide as the monocoque itself, exploiting the central part too.

Ferrari

Lotus

Mercedes

LOTUS AIRSCOOP
A new configuration for the two intake ears on the Lotus, set lower to create less disturbance of the flow towards the rear wing. Usually, the additional ducts were place either in the upper part (Ferrari 2014 and Mercedes 2013) or to the sides (Mercedes 2014). In theory, this new position should have permitted improved aerodynamic efficiency.

ulations. Force India, ever since its debut, had been one of the group of cars equipped with the S-Duct (Red Bull, Sauber and McLaren) as well as blowing front hubs like Red Bull, McLaren and Ferrari.

Again in Austria, there was a surprising number of new features introduced at the same time and concentrated in the high pressure zone ahead of the rear wheels, which has increasingly become the object of research and therefore a field for the development of new features. The double L-shaped longitudinal slots of the Toro Rosso were in fact new, while McLaren introduced four on Alonso's

car, again set longitudinally, and another two transversally just in front of the rear wheel. The aim was to reduce the lift effect generated at this point of the car with the complicity of the rotation of the rear tyres. In Singapore, again in this area of the car, Ferrari went even further, adopting nine slots in place of the

usual three, reducing on the one hand the lift effect mentioned and also improving the efficiency of the extractor profile that received detail modifications.

A trend-setting feature with McLaren presenting no less than 11 slots at Austin in place of the nine of the SF15T.

McLAREN REAR SUSPENSION

Another new rear suspension design on the 2015 McLaren following the new configuration introduced for 2014. In both cases it can be seen how aerodynamics influenced the adoption of this new configuration. The lower wishbone was set as far back as possible, beyond the rear axle, so as to have the rear arm working in synergy with the diffuser. For the first time its anchorage (indicated by the red arrows) was on the deformable structure rather than the gearbox casing.

The previous year in this zone McLaren had adopted the innovative "shutters" applied to the suspension arms (see the insert) to overcoming the outlawing of the beam wing.

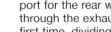

McLAREN

The new MP4-30 was painstakingly designed and began the season with a particularly long, low nose combined with the wing that had in part been seen in Abu Dhabi and which recalled the wings designed by Peter Prodomou for Red Bull. What was new above all was the shape of the brake cooling ducts that draw air from between the tyre and the

duct indented in the central section where there is a greater flow of air towards the interior of the wheel. It should be noted that the MP4-30 also presented blowing front hubs.

TORO ROSSO

On the STR10 the vertical support for the rear wing passes through the exhaust for the first time, dividing and accelerating the flow of hot air. This feature was destined to be copied by other teams.

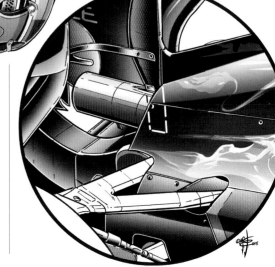

GIORGIO PIOLA

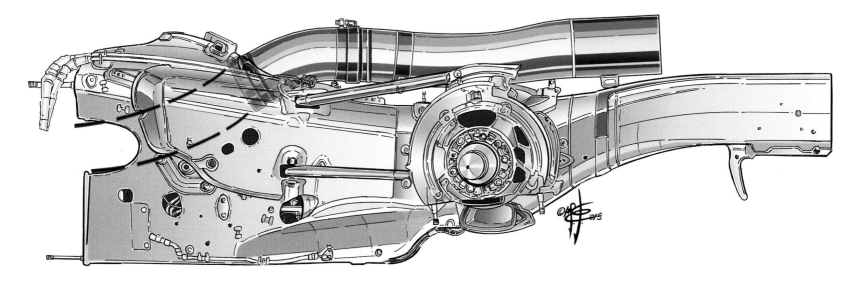

FERRARI EXHAUST IN GEARBOX

From the previous season, the wheelbase of the new generation cars had been increased, with the adoption of spacers and larger gearbox casings. On the F14T, Ferrari had used this space for both the MGU-K electric motor and the oil reservoir, thus occupying all of the free area. On the other cars, the room inside the gearbox spacer was instead exploited to create a passage for the exhaust that exited via a hole (visible in the drawing of the Sauber gearbox) in the upper part.

This feature permitted a more compact installation.

With the return of the oil tank between chassis and engine, the SF15T and the Sauber

also adopted this feature which permitted improved aerodynamics with the exhaust manifolds grouped low down, entering the gearbox spacer and exiting from the upper part, with the large terminal having dimensions imposed by the regulations.

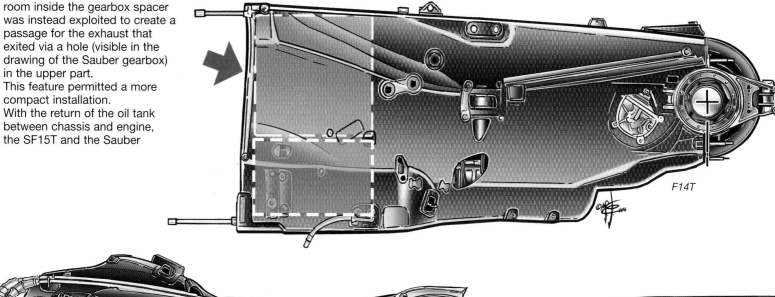

F14T

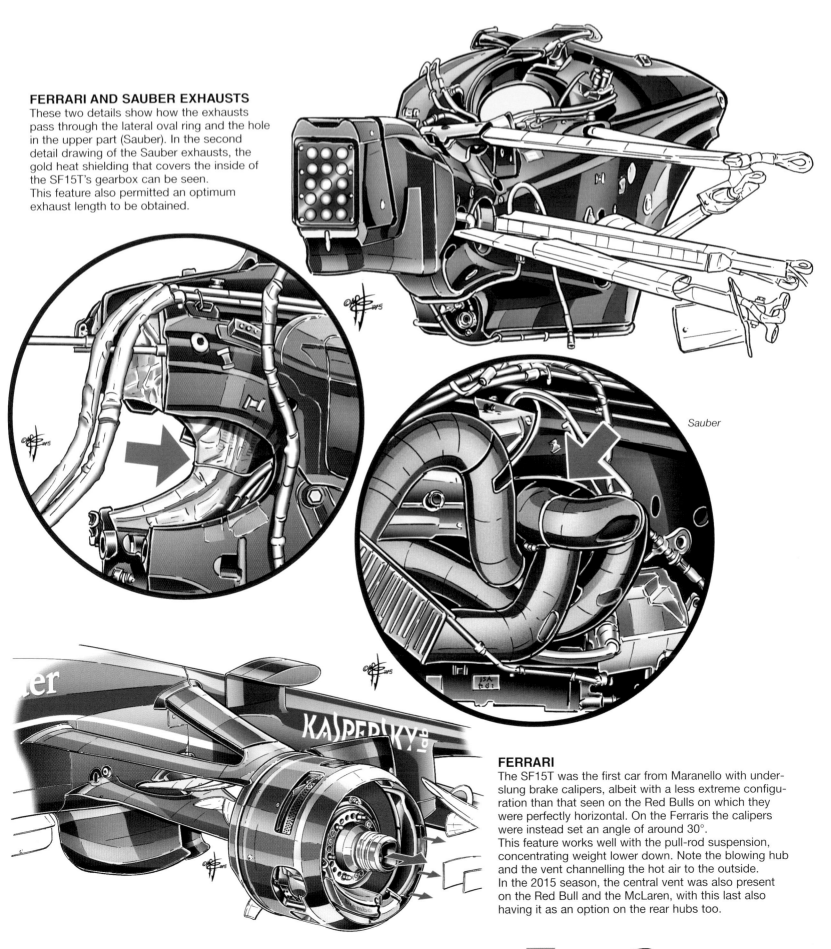

FERRARI AND SAUBER EXHAUSTS

These two details show how the exhausts pass through the lateral oval ring and the hole in the upper part (Sauber). In the second detail drawing of the Sauber exhausts, the gold heat shielding that covers the inside of the SF15T's gearbox can be seen. This feature also permitted an optimum exhaust length to be obtained.

Sauber

FERRARI

The SF15T was the first car from Maranello with under-slung brake calipers, albeit with a less extreme configuration than that seen on the Red Bulls on which they were perfectly horizontal. On the Ferraris the calipers were instead set an angle of around 30°.
This feature works well with the pull-rod suspension, concentrating weight lower down. Note the blowing hub and the vent channelling the hot air to the outside.
In the 2015 season, the central vent was also present on the Red Bull and the McLaren, with this last also having it as an option on the rear hubs too.

FORCE INDIA

Unexpectedly, at the races following the Austrian GP it was Force India that introduced a new feature destined to be copied elsewhere: that of the "nostrils" in the VJM 08's nose. The design was based on the nose with the long finger from the previous season to create two "tubes" that fed the lower part of the car. A perfectly legal design that respected the sectional dimensions and their progression and above all because, as prescribed by Para. 3.7.8, the ground could not be seen from a vertical point of view. The two ducts have an inclination of 45°. In the view from below a kind of scoop can be seen that not only prevents the ground from being seen but channels the flow towards the lower part of the car and increases the effect of the S-Duct visible in the drawing top left. In practice, this feature provides for greater loading of the front end like the long noses, without diminishing the efficiency of the flow towards the rear as with short noses.

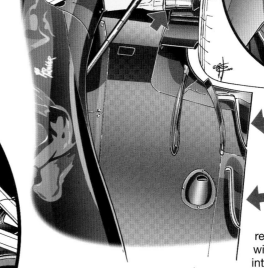

McLAREN RED BULL S-DUCT

At the second race of the season, McLaren introduced an S-Duct on its MP4-30 and did so by adopting a dual configuration in contrast with what firstl Sauber and then Red Bull had done with a single S-shaped duct like that on the Force India.

TORO ROSSO

A new more extreme feature was introduced to the rear suspension by Toro Rosso at the Austrian GP. Both the Mercedes-style raised upper arm and the lower wishbone reprised the new concept of the wide base in the front suspension introduced as a major innovation by the Stuttgart-firm during the previous season. This feature was copied at the front in 2015 by Ferrari and Force India and introduced for the first time at the rear on the STR 1 (highlighted in yellow in the drawing).

McLAREN ZELTWEG

In 2015, the high pressure zone in front of the rear wheels increasingly became the object of new features. Following the twin L-shaped longitudinal slots on the Toro Rosso, McLaren presented no less than four on Alonso's car, again longitudinal, and a further two transverse slots just in front of the rear wheels. The aim was to reduce the lift effect generated at this point by the rotation of the rear tyres.

FERRARI SINGAPORE

The latest detail modification in the high pressure area ahead of the rear wheels, this time introduced by Ferrari. Following the Toro Rosso's dual L-shaped slots and the multiple ones on the McLaren, in Singapore the SF15T presented no less than nine slots in place of the previous three. The aim was to reduce the lift effect generated at this point by the rotation of the rear tyres.

MERCEDES REAR SUSPENSION

Rather than a new feature, this was a more extreme interpretation of the regulations in order to improve rear aerodynamics. Mercedes had taken to extreme lengths the possibility of fixing the suspension wishbones not directly to the hub carrier but to a plate, in this case significantly raised so as to achieve both a different suspension geometry and for aerodynamic purposes to free the lower zone of the brake ducts that had increasingly become an element destined to create downforce (on the rear axle).

Talking about **BRAKES** and **TYRES**

Following the major changes to the regulations introduced in 2014, which led to a substantial modification of the braking systems with the introduction of Brake By Wire (BBW), in 2015 there was a further development of the assisted braking system and an even more extreme solution to the cooling of the braking systems.

Having come into F1 in 1975, last year Brembo celebrated 40 years in motorsport's blue ribbon category, supplying its braking systems to no less than five teams: Red Bull, Ferrari, Sauber, Mercedes and Toro Rosso. AP supplies four: Williams, Force India, Lotus and Manor, while the Japanese Akebono is exclusive to McLaren.

The Brembo client teams were provided with more efficient calipers thanks to the use of innovative features and they were better integrated with the corners of the car, a factor that also helped improved the cars' aerodynamic performance. Over 14 consecutive

hours are required to produce the new aluminium-lithium calipers and achieve the best weight-stiffness compromise.

Brembo in the design, simulation and configuration of the entire braking system as well as the individual Brake By Wire components, working on their installation and miniaturization. For certain teams only the actuator was developed, that is, the component that acts an interface between the car's hydraulics and the rear calipers. For the other teams Brembo provided a more comprehensive service that embraced much of the BBW circuit, such as the valves regulating the Brake By Wire switch from the condition of normal to emergency use or the simulator that reproduces the rigidity of the rear circuit, ensuring the driver has appropriate pedal feel.

In 2015, braking bias was shifted further to the front axle and over the course of the year we saw an increase of 15% in the maximum braking force.

This increase was as a result of the constant aerodynamic development of the cars and the consequent increase in grip.

For this reason, the rear axle was fitted with smaller discs than in 2014 (260 mm) and four-pot calipers (Red Bull and Sauber), with Mercedes instead returning to more conservative six-pot calipers. A path followed after the problems encountered during the Canadian GP 2014 when a problem with the ERS had affected the rear brakes that were no longer assisted effectively by the Brake By Wire system.

Again regarding the brake discs, the cooling was further increased and optimized given that in F1 the component can reach a maximum temperature of 1200°C, with work being done on the number of ventilation holes (which may exceed 1,200) and on the mounting of the components to the carrier in order to improve structural strength.

Increased perforation of the disc is only func-

BRAKE BY WIRE

In the 2015 season, the configuration of the Brake By Wire system applied to the rear brakes to recover energy (MGU-K) was practically unchanged and for this reason the diagram provided Brembo has been represented.

The basis is the traditional system with the brake pedal (1) commanding the two axles via two separate pumps (2 front – 3 rear). The driver can always adjust the brake bias between the two axles from the cockpit. Under braking the front system functions as always: the pump pres-

surises the liquid which acts via the pistons (six at the front) on the pads and then the discs, slowing the car.

The rear brakes are managed electronically with the system comprising a simulator known as a "compliance chamber" made by Brembo for its teams (6); this last guarantees brake feel for the driver when the rear axle is governed electronically, while the system is controlled by a CPU (7) that slows the motor-generator (7) and, via an actuator (8) pressurises the rear braking circuit (9).

Braking is therefore the combined effort of

the pressure of the fluid acting within the traditional brake circuit and the deceleration actuated by the motor-generator that depends on how much energy on wishes to recover to recharge the batteries. While at the front the classic six-pot calipers are retained (10), at the rear the discs are of a reduced diameter (up to 12 mm less) and smaller calipers are fitted, in some cases four-pot units. In the case of problems with the electronic management, the systems returns to the traditional configuration, albeit less effective at the rear.

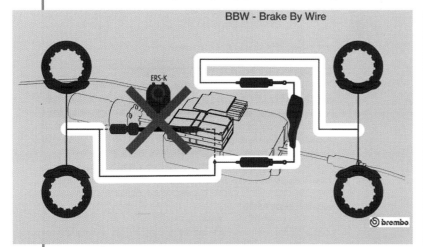

BBW - Brake By Wire

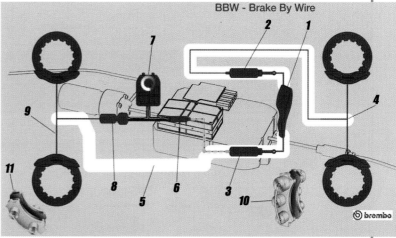

BBW - Brake By Wire

tional if the flow of air within the holes is sufficient to permit effective thermal exchange and this is guaranteed through careful CFD (Computer Fluid Dynamics) simulations and the synergy between the air intake, developed by each team for its car, and the brake discs supplied by Brembo.

The ventilation holes have as a consequence been increased in number but reduced in diameter, exponentially increasing the carbon surface exposed to the flow of air and consequently the thermal exchange.

Recognising the discs with over 1200 holes from the outside is possible by observing the oblique disposition of the five holes rather than the horizontal configurations of the rows of four (850 holes).

This structural evolution required much more complex and delicate machining, together with increased efforts regarding research into fluid dynamics. A fundamental contribution has been made by each team with the pairing and combination with the air intakes of the new cars.

The material used for the discs has also been the object of significant changes. While notably reducing wear and guaranteeing more efficient thermal conductivity, the CER carbonfibre used for the brake discs has offered reduced warm-up times, that is it rapidly reaches the optimum working temperature, a broad range of use in terms of pressure and temperature and a very linear response in terms of friction. All characteristics that permit the driver perfect modulation of the braking system.

The incredibly low wear also means performance is constant and repeatable throughout the race.

In the 2015 season the CER 300 disc material was identical for all teams supplied by Brembo, while new CCR 700 ventilated pads were also available.

In a full season on average Brembo supply a two-car team with 10 sets of calipers, between 140 and 240 discs and between 280 and 480 pads.

MERCEDES

Mercedes was one of the four teams that in the 2014 season had adopted four-pot calipers (in the circle, left) at the rear, combined with smaller discs with respect to the maximum permitted by the regulations.

A configuration that with the ERS failing during the 2014 Canadian GP

Montreal 2014

2015

penalised the performance and the two W05s, gifting victory to Red Bull, also fitted with a similar braking system but not suffering the same electronic management issues.

For this reason, in 2015 the W06s went back to a six-pot calipers (in the circle, right) at the rear.

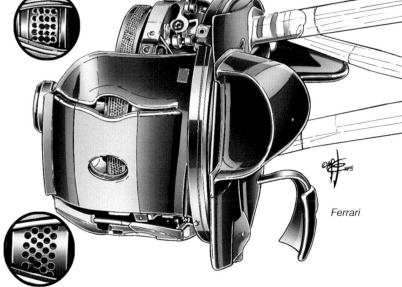

Ferrari

DISC EVOLUTION

The major progress with regard to the braking systems came in the forms of the disc material with which Brembo replaced the CCR that guaranteed maximum wear of 4-5 at the end of races on the tracks hardest on brakes. With CER 100, wear was reduced to 1 mm.

Great attention was paid to ventilation with the number of holes increased over the years, as documented in this sequence provided by Brembo. The drawing shows the disc with over 1,200 holes (5 in oblique rows giving more space between one hole and the next), compared with the version with four in-line holes (850 holes).

2005	2006/7	2008	2012	2014	2015
100	100	200	600	1000	1200

ⓑ brembo

GIORGIO PIOLA

BREMBO DISC
An exploded view of the Brembo disc with over 1,200 holes (in oblique rows); the cooling channels have a sophisticated funnel shape and are not perfectly radial, as seen in the section taken from the animation.

RED BULL AND FERRARI
Just two teams fitted underslung brake calipers, with Ferrari adopting the configuration Red Bull had been using since the 2008 season. Blowing front hubs were instead adopted for the first time by Ferrari and also used by McLaren as well as, of course, Red Bull, which had been using them since 2013. Newey had actually been the first to introduce the feature in 2012, but the Federation had banned them after seven race as the holes were in the rotating part of the hub (see the insert).

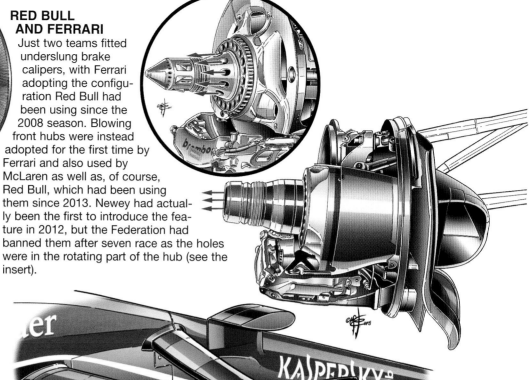

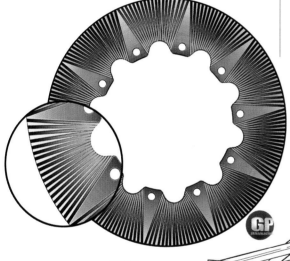

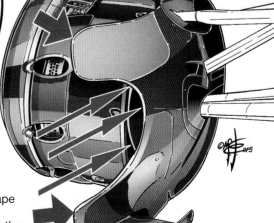

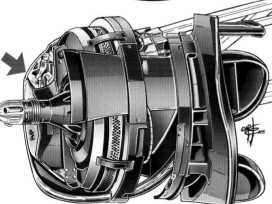

2010

FORCE INDIA
After no less than six season, at the Monaco Grand Prix Force India finally abandoned the absurd location of the brake calipers ahead of the front axle introduced in 2010, adopting the classic vertical position along the axis. A feature that also had a negative influence on the cooling of the calipers.

McLAREN
The McLaren brake air intakes had a new shape (an inverted C) introduced at the debut of the new MP4-30. The cooling air was drawn from the internal part of the large shield only.

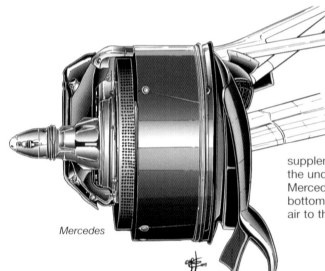

Mercedes

MONTREAL
The Montreal circuit is particularly hard on brakes and obliged the teams to adopt extreme configurations. For the first time Mercedes used completely open front brake shrouds to improve the thermal dumping of the Carbon brake discs with four in-line holes. Red Bull instead retained the small supplementary intake introduced at Monaco to cool the underslung caliper with the addition of a new Mercedes-style shield with a conspicuous curve at the bottom; all this with the aim of increasing the flow of air to the system.

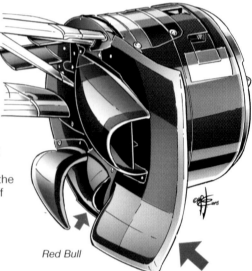

Red Bull

A question of TYRES

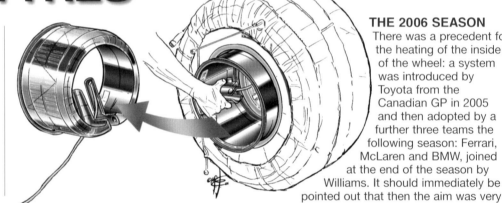

In contrast with the 2014 season in which it had helped enliven race strategies with very aggressive compounds that favoured pit stops during the various races, in 2015 Pirelli opted for more conservative solutions. The technicians at the Bicocca plant were well aware of the increased performance of the cars in the second year of the Power Units and therefore preferred not to run risks. The tyre manufacturer has always provided the teams with information regarding the optimum use of its tyres, but the teams have never been obliged to regard this information as binding as it was not part of the official FIA technical regulations.
The suggestions were therefore treated as nothing more than advice by all the teams. The significant increase in downforce during the course of the season thanks to the efficient aerodynamic development of the cars (there was talk of an extra 100 kg of aerodynamic loading for the leading cars) and the increased power from the six-cylinder turbo engines, which were producing over 900 hp thanks to significant combustion innovations, took the F1 cars to the limits of the tyres' capabilities. Moreover, the teams' engineers were well aware that lowering tyre pressure would augment the contact patch and therefore improve performance, albeit at a price... The issue "exploded" in dramatic fashion during the Belgian Grand Prix. In free practice Nico Rosberg suffered a blown tyre on his Mercedes: it initially appeared to be a structural failure but instead debris had caused a puncture. However, panic set in because it happened at Spa Francorchamps, the longest world championship circuit (over 7 km) and with the highest lateral loadings given that the compression at Eau Rouge and Raidillon can be tackled by the drivers flat out in sixth gear

THE 2006 SEASON

There was a precedent for the heating of the inside of the wheel: a system was introduced by Toyota from the Canadian GP in 2005 and then adopted by a further three teams the following season: Ferrari, McLaren and BMW, joined at the end of the season by Williams. It should immediately be pointed out that then the aim was very different. In that case, in fact, the increase in temperature within the wheel served to optimise both the temperature itself and the pressure for a single qualifying lap. In the case of Mercedes in 2015, the same increase in temperature served to be able to count on a lower tyre pressure during the race than that measured on the grid. The original feature was then banned in the 2007 season.

(in qualifying). Pirelli's specifications called for a minimum inflation pressure of 19.5 PSI at the front and 18.5 PSI at the rear, with a maximum camber of 3.5° and 2.5° front and rear. Following qualifying, the Milan firm's engineers stated that the Medium tyres could be used for 22 laps without durability being an issue.
Ferrari with Sebastian Vettel instead decided to adopt an aggressive strategy that would allow the German driver to eliminate a pit stop and taken him to the podium with an SF16-H that was struggling on the circuit through the Ardennes forest.
On the penultimate lap, after 28 covered on the Mediums, the Ferrari's right rear delaminated on the Kammel straight. Vettel was thus obliged to retire while Romain Grosjean took a podium place with the Renault that had been hustling the Ferrari. In the heat of

the moment Sebastian accused Pirelli of supplying unsafe tyres, while Paul Hembery instead attacked Ferrari for not having respected the safety measures.
An investigation was therefore initiated that eventually revealed the presence of a very high quantity of micro-debris in the tyres analysed by Ferrari and that the depth of 30% of the tread on the right rear tyre had undoubtedly made it more susceptible to damage caused by the latter. In short, in Sebastian Vettel's case too it had been a slow puncture rather than a catastrophic blow out.
The FIA nonetheless decided to intervene. At Monza the teams were presented with a "users' manual" for the tyres indicating a series of safety precautions: minimum inflation pressure, camber values and temperatures for the tyre blankets not exceeding

120°. The FIA reserved the right to make checks during practice and on the grid ahead of the start. Pirelli fixed the minimum pressures at 21 PSI at the front and 19.5 at the rear, significantly higher values than those recommended at Spa.

Lewis Hamilton won the Italian Grand Prix but his victory was subject to investigation as the pressure in his rear tyres was lower than the minimum values recommended by Pirelli. The scrutineers in fact found that the values were those indicated by Pirelli when the tyres were fitted to the Silver Arrow on the grid, but that when the tyre blankets were switched off, according to the normal procedure, they were at a significantly lower temperature than those of the other cars on the grid, which caused the slightly lower pressure.

In order to play down the disputes, in Singapore the FIA adjusted its aim: the scrutineers could make surprise checks on the starting grid five minutes before the formation lap to oblige those who were found to be outside the limits to make adjustments. Unfortunately, these were only palliative measures as there was no live monitoring of tyre pressures.

As a consequence of what had happened at Monza, in Singapore Mercedes used a carbonfibre cover over the rear brake shroud, while an electric heater warmed disc and caliper via the air intake so that heat would irradiate to the wheel and thus the tyre when the pressure was checked. An expedient that allowed the tyres of the W06 Hybrid to pass scrutineering while being able to count on lower pressure during the race. A trick that sparked the imaginations of other teams that came up with equally ingenious solutions…

DATA ON THE 2015 SEASON

In its fifth season as exclusive F1 tyre supplier, Pirelli brought a new rear tyre construction to the entire P Zero range, designed to distribute heat and stress more evenly in view of the enhanced performance expected from the Power Units. The engineers led by Paul Hembery worked to optimize the contact patch and guarantee better temperature distribution to the benefit of grip and the driveability of the cars. The Supersoft tyres presented an all-new and softer compound, designed to prevent blistering and graining. Over the course of the season the Milan-based company produced 35,964 tyres, of which 29,856 were used over the 19 race weekends and 6,108 in testing.

Of the total, 25,004 were slicks and 10,960 rain or grooved intermediates. It is curious to note that 17,580 covers were actually used, comprising 16,288 slicks and 1,292 rain tyres. Four slick compounds were available: two Low Working Range (operating within a temperature window of between 75° and 105°) and a further two High Working Range (at their best between 105° and 135°):
Supersoft (Red) - Low Working Range
Soft (Yellow) - High Working Range
Medium (White) - Low Working Range
Hard (Orange) - High Working Range.
There were two rain tyres: the Intermediates (green) and the Full Wets (Blue) that disperse respectively 25 and 65 litres of water per second at maximum speed.
Pirelli took two slick compounds to each race as well as the rain tyres: the most used were the Softs (15 GPs), followed by the Mediums (13 GPs) and the Supersofts (6 GPs), while the Hards were the least used (4 GPs).

In reality, the tyre that covered the greatest distance was the Medium (114,727 km), followed by the Soft (107,070 km), the Supersoft (39,007 km) and finally the Hard (33,842 km).
Among the wet weather tyres, there was a clear prevalence of the Intermediates (9,370) with respect to the Full Wets (4,781 km).
Each driver had 13 sets at his disposition: seven of the harder compound and six of the softest; the extra set of hard tyres was to be used in the first half hour of Free Practice 1 and then handed back to the Pirelli engineers: this was to incentivise the presence of the drivers on track even when it had yet to receive a coating of fresh rubber.
In qualifying each driver could count on seven sets: three of the hard compound and four soft.
The drivers making it through to Q3 could use an extra set of soft tyres that had to be returned after the timed session, with the race being started on the tyres with which the car had obtained the best time in Q2.
All the other drivers were allowed to choose which tyres they used at the start.
The provision of wet weather tyres was also restricted: four sets of Intermediates and three of Full Wets.
During the race each driver had to use the two compounds for at least a lap: during the 2015 season there were 697 tyre changes, with an average of 37.1 per races and 1.88 per driver in each GP.
The race with the most pit stops was the Hungarian GP with 60, while the one with least was the Australian GP with 17.

Franco Nugnes

	Mercedes AMG								Red Bull Racing Renault								Williams Mercedes									Ferrari										McLaren Honda								
	Hamilton				Rosberg				Ricciardo				Kvyat				Massa					Bottas				Vettel				Raikkonen					Alonso/Magnussen				Button				
Stint	1	2	3	4	1	2	3	4	1	2	3	4	1	2	3	4	1	2	3	4	5	1	2	3	4	1	2	3	4	1	2	3	4	5	1	2	3	4	1	2	3	4	5
Australia	Su	Mn			Su	Mn			Su	Mn			DNS				Su	Mn				DNP				Su	Mn			Su	Su	Mn	NC		DNs				Sn	Mn			
Malaysia	Mu	Hn	Mn	Hn	Mu	Hn	Hn	Mn	Mu	Mn	Mu	Hn	Mu	Mn	Hn	Hn	Mu	Mn	Mu	Hn		Mu	Mn	Mn	Hn	Mu	Mn	Hn		Mn	Mn	Mn	Hn		Hn	Mn	NC		Hn	Mn	Mn	Mu	NC
China	Su	Sn	Mn		Su	Sn	Mn		Su	Su	Mn		Mn	NC			Su	Mn	Mu			Su	Mn	Mu		Su	Sn	Mn		Su	Sn	Mn			Sn	Mn	Sn		Sn	Sn	Mn		
Bahrain	Su	Sn	Mn		Su	Sn	Mn		Su	Su	Mn		Sn	Mn	Sn		Su	Sn	Mn			Su	Sn	Mn		Su	Sn	Mn	Mn	Su	Mn	Sn			Su	Mn	Sn		DNS				
Spain	Mu	Mn	Hn	Mu	Mu	Mn	Hn		Mu	Mu	Hn		Mu	Mu	Hn		Mu	Mu	Hn	Mu		Mu	Mu	Hn		Mu	Mn	Hn		Mu	Hn	Mn			Mu	Hn	NC		Mu	Hn	Mn	Mu	
Monaco	SSu	Sn	SSu		SSu	Sn			SSu	Sn	SSu		SSu	Sn			SSn	Sn	SSu	SSu		Sn	SSn	SSn		SSu	Sn			SSu	Sn				Sn	SSn	NC		SSn	Sn	SSu		
Canada	SSu	Sn			SSu	Sn			SSu	Sn			SSu	Sn			Sn	SSn				SSu	Sn			SSn	Sn	Sn		SSu	Sn	SSu			SSn	Sn	NC		Sn	SSn	NC		
Austria	SSu	Sn			SSu	Sn			Sn	SSn			SSu	Sn	SSu		SSu	Sn				SSu	Sn			SSu	Sn			Sn	NC				SSn	NC			SSn	Sn	Su	NC	
Great Britain	Mu	Hn	In		Mu	Hn	In		Mu	Hn	Hu	NC	Mu	Hn	In		Mu	Hn	In			Mu	Hn	In		Mu	Hn	In		Mu	Hn	In	In		Mn	Hn	Hn	In	Mn	NC			
Hungary	Su	Su	Mn	Su	Su	Mn	Mn	Su	Su	Mn	Su	Su	Su	Mn	Su	Su	Su	Mn	Su	Su		Su	Su	Mn	Su	Su	Su	Mn		Su	Su	Mn	Su	NC	Su	Sn	Mn	Su	Sn	Sn	Mn		
Belgium	Su	Mn	Sn		Su	Mn	Sn		Su	Mn	NC		Su	Mn	Sn		Su	Mn	Mn			Su	Mix	Mu		Su	Mn			Sn	Sn	Mn			Mn	Sn	Sn	Sn	Mn	Sn	Sn	Sn	
Italy	Su	Mn			Su	Mn	DNF		Mn	Sn			Mn	Sn			Su	Mn				Su	Mn			Su	Mn			Su	Mn				Mn	Sn	Su	DNF	Sn	Mn			
Singapore	SSu	Sn	NC		SSu	Sn	Sn		SSu	SSn	Su		SSu	SSu	Sn		SSu	SSu	Sn	Su	NC	SSu	SSu	Sn		SSu	SSn	Sn		SSu	SSn	Sn			SSu	Sn	NC		SSn	Sn	Sn	SSu	NC
Japan	Mu	Mn	Hn		Mu	Mn	Hu		Mu	Hn	Hu		Mu	Hn	Mu	Hn	Mu	Hn	Mn	Mu		Mu	Mn	Hn		Mu	Hn	Hn		Mu	Hn	Hn			Mu	Mn	Hn		Hn	Mn	Mn		
Russia	SSu	Sn			SSu	NC			SSu	Sn	DNF		SSn	Sn			Sn	SSn				SSu	Sn			SSu	Sn			SSu	Sn				Sn	SSn			SSn	Sn			
USA	In	Sn	Sn		In	Sn	Sn		In	Sn	Sn	Sn	In	Sn	Mn	NC	In	Sn	NC			In	Sn	In	NC	In	Sn	Mn	Sn	In	Sn	Sn	NC		In	In	Sn	Sn	In	Sn	Sn	Sn	
Mexico	Su	Mn	Mn		Su	Mn	Mn		Su	Mn	Mn		Su	Mn	Mn		Su	Mn	Mn			Su	Mn	Mn	NC	Su	Mn	Mn	NC	Mn	NC				Mn	NC			Mn	Sn			
Brazil	Su	Mn	Mn	Mn	Su	Mn	Mn	Mn	Su	Mn	Mn	Su	Su	Mn	Mn		Su	Mn	Mu	Mu	EX	Su	Mn	Mu		Su	Mn	Su	Mn	Su	Mn	Mn			Sn	Mn	Sn	Su	Sn	Mn	Sn	Su	
Abu Dhabi	SSu	Sn	Sn		SSu	Sn	Sn		SSu	Sn	Sn		SSu	Sn	Sn		SSu	Sn	Sn			SSu	Sn	Sn	Su	Sn	Sn	SSn		SSu	Sn	Sn			SSn	Sn	Sn	SSn	SSn	Sn	Sn		

SS: super soft **S**: soft **M**: medium **H**: hard **I**: intermediate **W**: wet n: new u: used

MERCEDES

When tyre pressure checks on the starting grid were introduced, Mercedes had developed a strategy for use from the following race in Singapore, introducing firstly a kind of cap and then, in Sao Paulo, a second shroud for the rear brakes only, so as to warm the wheel and tyre with an electric heater. The operation was done on the grid after the formation lap: the warming phase occurred during the checking of the inflation pressures. An expedient that allowed the tyres of the W06 Hybrid to pass scrutineering while being able to count on lower inflation pressure during the race.

2015	Pressure						Camber	
	Slick		Inter		Xtreme Wet			
	Min Start		Min Start		Min Start			
Race	Front	Rear	Front	Rear	Front	Rear	Front	Rear
Australia	17	17	16	16	16	16	-4,25	-2,75
Malaysia	18	17	17	16	16	16	-3,75	-2,5
China	19	18	18	17	17	16	-3,5	-2,5
Bahrain	21,5	20,5	19	18	18	17	-3,25	-2,5
Spain	19	18	18	17	17	18	-3,75	-2,5
Monaco	16	16	16	16	16	16	-4,5	-3
Canada	19	18	18	17	17	16	-4	-2,5
Austria	18	17	17	16	16	16	-4	-2,5
Great Britain	19,5	18	18,5	17	17,5	16	-3,5	-2,5
Hungary	16	16	16	16	16	16	-4,5	-3
Belgium	19,5	18,5	18,5	17,5	17,5	16,5	-3,5	-2,5
Italy	21	19,5	20	18,5	19	17,5	-3	-2
Singapore	18	17	17	16	16	16	-3,75	-2,5
Japan	17	17	16	16	16	16	-4	-3
Russia	21,5	20,5	20,5	19,5	19,5	18,5	-3,25	-2,25
USA	20,5	19,5	19	18	18	17	-3,5	-2,5
Mexico	20,5	19,5	19	18	18	17	-3,5	-2,5
Brazil	21	20,5	19	18	18	17	-3,5	-2,25
Abu Dhabi	20	19	18	17	17	16	-3,75	-2,5

Talking about **COCKPITS**

F14T-SF15H STEERING WHEELS COMPARISON

The 2015 season represented an important step in the history of Ferrari steering wheels: for the first time since 1996, the lower part of the steering wheel rim was eliminated so as to create more space for the driver's legs.

This was requested by Sebastian Vettel, who was accustomed to driving the Red Bull with a butterfly steering wheel, cut away at the centre. In the comparison between the SF15H and F14T (2014) steering wheels you can immediately note the elimination of a knob but also a different and simpler arrangement of the various controls, designed in this case too on the basis of the drivers' requirements.

It should also be said that on occasion the arrangement of the knobs might vary as a function of the diverse demands of the tracks, for example locating in a more ergonomic position those functions that are used more often on a certain track. From the 2014 season the FIA has permitted the use of a larger display (9.5 cm wide and 5.4 cm high), indispensible for handling the quantity of information required and supplied during the race by the complex Power Units. In the upper part of the steering wheel is the traditional sequence of blue lights indicating the correct engine speed for gear changes, although the tendency is

F14T

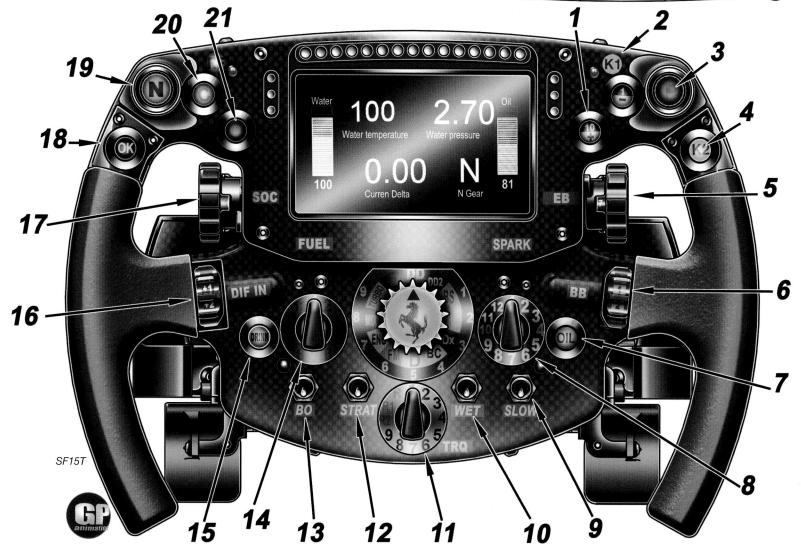

SF15T

F14T

SF15T

COMPARISON FROM BEHIND

Clearly, the most obvious difference in the view from behind is the cutaway in the lower part of the rim. The handling of gear changes was also different: on the F14T there were two separate paddles with the right-hand one allowing the driver to change up and the left-hand one to change down. On the SF15H there was a single wishbone, as at the time of Michael Schumacher, with the possibility of handling changes up and down with one hand.

now to receive an acoustic signal with the same function.

The driver can select several screen modes and types of information to visualise in the menu via the button (1), as well as via the knob (8). A very important button is the one Pit Limiter (3) engaged on entering the pit lane. Buttons (2-4) control the Kers, while engine braking is handled by another (5). Brake bias adjustment on the two axles (6) is extremely important and can be varied by the drivers, overriding electronic rear braking control. When necessary the driver can deliver more oil to the engine via a button (7). Power delivery in particular situations is controlled by a button (9) and in wet conditions by this one (10). There are also a number of adjustments for certain engine parameters such as torque (11) and different mappings to suit different strategies (12). Wheel spin ahead of the start can safely be effected by pressing the button (13) that prevents excessive engine speeds being reached.

There is also a multifunction dial.

The drivers' favourite button (15) is the one that engages a pump allowing them to drink mineral salts during the race.

Compared with the F14T, the differential control (16) was moved. Buttons 17 and 20 control the state of the battery charge while 18 allows the driver to confirm instructions received.

Neutral is found with button 19, while reverse is on the rib behind the wheel to the left; this button is protected by a ring preventing accidental engagement. Last but not least in terms of importance, the radio (21).

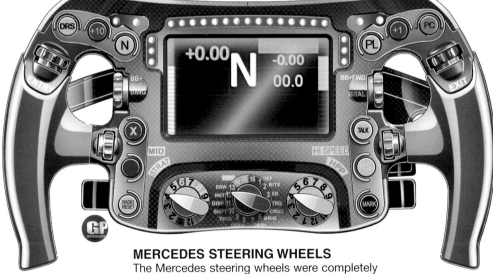

MERCEDES STEERING WHEELS

The Mercedes steering wheels were completely unchanged with respect to the 2014 season, both from the front and the rear; they were also notably simpler than the Ferrari wheels with just four levers at the rear. The colour differences and the arrangement of the dials in the front view including writing in English for Hamilton and German for Rosberg were also retained.

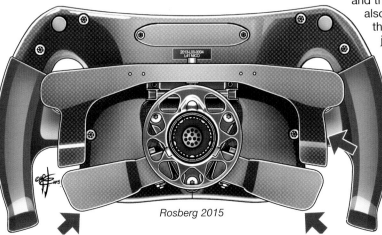

Rosberg 2015

GIORGIO PIOLA

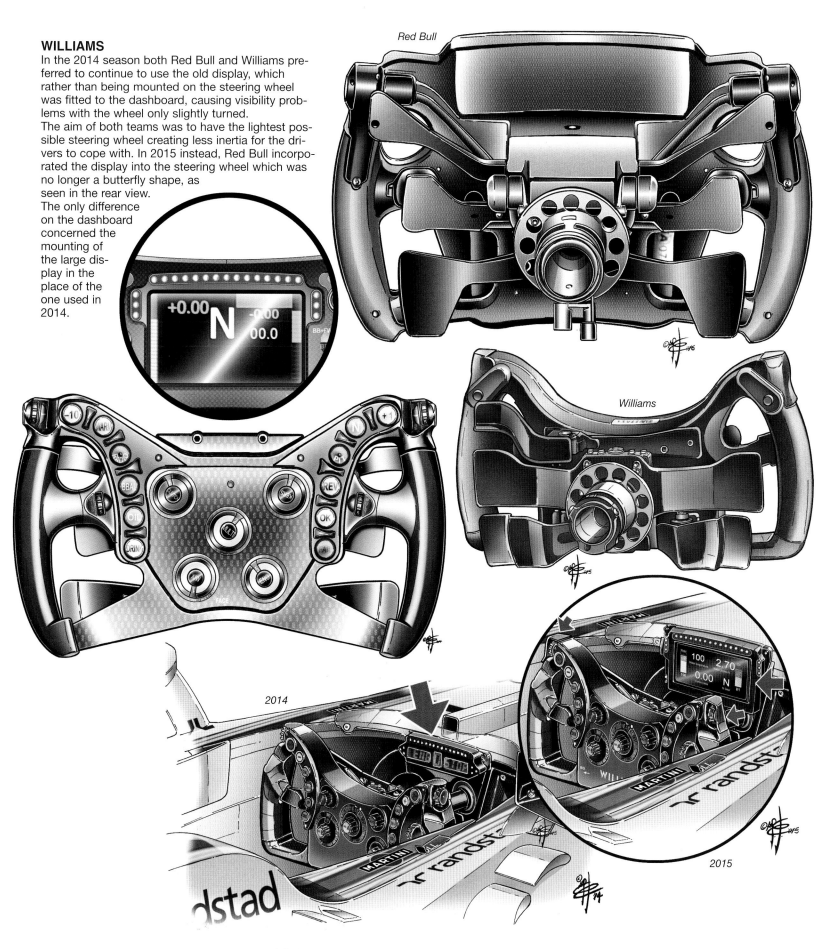

WILLIAMS

In the 2014 season both Red Bull and Williams preferred to continue to use the old display, which rather than being mounted on the steering wheel was fitted to the dashboard, causing visibility problems with the wheel only slightly turned.

The aim of both teams was to have the lightest possible steering wheel creating less inertia for the drivers to cope with. In 2015 instead, Red Bull incorporated the display into the steering wheel which was no longer a butterfly shape, as seen in the rear view.

The only difference on the dashboard concerned the mounting of the large display in the place of the one used in 2014.

Red Bull

Williams

2014

2015

Engines 2015

FIA's Power Unit regulations were substantially unchanged with respect to the 2014 season when the 2.4-litre naturally aspirated engines gave way to the complex six-cylinder, 1.6-litre units fitted with turbochargers and an ERS system composed of two electric motors (MGU-K for the recovery of kinetic energy under braking and MGU-H for the recovery of thermal energy from

the turbo). The most important variation concerned the number of units that each driver could use during the championship, which dropped from five to four units that were required to complete 19 Grands Prix. The only constructor that succeeded in respecting this limit was Mercedes: the Silver Arrows from the Brackley-based team and the client teams (Williams, Force India and Lotus)

all managed to complete the season with four Power Units per car. In fact, the three teams supplied by Brixworth actually "saved" a battery and a CPU from the available components, displaying a surprising reliability and the engineers led by Andy Cowell, Mercedes AMG High Performance Powertrains chief, can be proud of their PU106 B, capable completing six race weekends without the slight-

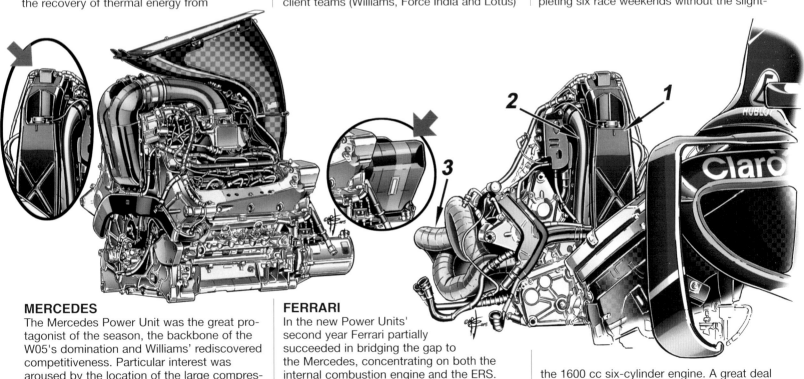

MERCEDES

The Mercedes Power Unit was the great protagonist of the season, the backbone of the W05's domination and Williams' rediscovered competitiveness. Particular interest was aroused by the location of the large compressor at the front of the engine (1), generally semi-concealed by the traditional oil tank (2). The turbine (3), also of a notable size, was located at the other end of the engine with the MGU-H electric motor set in the V. The exhausts (4) were brought together in a kind of niche and had very short pipes so as not to disperse heat.

FERRARI

In the new Power Units' second year Ferrari partially succeeded in bridging the gap to the Mercedes, concentrating on both the internal combustion engine and the ERS. The major change was the return of the oil tank (1) to a location between engine and chassis, rather than in the gearbox casing as on the F14T. The configuration with the compressor (larger in 2015) close to the turbine and set very low was unchanged. Both the MGU-H electric motor and the intercooler were found in the V of

the 1600 cc six-cylinder engine. A great deal of work was done on the exhausts (3) to avoid dispersal of the heat necessary for optimal MGU-H performance. The intercooler (2) remained in the V, as can also be seen in the profile view. The MGU-K in turn remained in the gearbox casing, mounted at the back of the engine.

GIORGIO PIOLA

est problem: just think that Power Unit No. 1 fitted to the W06 Hybrid in Australia was only removed following the Monaco GP. Nico Rosberg covered 4,389 km, while Lewis Hamilton reached 4,074 km. This is an unprecedented record for Formula 1 given that in the past engines were constructed for qualifying that were designed to survive just a handful of laps. Along with the two Drivers' and Constructors' World Championship titles, the spoils included 16 victories in 19 Grands Prix, 18 pole positions, 13 fastest laps, 38 podiums (with contributions from Valtteri Bottas and Felipe Massa with the Williams and Sergio Perez with the Force India) and 33 starts from the front row of the grid. A dominion that was not even dented by the growth of the Ferrari 059/4 Power Unit. The six-cylinder PU106 B was born with new impulse exhausts in place of the Birmann constant pressure system used in 2014. The reason? The adoption of the mobile intake trumpets prohibited the previous year: Cowell needed to "tune" the two phases and to contain the variable trumpets he had to widen the plenum chamber. The introduction of the new system added extra weight high up, negatively affecting the engine's centre of gravity. At Brackley they therefore tried to work on all the components in an attempt to bring the unit back to close to the minimum weight. Moreover, in collaboration with Bosch, the direct injection pressure was taken to close to 500 bar, adopting injectors capable of providing multiple fuel jets.

In Canada, Mercedes debuted its engine No. 2 which benefitted from certain modifications permitted by the FIA without spending any development tokens: detrimental vibrations were neutralised which allowed around 15 horsepower to be recovered, permitting the client teams to make significant progress, although the real leap forwards came on the occasion of the Italian Grand Prix when Mercedes spent all its seven available tokens on the third unit fitted to the Silver Arrows. Attention was focused on the combustion chamber, which was redesigned to favour the adoption of the Turbulent Jet Ignition System that allowed the compression ratio to be raised significantly with the pressure in the chamber thus simulating the self-ignition of the HCCI engine with a special spark plug equipped with a perforated "cap" capable of creating a kind of pre-ignition that could be used to adjust the advance and therefore influence performance. A new fuel was developed by Petronas for this configuration, further improving efficiency which now approached 50%. This feature, which was extended to the other teams from the Russian GP, restored the distance from Ferrari which had been closing in with the revised 059/4 run by Mattia Binotto and his team. Breaking through the 900 hp threshold opened new paths for development for the Brackley engineers who focussed above all on the internal combustion engine, after having got the bets out of the hybrid system.

While Mercedes maintained its power unit hegemony, much curiosity was aroused by Honda's return as an exclusive supplier to McLaren, in the hope of reviving the glory days of the late Eighties when the combination of the Japanese firm and Ron Dennis's team won four consecutive world titles (1989-1991). The Japanese manufacturer supported the Woking team by paying the wages of two World Champions, Fernando Alonso and Jenson Button, in the expectation that they would rapidly conquer the leading positions. The reality was instead unforgiving because McLaren slumped to the penultimate place in the Constructors Championship, followed only by Marussia which had raced with the previous year's car. The rash declarations by Yasuhisa Arai, Honda's F1 chief, who had promised podium performances, had fed unjustified expectations.
Firstly because the Japanese company rejoined the F1 circus a year after the other engine developers who had had the chance to gain invaluable experience with the Power Units, an innovative technical departure that brought together turbocharging and hybrid technology.
Secondly, Honda fielded staff with very little experience of racing and Formula 1.

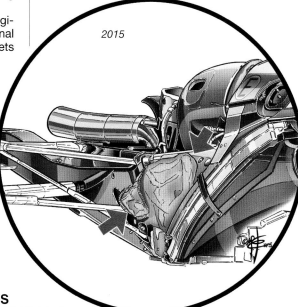

2015

MERCEDES
The drawing highlights the configuration of the Mercedes Power Unit. Clearly visible are the compressor (1) set at the front of the engine (within the chassis), with the oil tank (2) left in the conventional position. The MGU-H electric motor and the large turbine were located at the back of the engine. The position of the turbine (3) was unchanged, while the exhausts were completely revised (4) and no longer contained in a single envelope with very short manifolds but traditional in shape (see the detail drawing), with a notable increase in power. Ferrari instead fitted the compressor-turbine assembly (the turbine being smaller) together with the electric motor in exactly the same way as Renault. In the niche in the chassis, along with the classic oil tanks and the compressor (also present on the McLarens and the Force Indias), the Mercedes and the Williams also carried the intercooler in what was a new configuration for F1.

2

2014

3

4

1

Thirdly, all of the know how from the era of the turbos had been lost, with the firm consequently starting with a blank sheet of paper. Moreover, the new, extremely modern Tochigi Research Centre came on stream over six months late, hence development of the six-cylinder RA615 H was terribly slow and clumsy.

It has to be said that Honda did launch a very interesting project: in contrast with Mercedes which opted for a large turbo to guarantee optimum recharging energy for the hybrid system, the Japanese chose a very small turbocharger with the aim of extracting same power output of the Mercedes unit with a system spinning at over 125,000 rpm. This was the maximum speed of rotation permitted by the 2014 regulations which had yet to be reached by any constructor, with Brackley not having gone beyond 100,000 rpm. This incredible technical challenge was shared with the McLaren technical chiefs Tim Goss and Peter Prodromou who could count on what should have been significant aerodynamic advantages. At the rear the MP4-30 was a reduced-scale version of the 2014 car that earned a "size zero" nickname for the tapering of the engine cover and the pro-

nounced Coke bottle area ahead of the rear wheels. Among the peculiarities of the project was that the compressor was separate from the turbine, mounted almost centrally in an installation different to that of Mercedes. The Japanese equipped their unit with a variable geometry intake system, while Ferrari did without this technology. From the winter tests, first at Jerez and then Barcelona, serious reliability problems were evident and undermined the Japanese enthusiasm. Fernando Alonso collected no less than 12 Power Units in a single season, that is, triple the total provided for by the regulations. The fragility of the internal combustion engine was associated with a lack of turbo reliability which in turn compromised the durability of the MGU-H. In particular, the turbocharger was never run at its projected maximum capacity because there were no bearings on the market able to cope with 125,000 rpm. Honda had to significantly reduce the speed of rotation, encountering difficulties recharging the hybrid system that often deprived the MP4-30 of the necessary maximum speed on the straights. To all this was added a battery (designed by McLaren) that was only capable of functioning within a very restricted temperature window, suffering frequent overheating due to the "size zero" configuration of the car's rear end. Things certainly went no better for Jenson Button who in the Mexican GP

accumulated no less that 70 grid position penalties: the Japanese company had decided to homologate two new units, but had problems with both. The situation had wrong-footed the circus and after this episode it was decided to change the way of calculating the penalties that in the second half of the season had begun to arrive thick and fast for almost everyone. Honda refused to give up on the development of the RA615 H, spending two tokens in Canada, three at Spa for new injectors and camshafts and four at Sochi where a version of the engine was introduced that featured a new combustion chamber and different exhausts. The Japanese marque was given nine tokens over the season, despite having homologated an all-new engine in the February of 2015. This concession was made by the FIA to the manufacturer on its debut, calculating the average value of the tokens saved by the other power unit suppliers: Mercedes 7 (of the 32 allowed in 2015), Ferrari 10 and Renault 12. Moreover, McLaren also benefitted form a fifth engine with no penalty, on the understanding that the start up phase for a new constructor could be more difficult than for firms with experience with the Power Units. Rather than performance (at the end of the season a gap to Mercedes of almost 70 hp was suggested), Honda suffered from a lack of reliability. This was also a major issue

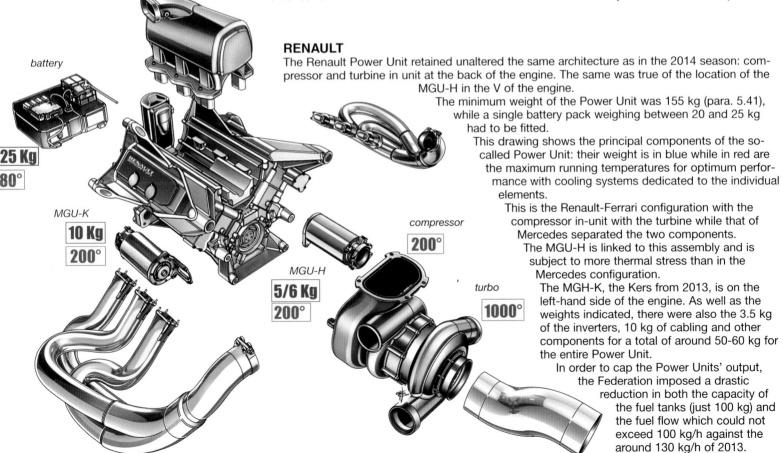

battery

25 Kg
80°

MGU-K

10 Kg
200°

MGU-H

5/6 Kg
200°

compressor

200°

turbo

1000°

RENAULT
The Renault Power Unit retained unaltered the same architecture as in the 2014 season: compressor and turbine in unit at the back of the engine. The same was true of the location of the MGU-H in the V of the engine.

The minimum weight of the Power Unit was 155 kg (para. 5.41), while a single battery pack weighing between 20 and 25 kg had to be fitted.

This drawing shows the principal components of the so-called Power Unit: their weight is in blue while in red are the maximum running temperatures for optimum performance with cooling systems dedicated to the individual elements.

This is the Renault-Ferrari configuration with the compressor in-unit with the turbine while that of Mercedes separated the two components.

The MGU-H is linked to this assembly and is subject to more thermal stress than in the Mercedes configuration.

The MGH-K, the Kers from 2013, is on the left-hand side of the engine. As well as the weights indicated, there were also the 3.5 kg of the inverters, 10 kg of cabling and other components for a total of around 50-60 kg for the entire Power Unit.

In order to cap the Power Units' output, the Federation imposed a drastic reduction in both the capacity of the fuel tanks (just 100 kg) and the fuel flow which could not exceed 100 kg/h against the around 130 kg/h of 2013.

for Renault, which used eight Power Units with the Red Bull drivers and the same number for Max Verstappen in the Toro Rosso, while Carlos Sainz "made do" with seven. The Viry-Châtillon engineers had a stressful season, under constant pressure from the powers that be at Red Bull who spared nothing in their ferocious criticism of the inadequate French engine, going as far as breaking their supply contract with a year still to run. However, they then had to backtrack and apologise to the French manufacturer in order to guarantee the Milton Keynes team the renamed Tag-Heuer Power Unit for 2016 given Mercedes and Ferrari's unwillingness to supply Christian Horner with their "core" technology. Toro Rosso instead reached an agreement with Maranello for a year's supply of the Prancing Horse's Power Unit in 2015 spec. Renault Sport F1, directed by Cyril Abiteboul, suffered a terrible season: on the one hand it was negotiating the acquisition of Lotus to return to the paddock as a chassis manufacturer too, intervening to save the Enstone team which was on the verge of bankruptcy; on the other it paid for the collaboration with Mario Illien, the Swiss consultant brought in by Red Bull who modified the cylinder head and the turbo (a larger unit) to create a more powerful engine but one that

proved more difficult to exploit and which required comprehensive and time-consuming reprogramming. This meant that only Ferrari remained to mount a challenge to Mercedes and in 2015 the Cavallino returned to the winner's circle after a disastrous 2014 in which it failed to win a single race: in his debut season with the Rossa, Sebastian Vettel won three races thanks to a 059/4 Poweer Unit revised under the technical direction of Mattia Binotto with Lorenzo Sassi as the chief designer. The oil tank that on the F14T was located in the gearbox casing, was placed between the engine and the chassis, setting

the six-cylinder unit a few millimetres further back to improve traction. Further developments concerned the direct fuel injection that reached a pressure of 500 bar thanks to the new Magneti Marelli injectors and a suitable fuel pump, while the previous year's six-cylinder turbo did not exceed 350 bar.
Other important modifications were made to the combustion chamber and the pistons, drawing on the collaboration with the AVL engineers in the Racing Department.
The were significant novelties in the turbocharging too: Ferrari adopted larger Honeywell turbines and compressors that

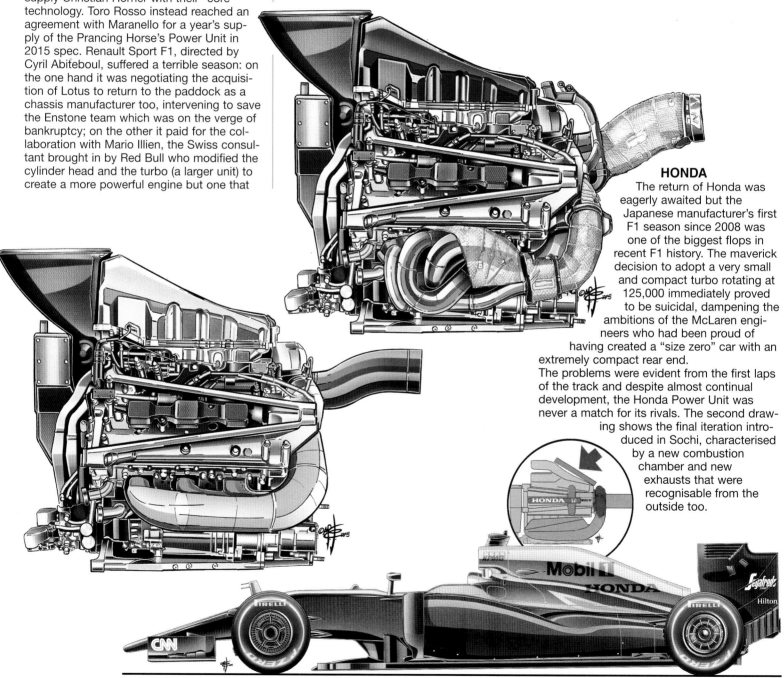

HONDA
The return of Honda was eagerly awaited but the Japanese manufacturer's first F1 season since 2008 was one of the biggest flops in recent F1 history. The maverick decision to adopt a very small and compact turbo rotating at 125,000 immediately proved to be suicidal, dampening the ambitions of the McLaren engineers who had been proud of having created a "size zero" car with an extremely compact rear end.
The problems were evident from the first laps of the track and despite almost continual development, the Honda Power Unit was never a match for its rivals. The second drawing shows the final iteration introduced in Sochi, characterised by a new combustion chamber and new exhausts that were recognisable from the outside too.

required an uprated intercooler that continued to be mounted in the V of the engine given that the Maranello engineers had decided against adopting variable length intake trumpets. The exhausts were redesigned and suitably insulated to avoid the dispersal of heat. In substance, the errors in terms of configuration that had penalised the 2014 Power Unit were corrected. The Prancing Horse team had to thank the technical director James Allison who found a loophole in the regulations that allowed the engineers to develop the Power Units with 32 tokens that were initially not provided for.

The 059/4 made remarkable progress, almost succeeding in closing the gap with respect to the Mercedes (at least until the Monza iteration), but did suffer from certain reliability issues that obliged the specialists at Binotto to programme the season around five units (Räikkönen actually used six), anticipating the rotations. Ferrari took only two iterations of the Power Unit to the track, using the first three tokens in Canada (combustion and camshafts), to which were added the two at Monza (combustion), while the final four were "spent" on a test bench with more of an eye to 2016 rather than the season's finale.

Sauber on the C34 had been using the 059/4, but used the tokens later than the works team, while Marussia raced the 2014 car equipped with the 059/3 Power Unit with modifications made to the exhausts only. Shell made an important contribution by accompanying Ferrari's developments with new fuels during the course of the season. Ferrari's tifosi were at least able to dream, a sign that the management of Sergio Marchionne and the team principal Maurizio Arrivabene had shaken up the team sufficiently for it to regain its pride…

Franco Nugnes

MERCEDES

A comparison between the configurations of the four Power Units raced in the 2015 season. The Mercedes maintained unchanged the layout with the large compressor at the front, the MGU-H in the middle and the large turbine at the back of the engine, with the MGU-K to the bottom left. The intercooler was inside the chassis.

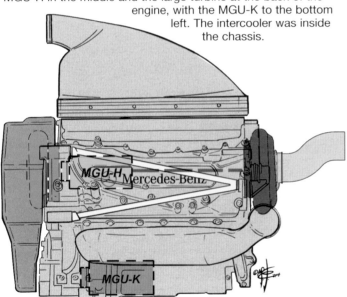

HONDA

Honda went against the tide with a very small compressor designed to spin at the maximum 125,000 rpm permitted by the regulations. Note the unusual position of the intercooler above the intake box, shifted during the season to the rear of the engine above the gearbox.

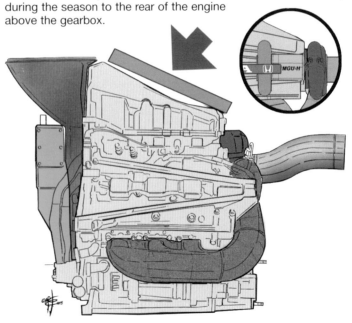

FERRARI AND RENAULT

Compared with the 2014 season, Ferrari relocated the oil tank between the engine and the chassis, like Renault retaining the compact compressor, MGU-H and turbo assembly. The location of the MGU-K was different with Ferrari leaving it inside the gearbox casing and Renault, like Mercedes, leaving it to the side of the engine, bottom left.

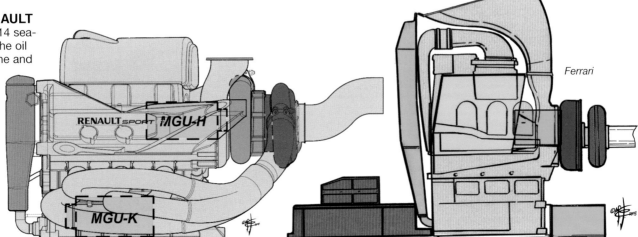

Ferrari

GIORGIO PIOLA

MERCEDES

Paddy Lowe was right when, on the launch of the W06, he pointed out that the car was not just the logical evolution of the W05 from 2014, but a true revolution. The aerodynamic configuration was in fact deceptive thanks to the family look with respect to the final version of the old car introduced at Suzuka, but under the skin everything was different. Beginning with the incredible process of rationalisation in the installation of the various components of the Power Unit and its cooling system which was redesigned from scratch with much better results in terms of heat dispersal with respect to the 2014 car. It was no coincidence that even on the "hot" tracks the W06 never needed bodywork with a greater number of apertures as was the case with the W05. All this entailed a significant improvement in terms of aerodynamics, with fluid dynamics inside the sidepods that were even cleaner and more efficient. Lowe himself admitted that, in terms of aerodynamic efficiency and downforce, the W06 began the season with values better than those of the W05 from late 2014, despite the FIA's new restrictions relating to the nose. The exhausts were thoroughly revised in order to privilege power delivery from the internal combustion engine, with longer manifolds that were no sacrificed as on the W05 where they were enclosed in a kind of lung to the detriment of power delivery. This was achieved without reducing the supply of heat for the electric motor attached to the turbo and without creating a blockage effect upstream of the radiators that were more inclined with respect to 2014.

In developing the Power Unit, the Stuttgart firm spent 24 of the 32 tokens available for the winter phase, not using the other eight until Monza where a new Petronas fuel was also introduced. In practice, a version that represented the basis for the 2016 unit, with modifications above all to the combustion chamber. One of the Mercedes' great advantages was that when necessary it could exploit the most extreme power delivery mode in Q3 beyond the 15-second limit with respect to the client teams. The position of the compressor at the front of the engine was unchanged, separated from the turbo that was mounted at the rear. The dual gearbox casing and the lower front suspension wishbone with the tuning fork-like narrow base were also retained.

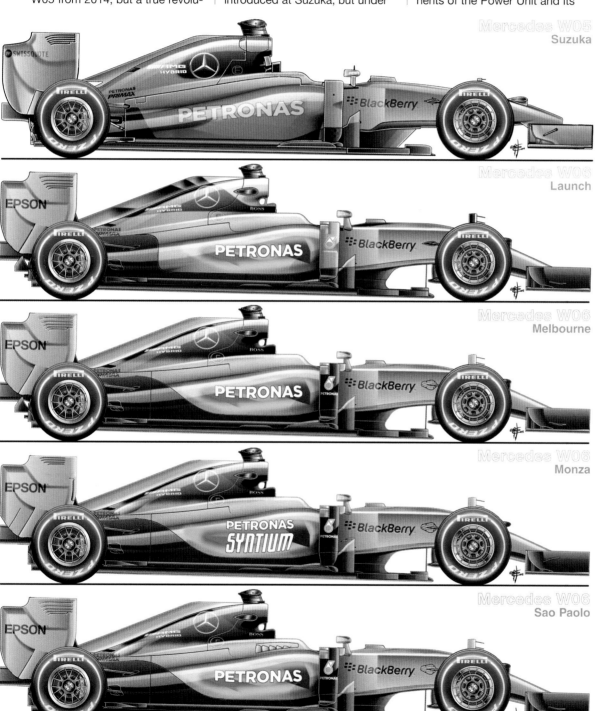

Mercedes W05
Suzuka

Mercedes W06
Launch

Mercedes W06
Melbourne

Mercedes W06
Monza

Mercedes W06
Sao Paolo

There were instead innovations in the braking system, which did however remain Mercedes' weakness, despite six pistons being adopted on the rear calipers rather than four. This was to guarantee reliability even in the case of the failure of the BBW electronic rear braking control system, as had happened during the 2014 Canadian GP. The four-pot configuration was instead retained by Sauber, McLaren and Red Bull, which had introduced it (together with the then Brawn GP) back in 2009.

With the W06, Mercedes again decided not to take advantage of neither the "rake" set-up that had been tested in in-door simulations nor the blown front hub feature. The advantage obtained by improved extraction of the flow from the front wing was foiled by the interference generated by the vortexes created by the blowing effect. Aerodynamic development was nonetheless constant, almost at every race, with the most important step coming in China with the appearance of a new front wing with the peripheral area adjacent to the endplates completely revised so as to better direct the flow towards the outside of the front wheels.

The arched area, equipped with no less than eight slots, had a more aggressive section, modified in the intermediate vanes and the endplates. This feature was gradually copied by Mercedes' rivals. In Canada, in order to improve ERS reliability, a larger radiator was mounted behind the Power Unit, a change that entailed a slight swelling in the engine cover.

In free practice on the Friday at Spa, Mercedes introduced an all new feature without even comparing it with the previous configuration. This was the rear wing designed specifically for the circuit that represented a clear break with the recent past: a "spoon" wing had never previously been seen on the cars from Stuttgart. However, once again the wing was actually a re-rehashing of a technical feature that had been fashionable for many years; we have to go back as far as 2006 to find the first dished rear spoon wing, when Adrian Newey created the wing for the McLaren MP4-21. This feature was then reprised by

Bar Honda, Williams and Sauber, and always used on the fast circuits of Bahrain, Montreal and Spa. Taken to scrutineering on the Thursday evening, this wing was retained on both cars while almost all the other teams preferred to run comparison tests before making their choices for the race.

A further evolution was seen at Monza, with a wing designed to guarantee maximum speed on the straights. A slightly waved main profile, combined with a flap with a small Gurney flap and a Monkey Seat were instead raced in Belgium. Although not evident to the naked eye, there was also a modification in the area of the lower front wishbone, subjected to a control with paint during practice on the Friday on both cars.

A specific aerodynamic package was introduced for Suzuka. The main modifications were concentrated at the rear with new endplates equipped with a Red Bull-style vertical slot on the leading edge, which was very long compared with the one used throughout the season, combined with a series of features seen on the medium-downforce tracks. Both the main profile and the flap were those from Bahrain with the trailing edge trimmed at 45° in the area adjacent to the endplates combined, however with the mono-profile Monkey Seat used at Spa. The horizontal U-shaped duct in the end part of the sidepod was widened.

There was a new front wing configuration with a kind of serrated trailing edge applied to the second flap that reprised the concepts of the dual serrations introduced by McLaren on the rear wing for the German GP in 2014 and applied to both the trailing edge of the main profile and the leading edge of the flap.

The shrouds hurriedly created to heat the rear tyres were also revised, while at the front in order to direct heat inside the wheels and therefore to the tyres, open brake ducts were used.

Surprisingly, Austin saw a return of the ears either side of the engine air intake in view of the Mexican GP where there was a greater need for heat dispersal. In order to compensate for the loss of power due to the altitude,

the maximum speed of rotation of the MGU-H in fact had to be increased.

The final decisive step came in Brazil with an on track verification of features to be transferred to the 2016 project. The salient points concerned: a simulation of the S-Duct and above all a new front suspension configuration with the rocker emerging from the upper part of the chassis. This experiment is to be seen in the light of the 2016 chassis which will be higher from the ground, with a different position for the driver and his feet and the suspension naturally raised, albeit by little. This is to allow a greater flow of air in the lower section. The complex operation to remove all the suspension elements and the pedal box suggested that the new configuration featured hydraulic interconnection with the braking system, with a stiffening of the assembly to maintain a constant ride height. At Abu Dhabi there was then a final experiment in view of the 2016 season with the use of a "magnetic" band on the back of the main profile and the flap, applied in both cases to the leading edge.

TOP VIEW COMPARISON

The Mercedes W06 was not so much the logical evolution of 2014's W05 but rather a true revolution. The family feeling in the appearance of the aerodynamic package concealed an all-new arrangement of the mechanical organs. The fluid dynamics within the sidepods were improved to the point that apertures at even hot tracks were reduced to a minimum, despite the much more tightly tapered bodywork in the Coke bottle area. (1) The nose of the W06 was very short (2) while the W05 had to dispute the first races with a long nose, the short version (dotted) only arriving at the Spanish GP. (3) The new front wing was very sophisticated with the peripheral area close to the endplates thoroughly revised so as to better direct the air flow towards the outside of the front wheels. The arched area adjacent to the endplates had no less than eight slots. (4) The steering arm of the W05 was found at the height of the upper wishbone and was lowered so as to increase the chord of the broad profile created together with the narrow-base lower wishbone.
(5) The aerodynamics at the front of the sidepods was very different, in particular with respect to the version of the W05 from the start of the year. (6) In the overhead view, the greatest difference can be seen in the particularly tapering rear section. (7) A great deal of work was done in the area ahead of the rear wheels.
(8) The end part of the sidepods comprised a kind of arch to better direct the flows towards the diffuser.
(9) Another very delicate zone was that of the diffuser near the tyres, with a kind of forward facing turning vane.

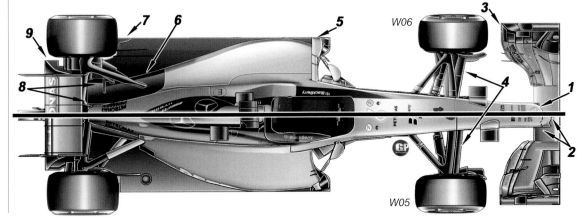

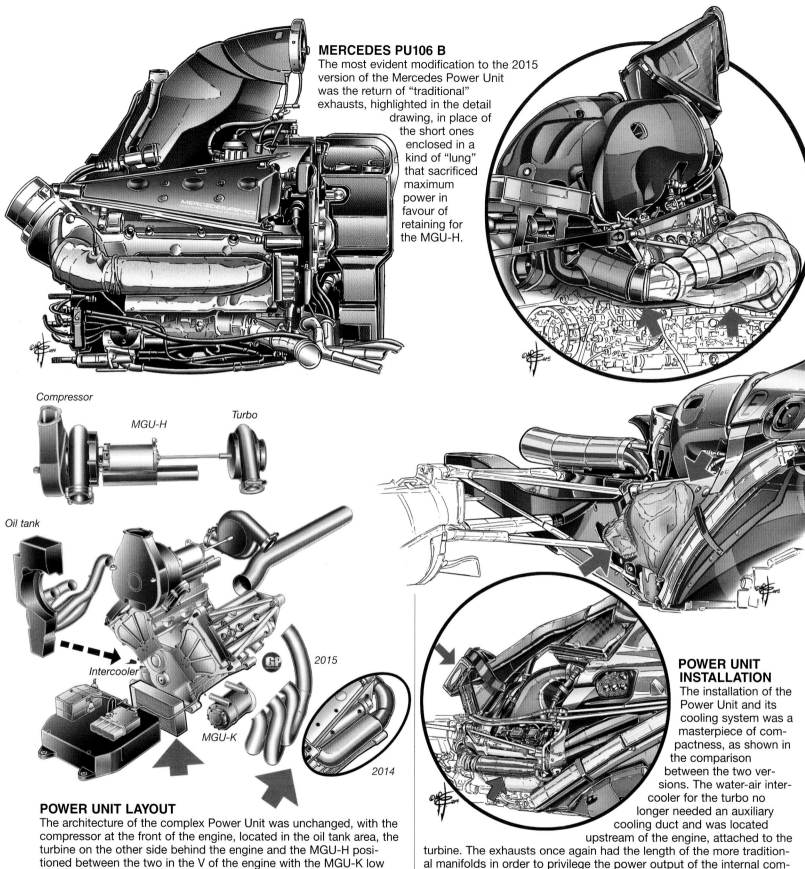

MERCEDES PU106 B

The most evident modification to the 2015 version of the Mercedes Power Unit was the return of "traditional" exhausts, highlighted in the detail drawing, in place of the short ones enclosed in a kind of "lung" that sacrificed maximum power in favour of retaining for the MGU-H.

Compressor

MGU-H

Turbo

Oil tank

Intercooler

2015

MGU-K

2014

POWER UNIT LAYOUT

The architecture of the complex Power Unit was unchanged, with the compressor at the front of the engine, located in the oil tank area, the turbine on the other side behind the engine and the MGU-H positioned between the two in the V of the engine with the MGU-K low down on the left-hand side. The location of the intercooler inside the chassis was also unchanged. The only difference that could be noted from the outside concerned the "traditional" exhaust manifolds. In the insert, the sacrificed 2014 feature.

POWER UNIT INSTALLATION

The installation of the Power Unit and its cooling system was a masterpiece of compactness, as shown in the comparison between the two versions. The water-air intercooler for the turbo no longer needed an auxiliary cooling duct and was located upstream of the engine, attached to the turbine. The exhausts once again had the length of the more traditional manifolds in order to privilege the power output of the internal combustion engine without affecting the efficiency of the MGU-H. Also of note was the shape of the gearbox casing with the raised differential assembly freeing up the whole of the lower area and creating what, from the outside, may be defined as kind of keel.

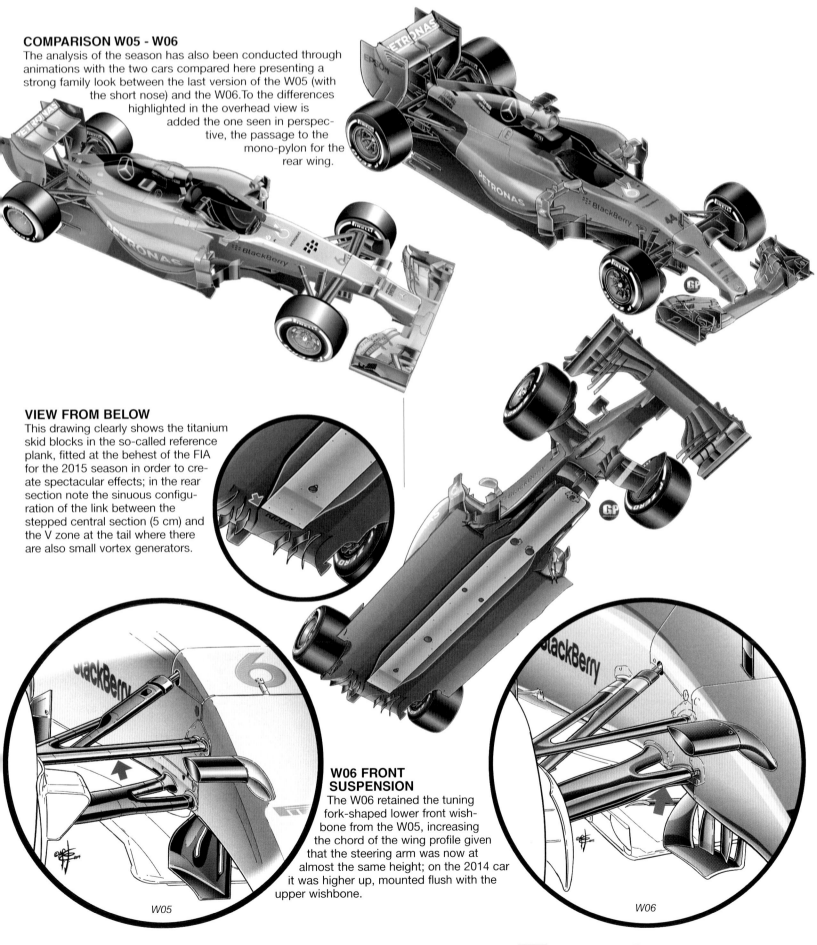

COMPARISON W05 - W06

The analysis of the season has also been conducted through animations with the two cars compared here presenting a strong family look between the last version of the W05 (with the short nose) and the W06. To the differences highlighted in the overhead view is added the one seen in perspective, the passage to the mono-pylon for the rear wing.

VIEW FROM BELOW

This drawing clearly shows the titanium skid blocks in the so-called reference plank, fitted at the behest of the FIA for the 2015 season in order to create spectacular effects; in the rear section note the sinuous configuration of the link between the stepped central section (5 cm) and the V zone at the tail where there are also small vortex generators.

W06 FRONT SUSPENSION

The W06 retained the tuning fork-shaped lower front wishbone from the W05, increasing the chord of the wing profile given that the steering arm was now at almost the same height; on the 2014 car it was higher up, mounted flush with the upper wishbone.

W05

W06

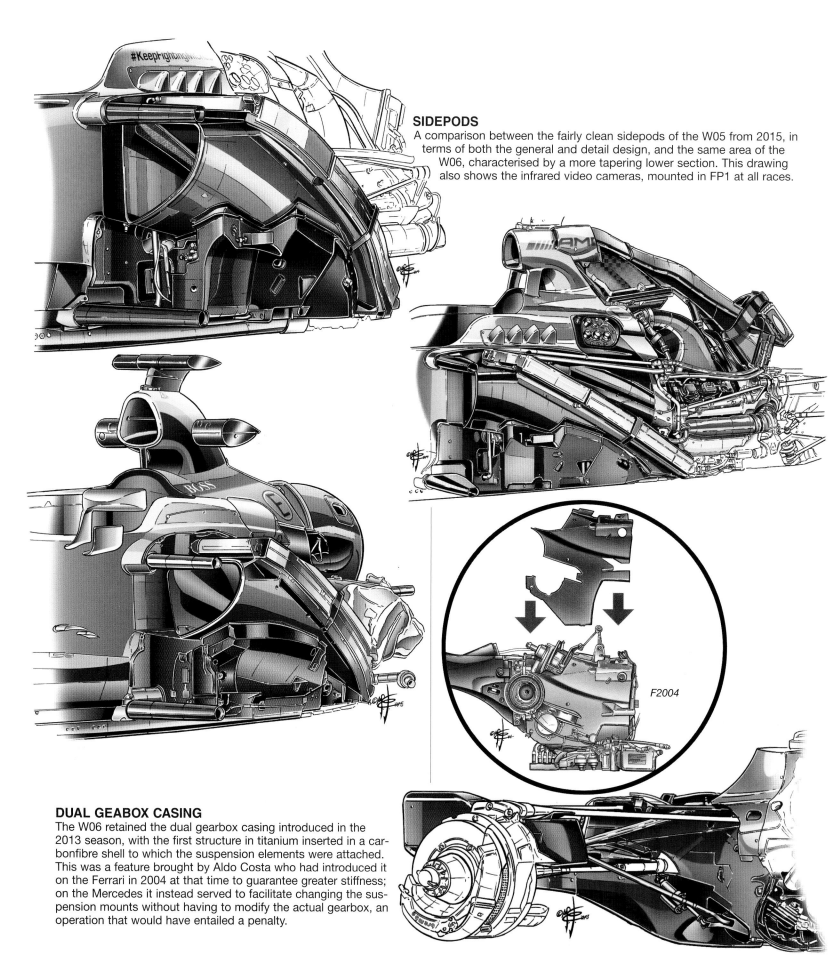

SIDEPODS

A comparison between the fairly clean sidepods of the W05 from 2015, in terms of both the general and detail design, and the same area of the W06, characterised by a more tapering lower section. This drawing also shows the infrared video cameras, mounted in FP1 at all races.

F2004

DUAL GEABOX CASING

The W06 retained the dual gearbox casing introduced in the 2013 season, with the first structure in titanium inserted in a carbonfibre shell to which the suspension elements were attached. This was a feature brought by Aldo Costa who had introduced it on the Ferrari in 2004 at that time to guarantee greater stiffness; on the Mercedes it instead served to facilitate changing the suspension mounts without having to modify the actual gearbox, an operation that would have entailed a penalty.

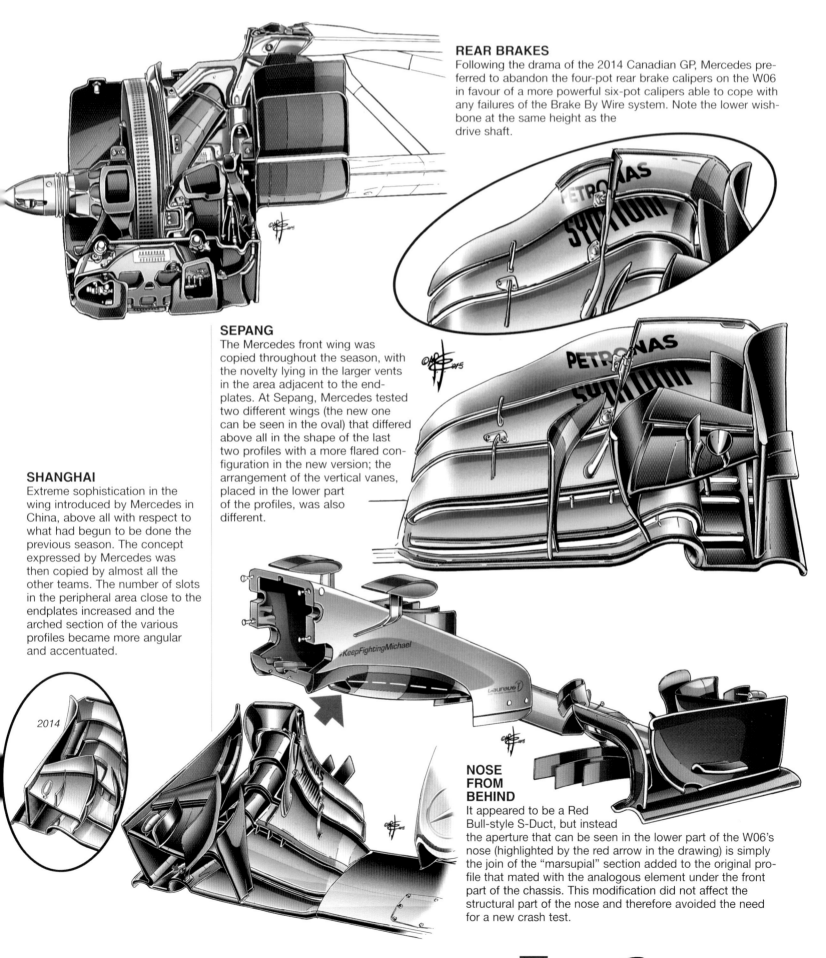

REAR BRAKES

Following the drama of the 2014 Canadian GP, Mercedes preferred to abandon the four-pot rear brake calipers on the W06 in favour of a more powerful six-pot calipers able to cope with any failures of the Brake By Wire system. Note the lower wishbone at the same height as the drive shaft.

SEPANG

The Mercedes front wing was copied throughout the season, with the novelty lying in the larger vents in the area adjacent to the endplates. At Sepang, Mercedes tested two different wings (the new one can be seen in the oval) that differed above all in the shape of the last two profiles with a more flared configuration in the new version; the arrangement of the vertical vanes, placed in the lower part of the profiles, was also different.

SHANGHAI

Extreme sophistication in the wing introduced by Mercedes in China, above all with respect to what had begun to be done the previous season. The concept expressed by Mercedes was then copied by almost all the other teams. The number of slots in the peripheral area close to the endplates increased and the arched section of the various profiles became more angular and accentuated.

2014

NOSE FROM BEHIND

It appeared to be a Red Bull-style S-Duct, but instead the aperture that can be seen in the lower part of the W06's nose (highlighted by the red arrow in the drawing) is simply the join of the "marsupial" section added to the original profile that mated with the analogous element under the front part of the chassis. This modification did not affect the structural part of the nose and therefore avoided the need for a new crash test.

GIORGIO PIOLA

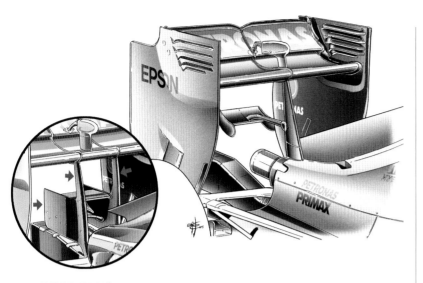

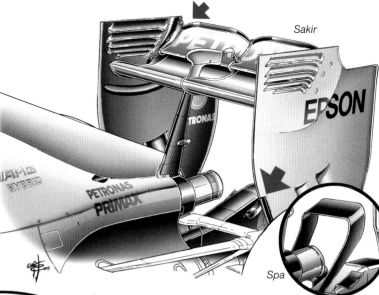

Sakir

Spa

REAR WING
Together with the appearance of the mono-pylon rear wing support arrived a simpler Monkey Seat fitted from the debut. In the detail, the dual pylon and the old Monkey Seat with large, square-cut endplates.

SAKHIR
In Bahrain, Mercedes retained the medium-low downforce wing introduced in China and characterised by the flap trimmed in proximity to the endplates (red arrow).

BARCELONA
The most important feature introduced in Spain concerned this air intake that might not have been devoted solely to the cooling of the rear end, which was even more tapered especially in the lower area. In many ways it resembled the vent in the central area of the Red Bull diffuser seen two years ago.

BARCELONA
In Spain, Mercedes introduced a package of micro-developments, with small fins applied at various points of the car, such as these either side of the deformable structure, all designed to recover downforce.

2014

MONACO
At Monaco there was a maximum downforce rear wing with the reappearance of the twin profile Monkey Seat introduced at this track in 2014.

MONTREAL

A new engine cover was seen in Canada with this swelling in the lower section that revealed an important modification affecting reliability: the presence of a larger ERS radiator to avoid the issues that arose in 2014.

EXPOSED DISCS

At Monaco and then in Canada, Mercedes used completely open front brake ducts so as to improve heat dispersal from the Carbon Industrie discs with four aligned holes.

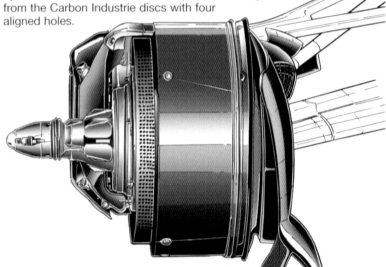

MONTREAL

Seen at Montreal but effectively adopted in the tests following the Spanish GP, this long turning vane resembled those placed laterally at the front of the sidepods and until then never applied to the brake ducts.

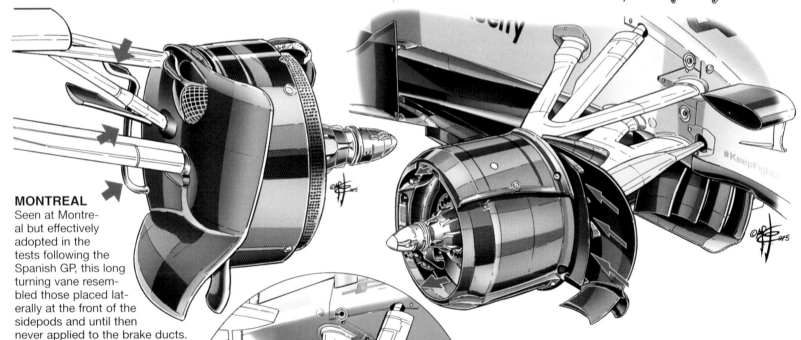

COMPARISON
OPEN AND CLOSED BRAKE DUCTS

This drawing illustrates the front brake duct used most often: the closed version, with the vent towards the outside. Highlighted in yellow is the aerodynamic profile around the steering arm that joined the enormous profile of the narrow-base lower wishbone.

A comparison with the open brake ducts with the air all venting towards the outside, used on the tracks particular hard on the braking systems.

Note the fairing that channelled air to the Brembo six-pot calipers.

ZELTWEG

Mercedes took to the extreme the possibility of mounting the rear wishbone son a plate rather directly on the hub, in this case it was relatively high to create both a different suspension geometry and to free up in aerodynamic terms the lower area of the brake ducts, which had become increasingly important in creating rear axle downforce.

BUDAPEST

On the Friday at Budapest, Mercedes tested a new very simple Monkey Seat with a single profile that was then shelved ahead of qualifying and the race in favour of the version with no profile (insert).

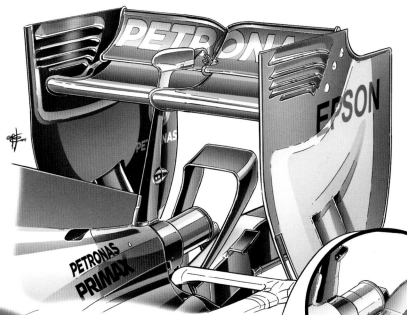

SPA

There was a surprise at Spa with Mercedes using throughout the weekend a brand new feature without even conducting a brief comparison test with the Montreal rear wing. This was a new spoon wing, a feature first seen in 2006 on Newey's McLaren MP4/21 and since then copied by other teams such as Williams (2011), Bar Honda and Sauber. It was not seen on any other car in 2015, however.

McLaren 2006/2007

Williams 2011

MONZA

Another new wing for the Mercedes after the spoon wing introduced in Belgium. This one specifically for Monza was used to reduce still further the downforce; as in Belgium it was used from the first lap of the track without any comparative testing.

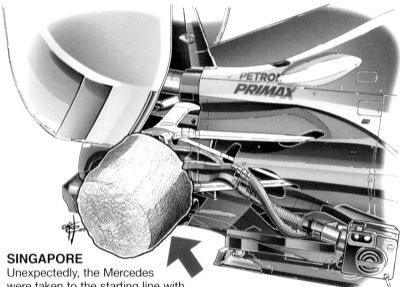

SINGAPORE

Unexpectedly, the Mercedes were taken to the starting line with rudimentary shrouds to warm the rear brakes and allow the starting pressure of the tyres to be increased, getting around the pressure check at the start introduced at Monza.

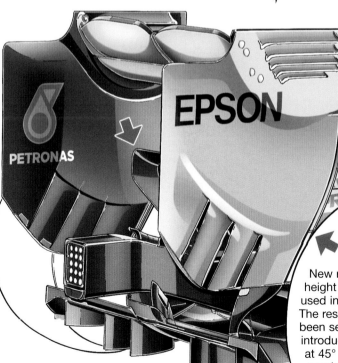

SOCHI

Sochi saw the debut of the definitive carbonfibre shrouds for warming the rear brakes at the start, introduced in provisional form in Singapore.

SUZUKA

New rear wing endplates, with a Red Bull-style full height vertical slot in place of the much shorter one used in the previous races.
The rest was a blend of features that had already been seen: the main profile and the flap were those introduced in Bahrain with the trailing edge trimmed at 45° in the area in proximity to the endplates, combined with the small single profile Monkey Seat used at Spa.

GIORGIO PIOLA

SOCHI FRONT WING

At Sochi Mercedes introduced the small tooth-like vortex generators seen the previous season on the McLaren. The novelty was that on the Silver Arrows the feature was mounted on the second flap of the front wing, while on the cars from Woking it was on the two rear wing profiles from the 2014 German GP.

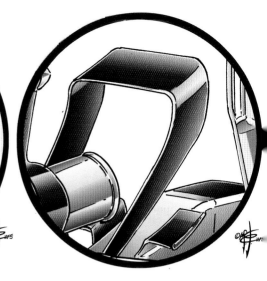

MEXICO

In the Friday morning practice session in Mexico, Mercedes tested the two versions of the Monkey Seat, adopting the higher downforce version for the rest of the weekend.

SAO PAOLO

In Brazil, Mercedes conducted an experiment with an eye to the 2016 season. The S-Duct-type intake seen on the Friday morning in reality concealed a much more important experiment: the simulation of a chassis with a higher ground clearance to allow a greater flow of air in the lower section and, above all, a new front suspension configuration

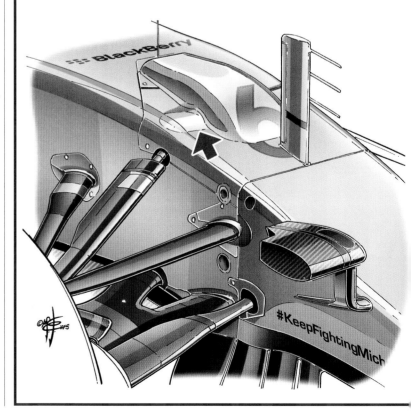

AIRBOX INTAKES

In the detail drawing the ducts added to the Mercedes engine cover in Mexico to compensate for the rarefied atmosphere and to provide additional cooling for the MGU-H; this feature had already been tested on the Friday at Austin.

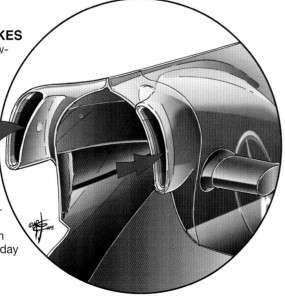

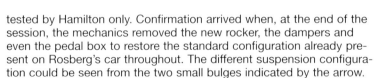

ABU DHABI

Testing of the front suspension continued at Abu Dhabi too. The two drawings show a comparison between the traditional version and the one that had first been tested in Brazil by Hamilton and then adopted at Abu Dhabi by both drivers. The traditional version was equipped (the only example in the current F1 field) with a large coaxial spring in place of the smaller disc springs or Bellville discs used by all the other teams. The 2016 feature was easily recognisable thanks to this large hydraulic damper interconnected between the two wheels.

tested by Hamilton only. Confirmation arrived when, at the end of the session, the mechanics removed the new rocker, the dampers and even the pedal box to restore the standard configuration already present on Rosberg's car throughout. The different suspension configuration could be seen from the two small bulges indicated by the arrow.

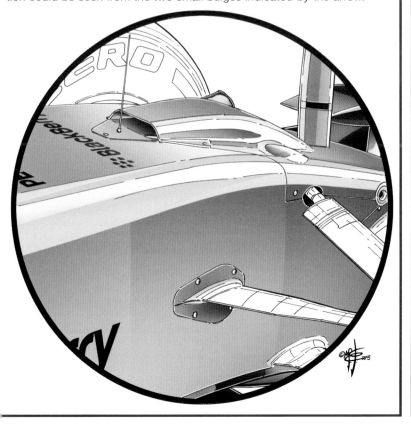

HALO

The Mercedes team designed on behalf of the FIA the Halo protection structure at the sides of the cockpit, of which a frame from the animation created for the Chinese GP is published here.

FERRARI

CONSTRUCTORS' CLASSIFICATION			
	2014	2015	
Position	4°	2°	+2▲
Points	216	428	+212▲

Under the direction of Sergio Marchionne and Maurizio Arrivabene, Ferrari was once again a protagonist in the 2015 season, finishing as the second force in the field behind Mercedes and immediately cancelling the disappointing 2014 campaign that failed to produce a single victory (for the first time since back in 1993) and finished with 4th place in the constructors' championship as in 2009.

The promise of two victories made on the occasion of the launch of the SF15T was exceeded with a total of three wins (Malaysia, Hungary and Singapore) and a pole position – all results achieved by Sebastian Vettel – in a year once again dominated by Mercedes. Much of the merit for this up turn in fortunes is to be attributed to the internal restructuring initiated by the new manage but above all

to the overhauling of the entire 2015 project. In practice, all the weaknesses of the F14T were eliminated, starting with the extravagant new location of the oil tank at the back of the engine, more precisely inside the gearbox casing. This feature had been abandoned in 1999 as from the previous year Stewart and Arrows had located the tank at the front of the engine in niche created in the chassis.

The F14T therefore stepped back no less than 16 years, but without obtaining the success that in 2009 Adrian Newey had had when he reprised the pull-rod layout for the rear suspension, which subsequently became generalised on the current F1 cars. Just a year later what had seemed a winning feature was rightly abandoned in favour of the standard configuration with the tank between engine and chassis. This decision permitted a cleaner installation of the cooling system, another area in which the SF15T made a clean break with the features adopted on the previous cars from Maranello. The radiators became very long and narrow, favouring the sidepod sections. This feature, together with others, led to a slight lengthening of the wheelbase (around 5-6 cm) without affecting other characteristics of the SF15T such as the location within the V of the engine of the intercooler and the MGU-H electric motor that in practice formed a single "package" with the compressor and the turbine, suitably oversized with respect to the 2014 version. A great deal of work was also done on the internal combustion engine and the so-called electrical part with improved interaction between the two components. The exhausts remained fairly traditional and not sacrificed as on the 2014 Mercedes. They were, however, integrated with the gearbox spacer, adopting the internal passage configuration already introduced by Mercedes and its client teams in 2014. They were, above all, designed so as to avoid dispersal of the heat that would be used for the MGU-H. The front brake calipers were underslung, albeit not in the extreme configuration seen on the Red Bull, with a slight angle upwards at the rear. The Mercedes-style front suspension was very interesting with the difference that on the SF15T the steering arm was incorporated in

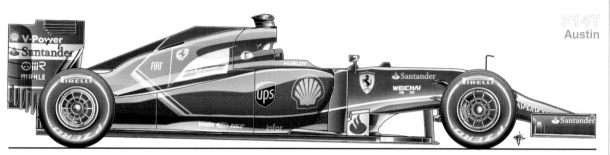

F14T
Austin

SF15T
Melbourne

SF15T
Sepang

SF15T
Barcelona

the upper wishbone so as to create a wide aerodynamic profile working in synergy with the even more extreme lower wishbone. The brake air intakes were also new with the shrouds blowing to the outside.

It should be noted that Ferrari, Red Bull and McLaren had the wide front wheel hub venting towards the outside.

The evolution of the car saw a fundamental step at the Spanish GP with the appearance of what was almost a "B" version, with novelties not only in the wings but also the body of the car, the sidepods being "stepped" at the front, new turning vanes both in the lower section of the car and the front part of the sidepods where vertical turning vanes were introduced. This type of sidepod was retained on the medium/high downforce tracks, alternating with the "base" version instead used on the fast circuits.

The novelties in any case arrived in small doses at almost every race and, importantly, always passed the track test.

Another major step came in Singapore, with the race seeing a third victory for Sebastian Vettel who was able to get the best out of the "rake" set-up thanks in part to the introduction of an advanced aerodynamic package. Much interest was aroused by the nine slots in the area of the stepped bottom ahead of the rear wheels and were immediately copied. The final evolution of the car was presented at Austin with a new front wing, turning vanes under the chassis, brake air intakes and modifications to the diffuser.

With regard to the engine, the 059 represented a major step forward thanks to the adoption of Magneti Marelli injectors capable of working at a pressure of 500 bar, together with a suitable fuel pump (the six-cylinder turbo from 2014 ran a maximum of 350 bar). Other major interventions concerned the combustion chambers, the pistons and above all the tur-

bocharging, with larger Honeywell turbine and compressor. This required a larger intercooler, as ever mounted in the V of the engine, thanks to the decision not to fit variable length intake trumpets. The exhaust were also redesigned and suitably insulated so as to avoid heat dispersal. During the course of the season Ferrari raced only two evolutions of the Power Unit, using the first three tokens in Canada (combustion and camshafts) then two more at Monza (combustion), while the last four were "spent" on an evolution that was bench tested at the time of the Sochi GP, ahead of the 2016 season and therefore not taken to the track for the last four races.

FRONT COMPARISON

The SF15T abandoned the short, square-cut nose of the F14T in favour of a very long ogival shape with a slight V in the lower section. The front wing elements were all new, profiles, flaps, raised flaps and endplates.

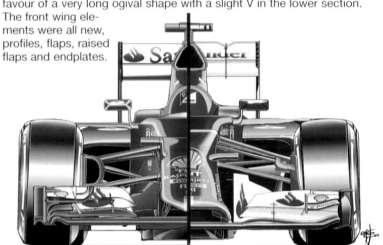

SF15T
Budapest

SF15T
Monza

SF15T
Singapore

SF15T
Austin

OVERHEAD VIEW

The SF15T distinguished itself as the car with the longest nose in the field (1), with a fairly sophisticated shape in the lower section: a kind of V-shaped droplet designed to direct the flows in the lower part of the car. This configuration was retained throughout the season. The entire front wing as seen at the presentation was new, starting with the simpler endplates. Interesting novelties were immediately apparent in the area of the front suspension with the adoption of a very narrow lower wishbone (3) similar to that introduced by Mercedes in 2014. A great deal of work was done on the cooling, with the sidepods more voluminous at the front (4) but tapering sharply (5) in the so-called Coke bottle area, channelling all the hot air to the rear (6). The wheelbase was extended by a few centimetres (7). Both the rear (8) and the front suspension were designed with an eye to aerodynamics.

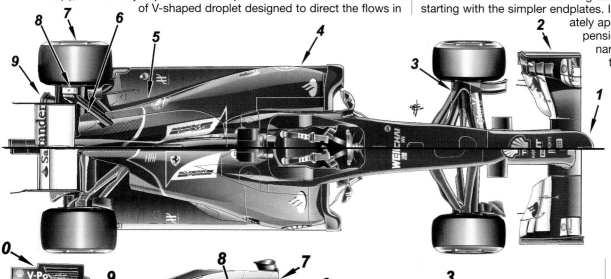

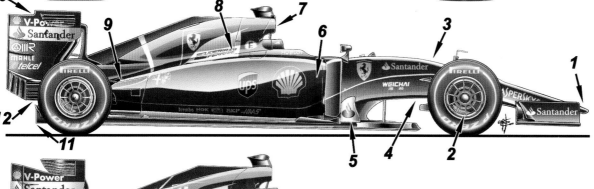

POWER UNIT COMPARISON

The great difference between the F14T and the SF15T was the return of the oil reservoir (1) to a location between engine and chassis rather than inside the gearbox spacer. The MGU-K (2) instead remained in the gearbox upstream of the engine. The position of the turbine-compressor assembly (3) was unchanged as was that of the intercooler (4) within the V of the engine.

SIDE VIEWS

The virtually clean break with the previous F14T can also be seen in stylistic terms with a darker red and the Alfa Romeo instead of Fiat badging re-establishing the link between the cars from Maranello and the origins of the Scuderia Ferrari. The droplet-shaped nose (1) was very long and the endplates were also a new design. For the first time, the front brake calipers were underslung so as to exploit to the full the lowering of the centre of gravity of the pull-rod suspension.

3-4) The chassis had softer lines low down like that of the 2014 Mercedes, with the monocoque descending earlier compared with the F14T, as can be seen in the profile comparison. There were also new turning vanes (5), located ahead of the sidepods like the vertical ones. 6) The sidepods started higher and were rounded, with the lower part sharply cut away. The air intake (7) had a second mouth in the lower section as on the 2014 Toro Rosso. Much work was also done on the Power Unit (8) with the adoption of a larger turbine-compressor assembly to better exploit the MGU-H which was also associated with a new exhaust configuration. The whole of the rear end (9) was very close-coupled and tapering. The new rear wing introduced in Austin (10) had a new feature in the lower section. Immediately behind the rear wheels horizontal fringes (12) were applied that were designed to optimize the negative lift generated by the Red Bull-style new diffuser (11).

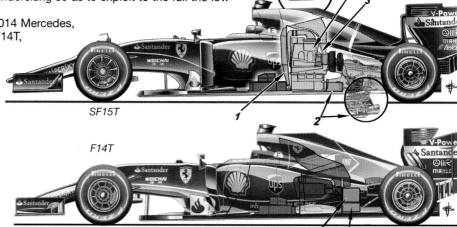

SF15T

F14T

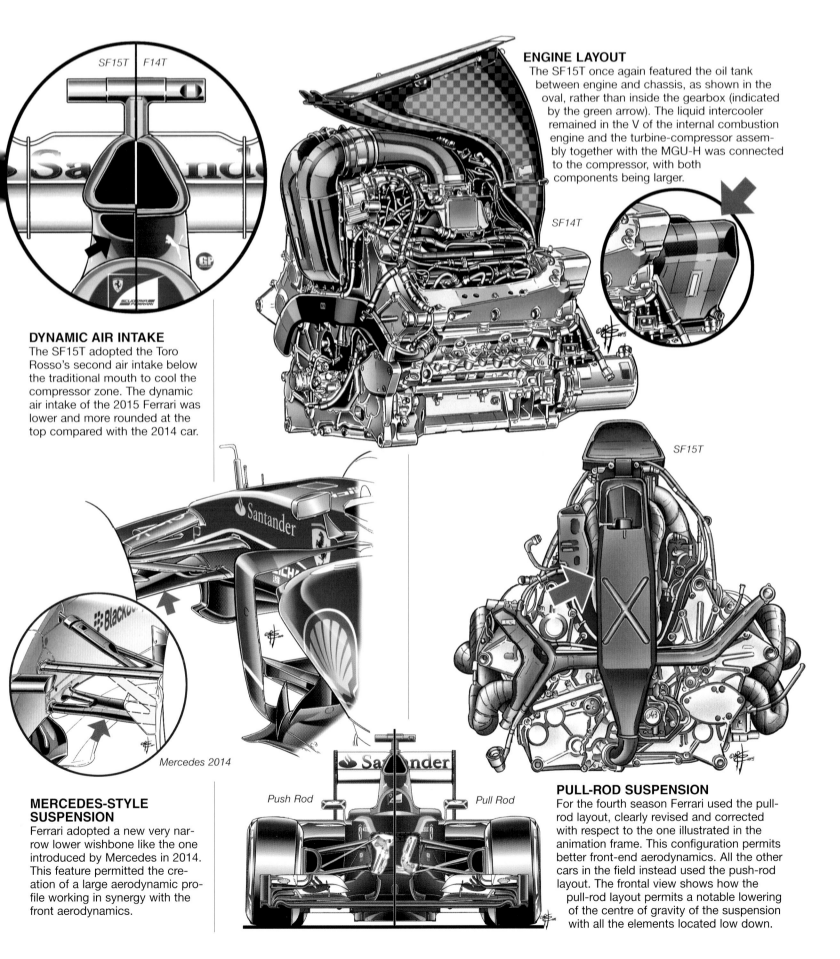

DYNAMIC AIR INTAKE

The SF15T adopted the Toro Rosso's second air intake below the traditional mouth to cool the compressor zone. The dynamic air intake of the 2015 Ferrari was lower and more rounded at the top compared with the 2014 car.

ENGINE LAYOUT

The SF15T once again featured the oil tank between engine and chassis, as shown in the oval, rather than inside the gearbox (indicated by the green arrow). The liquid intercooler remained in the V of the internal combustion engine and the turbine-compressor assembly together with the MGU-H was connected to the compressor, with both components being larger.

SF14T

SF15T

Mercedes 2014

MERCEDES-STYLE SUSPENSION

Ferrari adopted a new very narrow lower wishbone like the one introduced by Mercedes in 2014. This feature permitted the creation of a large aerodynamic profile working in synergy with the front aerodynamics.

Push Rod

Pull Rod

PULL-ROD SUSPENSION

For the fourth season Ferrari used the pull-rod layout, clearly revised and corrected with respect to the one illustrated in the animation frame. This configuration permits better front-end aerodynamics. All the other cars in the field instead used the push-rod layout. The frontal view shows how the pull-rod layout permits a notable lowering of the centre of gravity of the suspension with all the elements located low down.

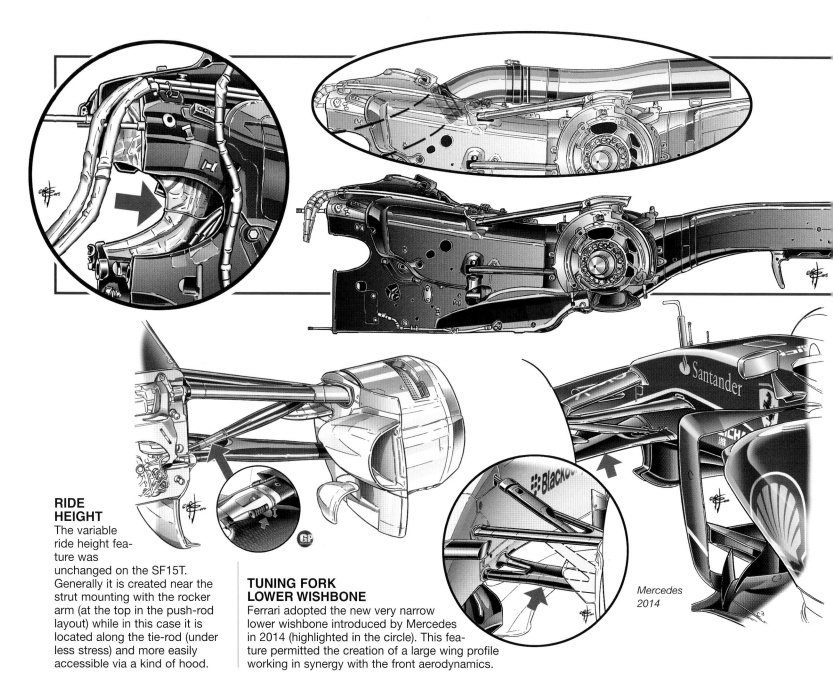

RIDE HEIGHT

The variable ride height feature was unchanged on the SF15T. Generally it is created near the strut mounting with the rocker arm (at the top in the push-rod layout) while in this case it is located along the tie-rod (under less stress) and more easily accessible via a kind of hood.

TUNING FORK LOWER WISHBONE

Ferrari adopted the new very narrow lower wishbone introduced by Mercedes in 2014 (highlighted in the circle). This feature permitted the creation of a large wing profile working in synergy with the front aerodynamics.

Mercedes 2014

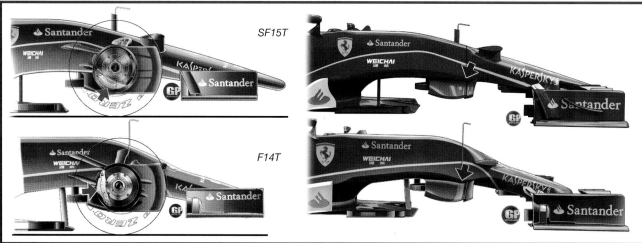

SF15T

F14T

UNDERSLUNG BRAKES

On the SF15T for the first time, the front brake calipers were underslung so as to exploit to the full the lowering of the centre of gravity offered by the pull-rod suspension. This was in reality a feature already in use for

GEARBOX SPACER

The Ferrari SF15T adopted the exhaust configuration with the pipe passing through the long gearbox spacer as on the 2014 cars with Mercedes Power Units.
To improve the aerodynamics, the exhaust pipes were compacted low down and entered the gearbox spacer before exiting from the upper part, with the large tail pipe dimensioned according to the regulations. In practice, the exhausts of the SF15T pass through the space left vacant by the moving of the oil tank from the spacer to between the chassis and the engine, as was the case with the F14T and highlighted in the comparison.
This feature also permitted the optimization of the exhaust manifold lengths.

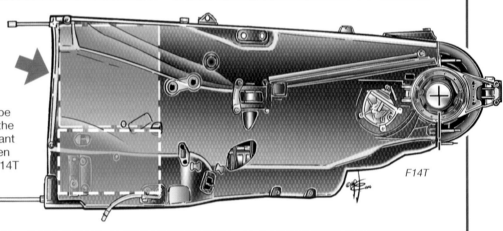

F14T

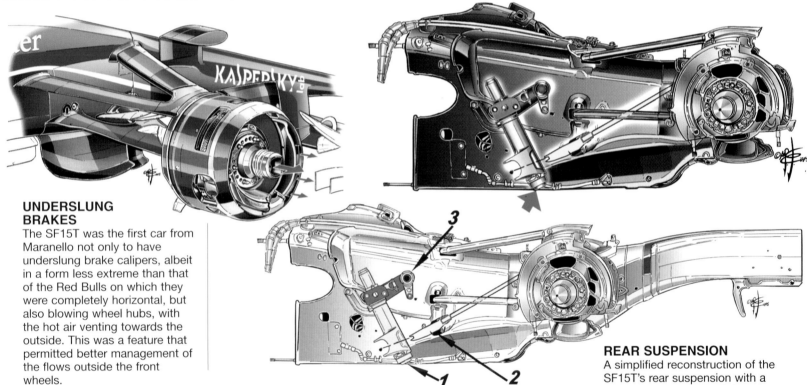

UNDERSLUNG BRAKES

The SF15T was the first car from Maranello not only to have underslung brake calipers, albeit in a form less extreme than that of the Red Bulls on which they were completely horizontal, but also blowing wheel hubs, with the hot air venting towards the outside. This was a feature that permitted better management of the flows outside the front wheels.

REAR SUSPENSION

A simplified reconstruction of the SF15T's rear suspension with a pull-rod layout as on all the other cars and with the torsion bar (1) removable from the bottom; the suspension tie-rod was linked to the rocker arm by a second element (2). The anti-roll bar was instead easily removable (3).

many seasons not just by Red Bull. Note also the blowing wheel nut with a more extreme configuration than that of the F14T.
The comparison without wheels instead highlights the less stepped configuration of the lower part of the chassis offering aerodynamics less sensitive to ride height variations.
This stepped configuration is visible in the detail drawing of the F14T, highlighted by the red arrow.

GIORGIO PIOLA

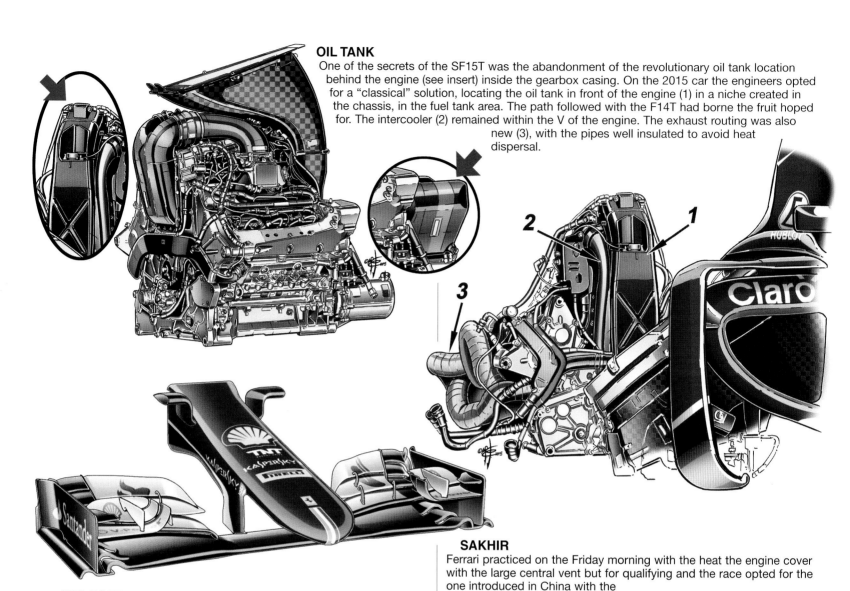

OIL TANK

One of the secrets of the SF15T was the abandonment of the revolutionary oil tank location behind the engine (see insert) inside the gearbox casing. On the 2015 car the engineers opted for a "classical" solution, locating the oil tank in front of the engine (1) in a niche created in the chassis, in the fuel tank area. The path followed with the F14T had borne the fruit hoped for. The intercooler (2) remained within the V of the engine. The exhaust routing was also new (3), with the pipes well insulated to avoid heat dispersal.

MELBOURNE

Without making comparisons, Ferrari mounted the front wing introduced in the last Barcelona test session which differed from the previous assembly in all its components and not just in the abolition of the "horn" camera mountings, as was the case with Mercedes at the Federation's request. Also new were the main profile with the peripheral area revised, the raised flaps, the vertical fin mounted inside them, as well as the addition of a slim flap on the external part of the endplates.

SAKHIR

Ferrari practiced on the Friday morning with the heat the engine cover with the large central vent but for qualifying and the race opted for the one introduced in China with the central vent very narrow around the exhaust. Note that the driveshafts that on the F14T were fully faired were here partially exposed (indicated by the red arrow).

BARCELONA

The most important novelties in the aerodynamics package introduced by Ferrari were focussed on the area at the start of the strongly flared sidepods (1), with a new horizontal winglet (2) and the boomerang-shaped vertical turning vane no longer in a single element. The turning vanes ahead of the sidepods received two vents (3) while the vertical ones (4) also presented a new shape.

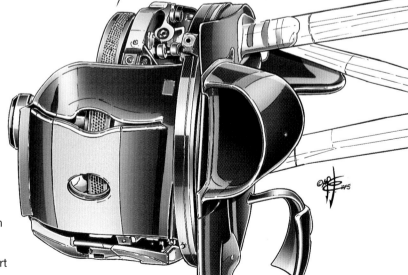

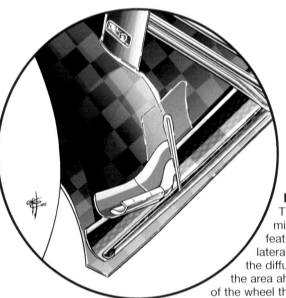

MINIFLAP

These L-shaped mini-flaps was a new feature, located in the lateral ramp of the diffuser in the area ahead of the wheel that attracted the attention of the engineers, as can be seen from the innovations introduced in Bahrain on the McLaren, with the trailing edge of the diffuser flipped up in an L.
The mounting of the vertical fringe on the extractor profile was also new. In the detail, these mini-flaps seen from above created small vortexes in this area.

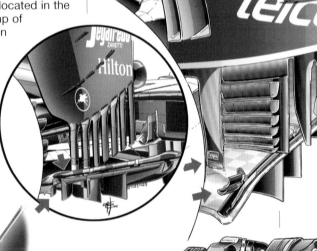

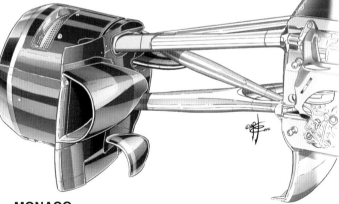

MONACO

Vettel debuted these oval holes on the brake shrouds of his SF15T (in the Ferrari drawing partially dismantled), which McLaren had introduced at the start of the season on the MP4-30. In the comparison, the feature used prior to the Monaco GP with the closed shroud, apart from a vertical slot for warming the wheel rims.

GIORGIO PIOLA

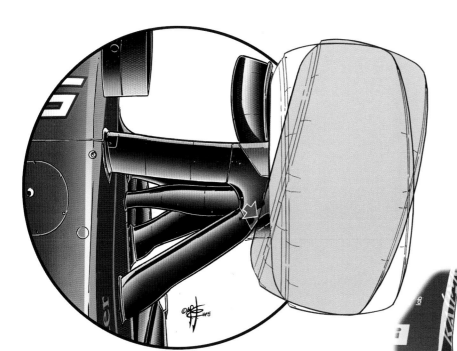

MONACO STEERING

In order to be able to negotiate the Principality's streets, all the teams increased their car's steering angle from 14° to 22°.
At this point, however, it was necessary to cut a small portion of the front suspension wishbones so as to prevent the wheel fouling the wishbone and effectively blocking the steering.

MONTREAL

A new front wing for the Ferraris with reduced chord flaps and a different position, as well as a different shape for the small winglet, shifted slightly towards the centre of the car and inclined more to outside.

ZELTWEG

The aerodynamic package introduced in Austria began around the front of the stepped bottom (T-Tray) with the addition of two small vertical fins.

REAR BRAKE INTAKE

A further modification to the rear brake intake with three small vortex generators positioned on the vertical fin introduced in Monaco. In the critical area of the bottom of the car, ahead of the rear wheel, there was another small step in addition to the three already seen in previous races, again designed to improve the efficiency of the flow in this area.

SILVERSTONE

A completely different wing in all its details was seen at Silverstone (bottom), beginning with the main profile that presented an area with a more pronounced upwards curve (1). The raised flaps were also wider and had an additional fin (2) to direct the flow to the outside of the front wheels. The endplate lost the external fin (3) and the final flap was also modified (4).

REAR WING

A low, albeit not extreme, downforce wing for Ferrari, with endplates featuring just two and a half slots at the top and profiles with reduced chord and incidence combined with the new front wing introduced in Belgium.

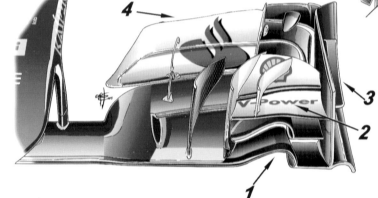

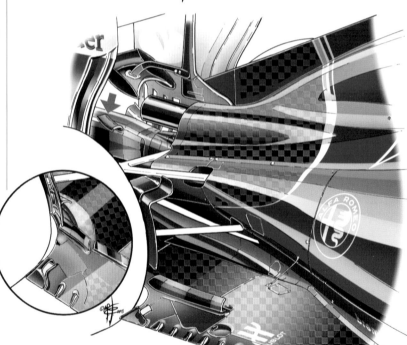

SPA-FRANCORCHAMPS

A comparison between the Silverstone and Budapest front wing (right) and the one designed for Spa: in practice, the raised flaps were eliminated and in their place two vertical fins curving outwards were introduced. The two traditional flaps were also eliminated in favour of a single element with a notably wider internal chord.

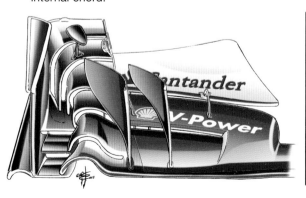

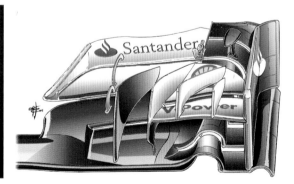

SINGAPORE

In Singapore, Ferrari introduced the more interesting novelties in the high pressure area ahead of the rear wheels which increasingly became the object of new features. Following the double L-shaped longitudinal cuts of the Toro Rosso and the multiple one of the McLaren, on the SF15T no less than nine appeared in place of the usual three. The aim was to reduce the lift generated at this point by the rotation of the rear wheels.

GIORGIO PIOLA

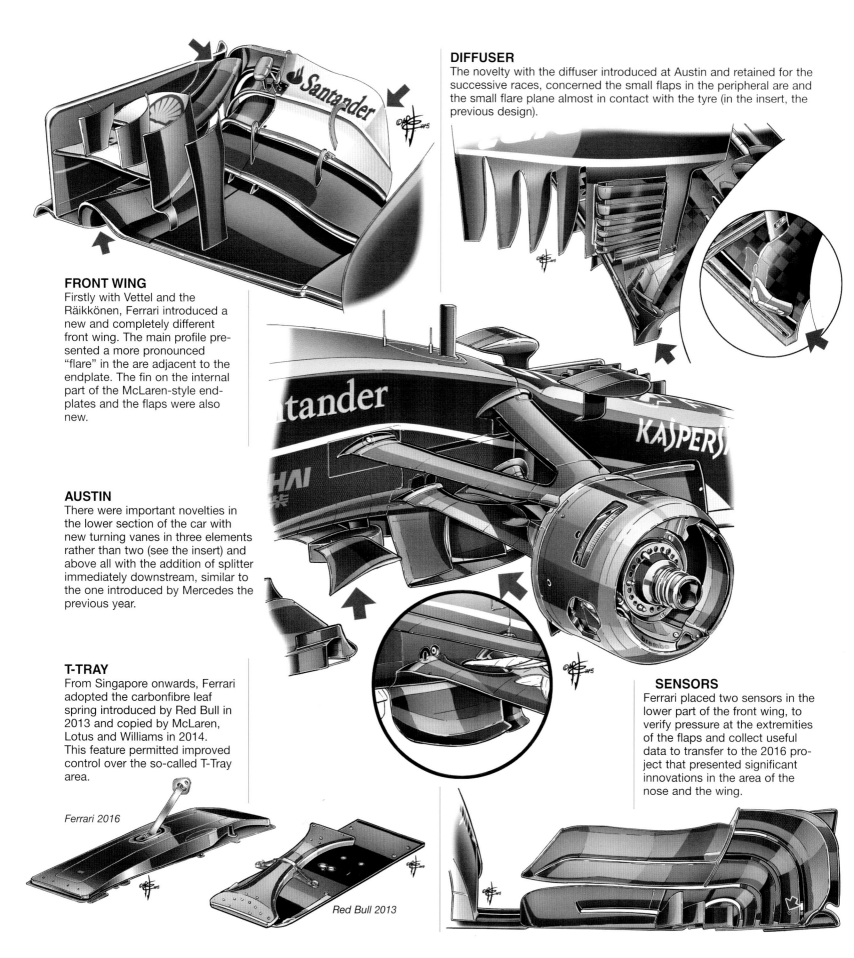

DIFFUSER

The novelty with the diffuser introduced at Austin and retained for the successive races, concerned the small flaps in the peripheral are and the small flare plane almost in contact with the tyre (in the insert, the previous design).

FRONT WING

Firstly with Vettel and the Räikkönen, Ferrari introduced a new and completely different front wing. The main profile presented a more pronounced "flare" in the are adjacent to the endplate. The fin on the internal part of the McLaren-style endplates and the flaps were also new.

AUSTIN

There were important novelties in the lower section of the car with new turning vanes in three elements rather than two (see the insert) and above all with the addition of splitter immediately downstream, similar to the one introduced by Mercedes the previous year.

T-TRAY

From Singapore onwards, Ferrari adopted the carbonfibre leaf spring introduced by Red Bull in 2013 and copied by McLaren, Lotus and Williams in 2014. This feature permitted improved control over the so-called T-Tray area.

Ferrari 2016

Red Bull 2013

SENSORS

Ferrari placed two sensors in the lower part of the front wing, to verify pressure at the extremities of the flaps and collect useful data to transfer to the 2016 project that presented significant innovations in the area of the nose and the wing.

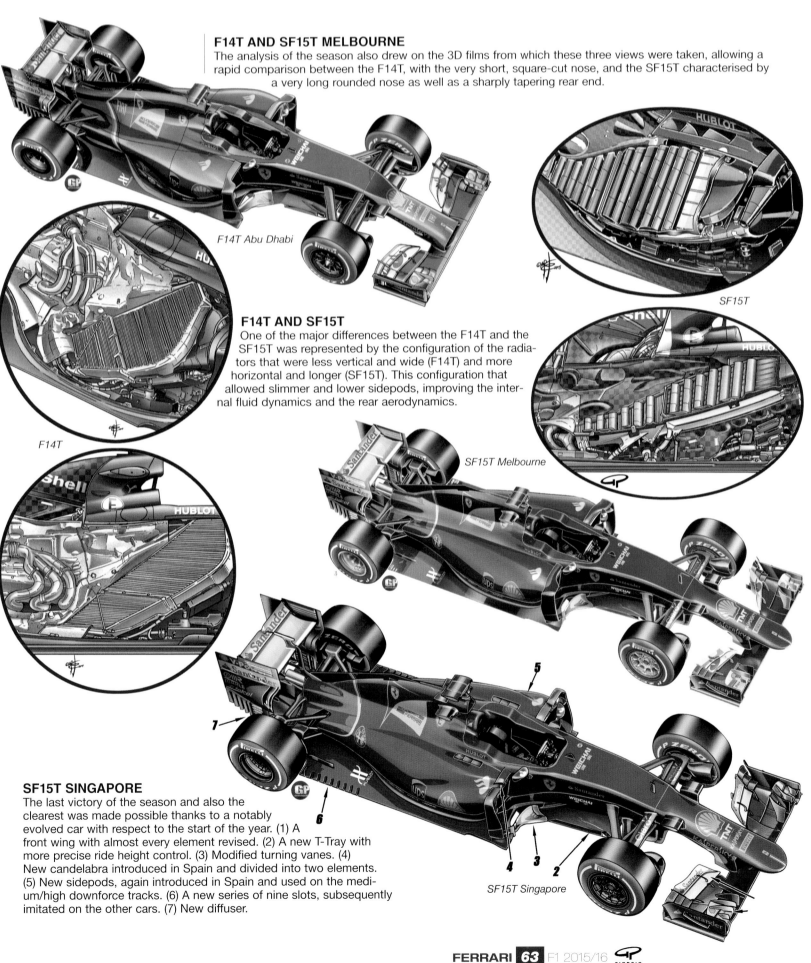

F14T AND SF15T MELBOURNE

The analysis of the season also drew on the 3D films from which these three views were taken, allowing a rapid comparison between the F14T, with the very short, square-cut nose, and the SF15T characterised by a very long rounded nose as well as a sharply tapering rear end.

F14T Abu Dhabi

SF15T

F14T AND SF15T

One of the major differences between the F14T and the SF15T was represented by the configuration of the radiators that were less vertical and wide (F14T) and more horizontal and longer (SF15T). This configuration that allowed slimmer and lower sidepods, improving the internal fluid dynamics and the rear aerodynamics.

F14T

SF15T Melbourne

SF15T SINGAPORE

The last victory of the season and also the clearest was made possible thanks to a notably evolved car with respect to the start of the year. (1) A front wing with almost every element revised. (2) A new T-Tray with more precise ride height control. (3) Modified turning vanes. (4) New candelabra introduced in Spain and divided into two elements. (5) New sidepods, again introduced in Spain and used on the medium/high downforce tracks. (6) A new series of nine slots, subsequently imitated on the other cars. (7) New diffuser.

SF15T Singapore

GIORGIO PIOLA

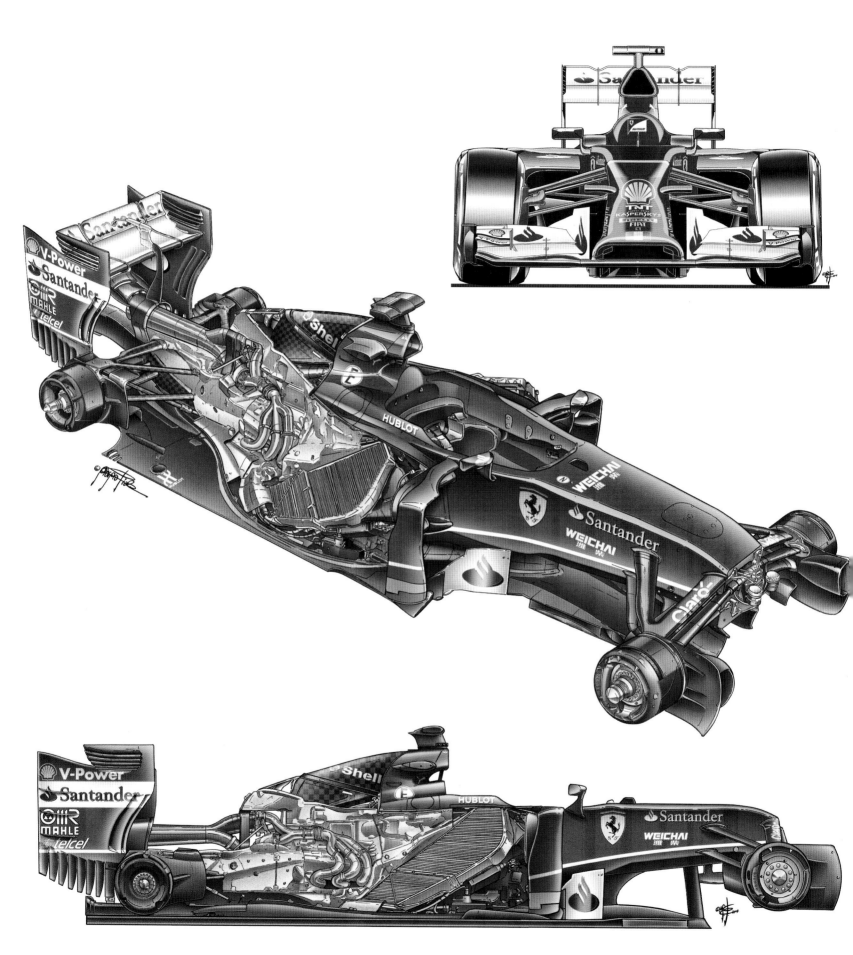

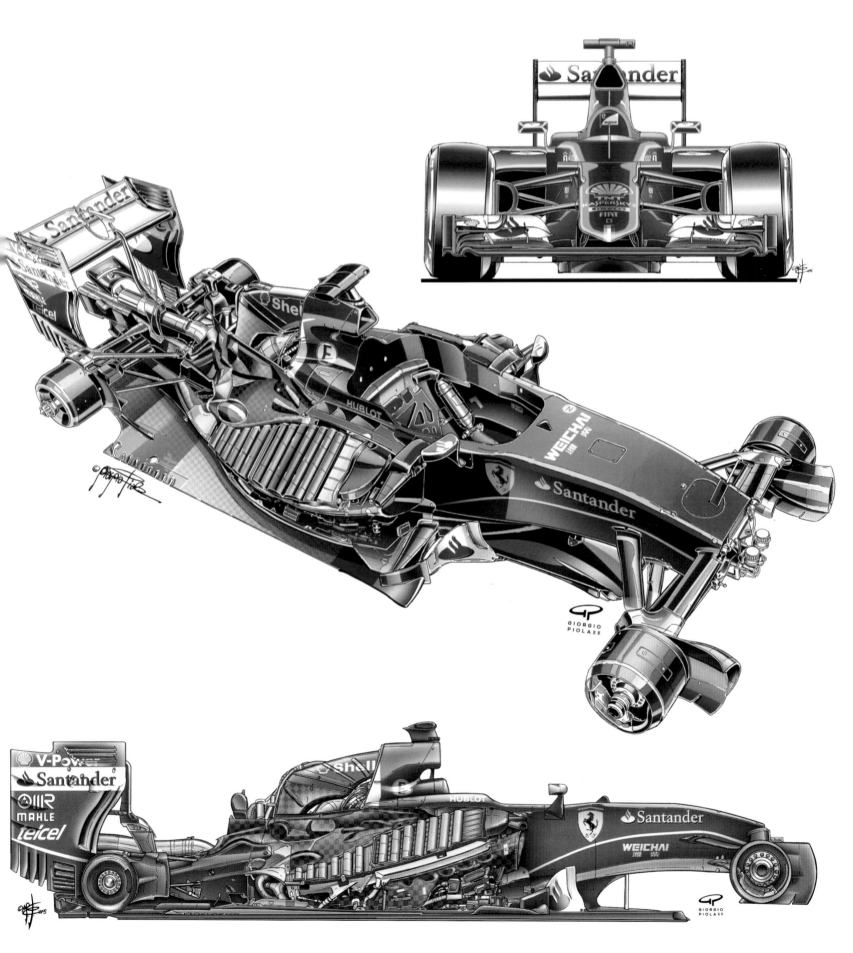

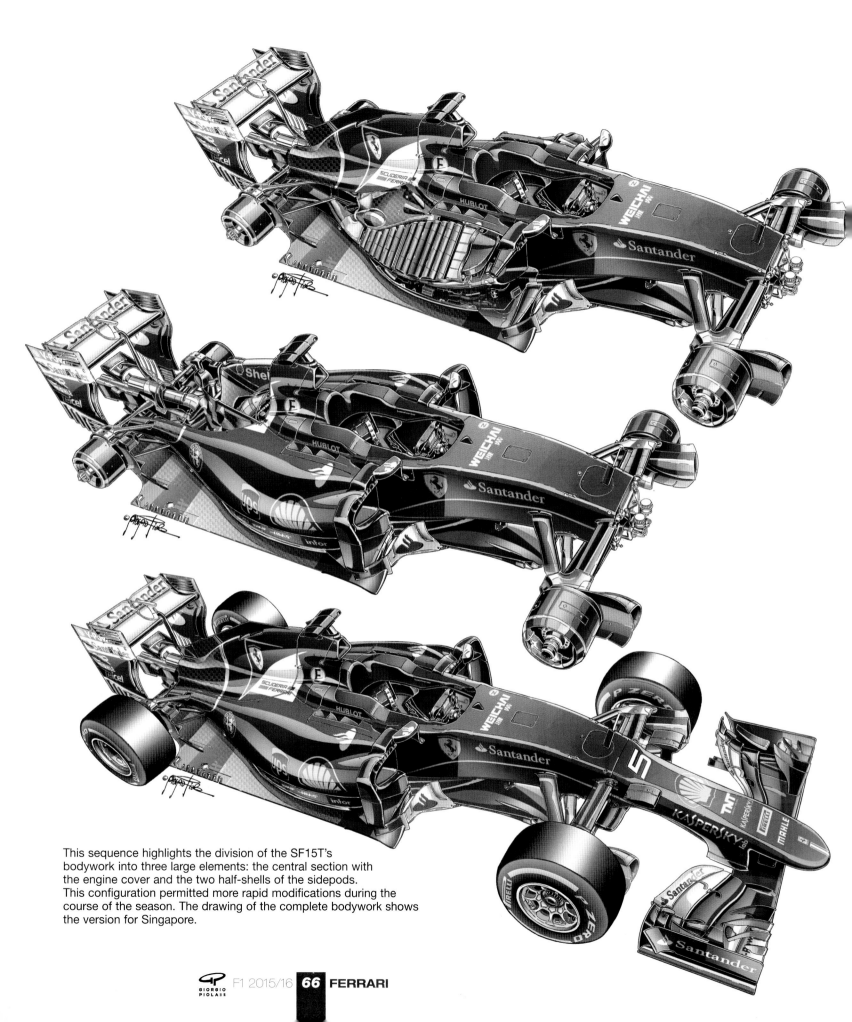

This sequence highlights the division of the SF15T's
bodywork into three large elements: the central section with
the engine cover and the two half-shells of the sidepods.
This configuration permitted more rapid modifications during the
course of the season. The drawing of the complete bodywork shows
the version for Singapore.

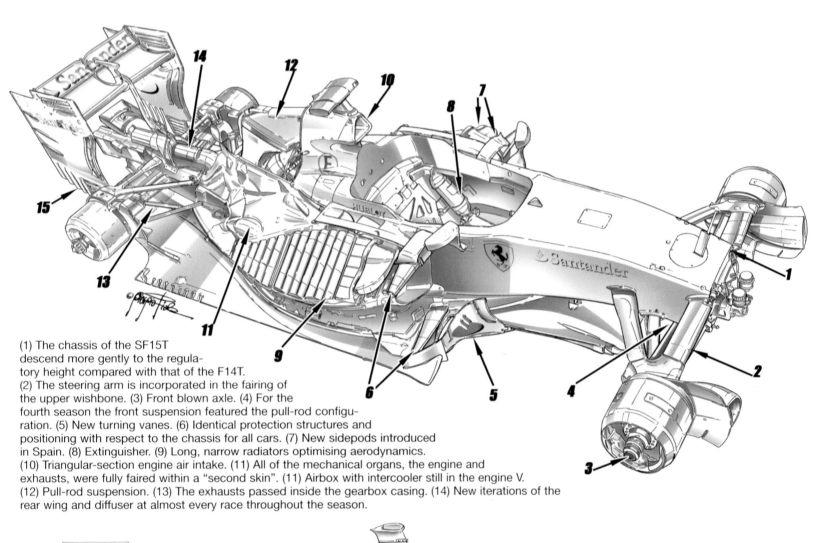

(1) The chassis of the SF15T descend more gently to the regulatory height compared with that of the F14T.
(2) The steering arm is incorporated in the fairing of the upper wishbone. (3) Front blown axle. (4) For the fourth season the front suspension featured the pull-rod configuration. (5) New turning vanes. (6) Identical protection structures and positioning with respect to the chassis for all cars. (7) New sidepods introduced in Spain. (8) Extinguisher. (9) Long, narrow radiators optimising aerodynamics. (10) Triangular-section engine air intake. (11) All of the mechanical organs, the engine and exhausts, were fully faired within a "second skin". (11) Airbox with intercooler still in the engine V. (12) Pull-rod suspension. (13) The exhausts passed inside the gearbox casing. (14) New iterations of the rear wing and diffuser at almost every race throughout the season.

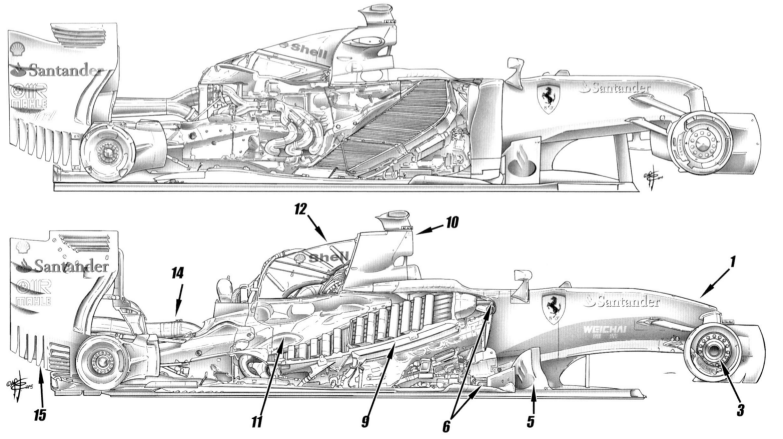

WILLIAMS

CONSTRUCTORS' CLASSIFICATION			
	2014	2015	
Position	3°	3°	=
Points	320	257	-63▼

Williams repeated its third place in the Constructors' World Championship from 2014, although its points total fell by 63 with respect to the previous year. However, for two years the Grove-based team had been performing a minor miracle, cementing its position as the championship's third force ahead of teams with much larger budgets such as Red Bull Racing and McLaren. With the Mercedes-powered FW37, Bottas took two third place finishes in Canada and Mexico, while Massa was on the podium in Austria and at Monza. Pat Symonds' car was at its best on the fast circuits but displayed its limits on the slower tracks and in particular in the wet. Williams scored points in 16 of the 19 scheduled races, missing out only at Monaco, the Hungaroring and Austin. The FW37 was also the first 2015 car to be revealed to the press and public as well as the first with the short nose: "I'm very proud of the work we've done", said the technical director Symonds, "because we passed the homologation crash test first time, while others have had to repeat it multiple times."

The Grove team had chosen the right line of development, even though it did present a nose with a protuberance 25 mm longer than the minimum permitted by the FIA regulations. Sir Frank's engineers did not throw out the basic concepts of the FW36, retaining the long wheelbase. There was however fine-tuning to lower the masses and improve the centre of gravity and the weight distribution.

The car proved to be the one with the most ballast and as such the lightest in the field. The rear suspension was fully redesigned with the raising of the arms to benefit aerodynamics, while the redesigned gearbox casing was again in metal for reasons of cost.

The car was presented with the two wing profiles almost attached to the floor in order to support the endplates and the rear wing, as on the previous FW36, but in winter testing it was converted to a mono-pylon set-up that permitted significant weight saving.

One of the FW37's major defects emerged during the pit stops: the Williams ruined a number of decent performances with lengthy stops caused by frequent problems with the wheel nuts. The team then launched a specific inquiry to resolve the problem and actually became the point of reference for the other teams within the circus.

Another curiosity: in contrast with the majority of the other cars that incorporated the digital display in the top part of the steering wheel-computer, William chose to mount a new, large type (not used in 2014) directly on the chassis which meant that the half-moon steering wheel was unchanged and also lighter.

In Australia, Williams presented two front wing flap configurations that differed in the upper flaps; the front brake ducts were also modified.

In Malaysia, in order to counter the humidity, the Grove team decided to open two rows of "gills" in the bodywork, alongside the cockpit and in the proximity of the roll bar so as to extract hot air from the sidepods.

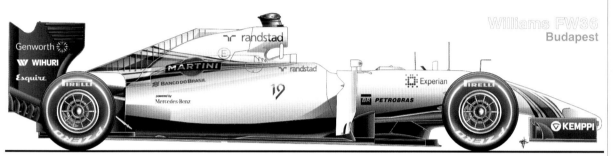

Williams FW36
Budapest

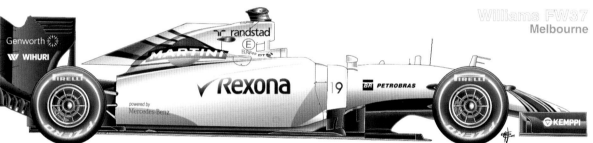

Williams FW37
Melbourne

Williams FW37
Monza

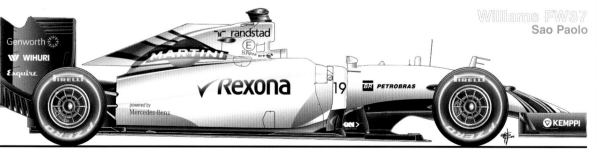

Williams FW37
Sao Paolo

In China the maximum aerodynamic efficiency was sought: for this reason part of the exhaust was faired through to the rear wing pylon.

This feature was not convincing, however, and in qualifying the Williams reappeared in standard form, with an overall improvement in heat dispersal; only a small slot on the back of the engine cover was opened.

The Monkey Seat also appeared at the rear in the hope of giving the drivers more grip in the twisting sections of the Chinese track. In the accident on the Saturday Massa destroyed one of the two new wings, that is the one with greater flap incidence and three turning vanes in place of the usual two in the lower section.

In Bahrain too cooling was of primary importance, with coachwork trapezoidal in shape at the rear with a larger vent than normal.

For the European debut in Barcelona three McLaren-style vertical fins were installed above the radiator mouths: previously there was just one other than the "bridge" linked to the turning vane; there was also a modification to the rear diffuser.

At Monaco, Williams adopted more open brake shrouds in the area of the discs in order to improve cooling given that the Principality's street circuit with its low average speeds does not provide the usual flow of air.

In Canada, together with Sauber, the Grove team was the only one to use a Monkey Seat in order to prevent the rear wing from stalling. The brake ducts were enlarged, while Carbon Industrie discs were adopted.

The Red Bull Ring saw the debut of a new development package with a more all-embracing engine cover that extended considerably towards the rear.

The rear wing was also fitted with new endplates with five slots rather than the four from Canada as well as straighter configuration.

The flap on the mobile wing had a V in the central section to reduce drag.

The brake ducts were also new. Williams then followed Ferrari's lead in developing the lateral section of the diffuser.

The lateral turning vane was also different with two slightly different vents, while the part that connected to the vertical candelabra was also modified.

The work conducted in the tests following the Austrian GP was interesting: the British team ran a test for the FIA, fitting sideskirts to the floor (strictly forbidden by the 2016 regulations) and a Monkey Seat ahead of the rear wheels. In Hungary Bottas was benefitted from a new front wing representing a clear break with the past and inspired by the Mercedes designs.

In proximity to the endplates in fact a conspicuous step with arched vents useful in deviating the air flows in order to reduce the turbulence generated by the front wheels.

A new winglet also appeared on the outside of the endplate.

At Spa a mobile flap was fitted with a large central V to reduce drag, while it was discovered that the T-Tray contained not the usual leaf-spring but a beam.

At Monza, the FW37 adopted a very low downforce rear wing, with the chord of the flap reduced by 4 cm with respect to the maximum permitted by the FIA.

This entailed a revision of the mobile wing control.

For Singapore, a new front wing was developed with a larger step on the inside of the endplate.

The upper flap instead remained composed of three elements with two slots, while there were two vertical turning vanes flared towards the outside on the main profile.

SHORT NOSE

Williams was the first team to present a short, square nose that was to be copied during the course of the season by other teams such as Force India (from the first race), Toro Rosso, Red Bull, McLaren and Sauber. A comparison with the FW36 nose from 2014 with the long proboscis. Note instead that the wing reprised the concepts express in the front wing/endplates assembly used in the 2014 season.

FW36

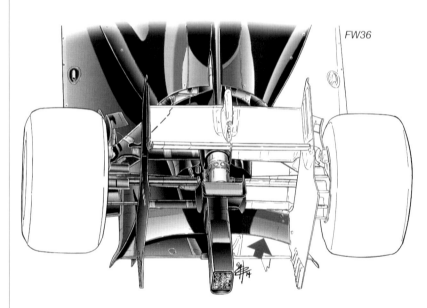

FW36

In Russia, Williams presented a turning vane composed of three elements with two vertical slots. What was unusual was the small step at the base, itself characterised by two small slots.

In Mexico the vents either side of the cockpit were revised.

For qualifying and the race the two drivers chose the new wing and the larger central vent.

In Abu Dhabi the car was equipped with the necessary instrumentation for collecting data: in particular there was a video camera for measuring and checking the tyres.

WING SUPPORT

At its launch the FW37 did not have a central rear wing support pylon but rather the feature used on the 2014 car.

The endplates were connected to the deformable structure via a wide profile placed above the diffuser but below the 150 mm limit from the reference place where the ban on bodywork elements came into play.

This feature entailed extra weight and was abandoned from the second race of the season in favour of a single central pylon.

GEARBOX

The gearbox of the FW37 was completely redesigned to integrate with the rear aerodynamics, but was still in metal for reasons of cost. The rear suspension was also completely revised in the interests of aerodynamics, with the raising of the arms (4). Note among the other features the accentuated anti-squat adopted on the FW37, while the suspension tie-rod (3) was set further back with respect to other cars.
The exhaust passed through the gearbox casing (1-2) as on the 2014 car.
The central wing pylon embraced the exhaust with a kind of inverted U-shaped bridge (5).
The AP brake callipers were underslung (6).

BRAKE DUCTS

While a revised and legal version (with respect to the Red Bull version prohibited in 2012) of the blowing front hub had been introduced in 2013, on the FW37 Williams abandoned the feature that slowed tyre changes in order to focus on optimising this operation so often critical to race strategies.

MERCEDES EXHAUSTS

The Mercedes PU106B for the 2015 season differed with respect to the 2014 version above all in the exhausts that no longer featured the scarified terminals enclosed in a kind of lung, but rather more traditional elements shrouded in an insulating material that prevented a loss of heat that could be used to recharge the MGU-H. The second red arrow in the insert drawing represents the hydraulic circuit radiator.

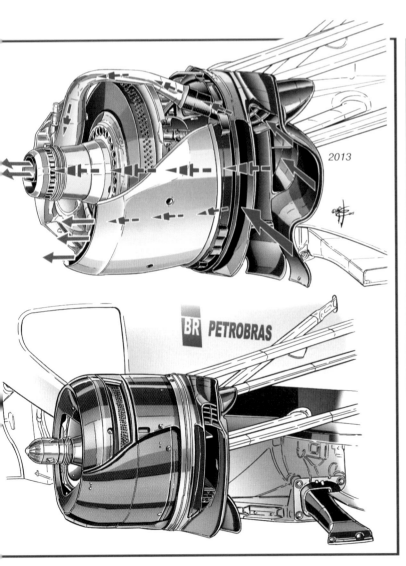

2013

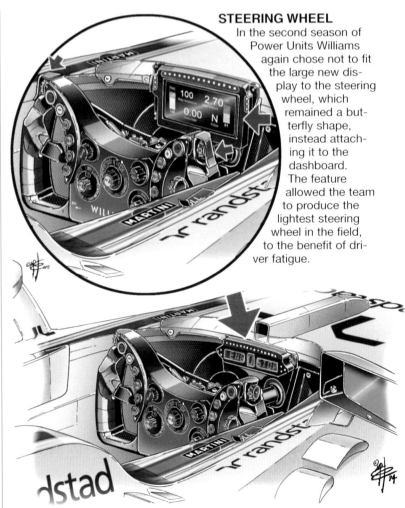

STEERING WHEEL

In the second season of Power Units Williams again chose not to fit the large new display to the steering wheel, which remained a butterfly shape, instead attaching it to the dashboard. The feature allowed the team to produce the lightest steering wheel in the field, to the benefit of driver fatigue.

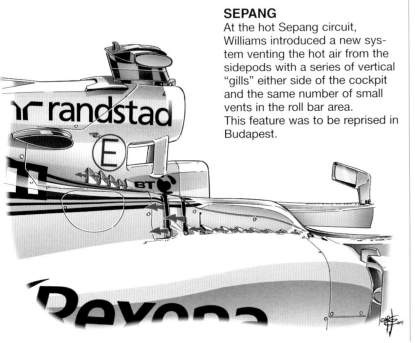

SEPANG

At the hot Sepang circuit, Williams introduced a new system venting the hot air from the sidepods with a series of vertical "gills" either side of the cockpit and the same number of small vents in the roll bar area.
This feature was to be reprised in Budapest.

SHANGHAI

At Shanghai a new engine cover was tested that had the end section completely closed and the exhaust faired to improve aerodynamic efficiency but in the end this feature was not raced given the higher ambient temperatures. The Monkey Seat was also introduced.

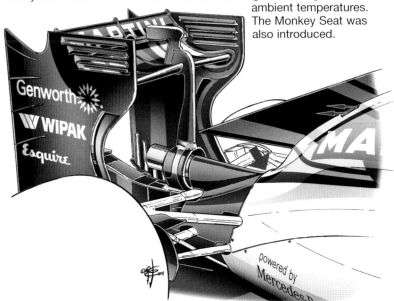

SIDEPODS

The sidepods and the turning vanes either side of the FW37 derived from those of the preceding FW36. At the 2014 Spanish GP the team had abandoned the innovative fairing of the wing mirror area and at the start of the season the FW37 also adopted the two small fins, replaced at the Austrian GP with a single wedge-shaped element (4). There were new bargeboards (1) with three vertical slots and different lower sections (2) for the turning vanes. On the upper part, three turning vanes (3) appeared in place of the single element.

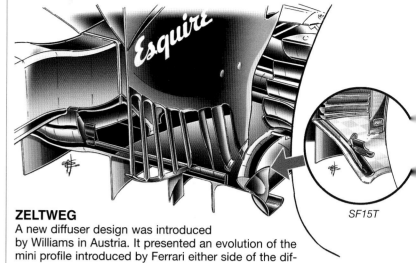

SF15T

ZELTWEG

A new diffuser design was introduced by Williams in Austria. It presented an evolution of the mini profile introduced by Ferrari either side of the diffuser, in the area close to the tyres. In practice they created a true vortex generator.

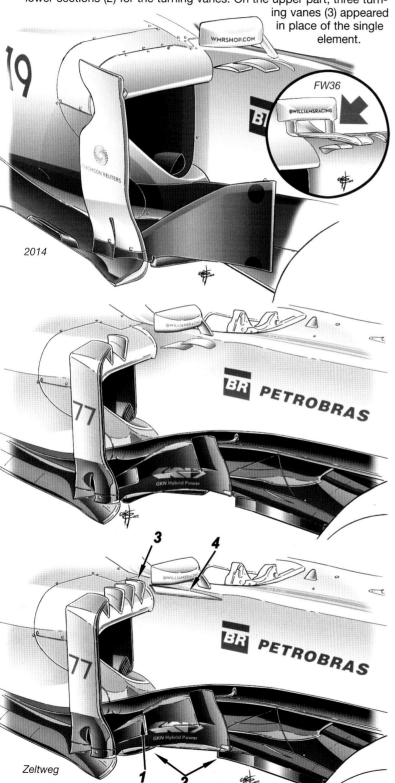

2014

Zeltweg

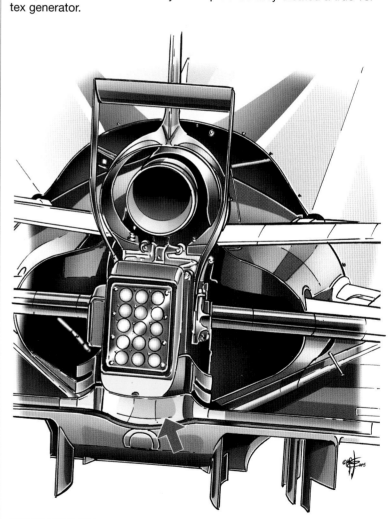

SILVERSTONE

At the following race at Silverstone, Williams presented a further development of the diffuser introduced in Austria, with modifications to the central zone with this additional flap making the extractor profile more efficient and guaranteeing more downforce.

FRONT WING

The front wing fitted to Bottas's car from the Friday morning at Silverstone was practically a photocopy of the Mercedes design. The endplates were virtually identical with the semi-horizontal external mini fins but a different management of the flows in the end section. The main profile featured a flat section (in yellow) inside the endplates with a series of slots as on the W05. The flaps were also new.

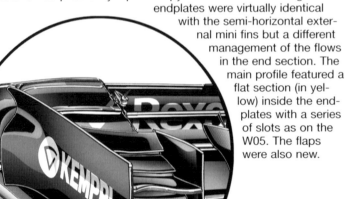

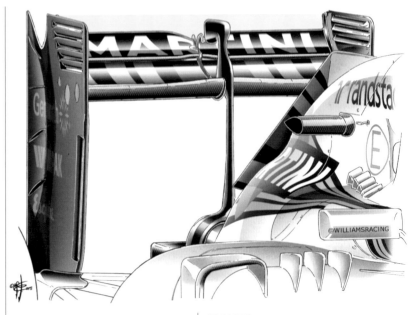

MONZA

There was no new wing for Monza with the Williams using the same wing as at Spa albeit with the trailing edge of the flap trimmed by no less than 4 cm to give a higher maximum speed by reducing drag. This reduction was much greater than seen in the past and with respect to the similar feature adopted by Toro Rosso.

ABU DHABI

Nothing new at the last race of the season but the car was crammed with sensors such as these mini-pitot tubes in the critical area ahead of the rear wheels collecting data useful for the design of the 2016 car.

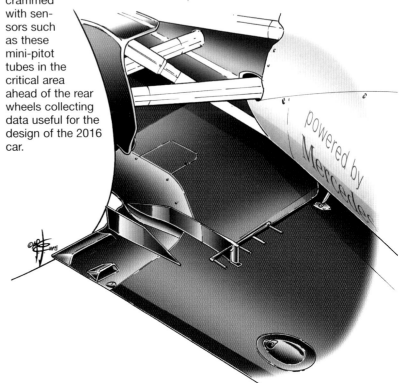

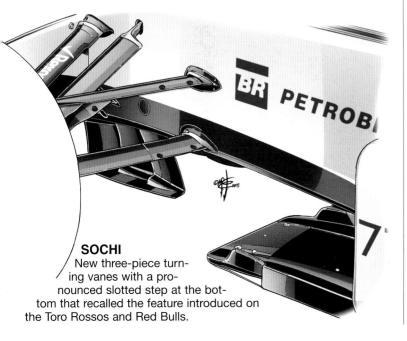

SOCHI

New three-piece turning vanes with a pronounced slotted step at the bottom that recalled the feature introduced on the Toro Rossos and Red Bulls.

RED BULL

CONSTRUCTORS CLASSIFICATION

	2014	2015	
Position	2°	4°	-2=▼
Points	405	187	-218▼

2015 was the worst season in the recent history of Red Bull: the team slipped two places in the Constructors' Championship and above all failed to score a single victory for the first time in seven years. Moreover, it was also a year of disputes and uncertainties relating to the continuation of the relationship with the Power Unit supplier Renault. The decision to add Mario Illien as a support for the development of the French six-cylinder engine was not particularly well received. However, the Renault Power Unit had proved to be the least effective in the field.

In any case, the RB11, especially at the start of the season, was not up to the standards of the recent cars by Adrian Newey. As is frequently the case when there is a technical upheaval, the team most severely penalised is the one that had achieved the greatest efficiency in the specific area affected by the new regulations. All it took was a modification to the regulation regarding the dimensions of the nose and the imposition of titanium sliders on the stepped floor to wreck the competitiveness of the RB11. The design of this car was based on a short nose configuration that unfortunately could only be introduced at the fifth race of the season in Spain, as it failed no less than four crash tests.

The rest of the car proved ill at ease with the long nose that had to be adopted in the meantime. With regard to the titanium sliders, their greater wear severely restricted full use of the rake set-up based on perfect control of the minimal ground clearance of the so-called T-Tray.

The first handicap was resolved in Spain when the short nose tested on the Friday morning by the two drivers was then adopted by both for qualifying and the race. The shortening by around 10 cm could be seen in relation to the forwards inclination of the vertical pylons and the position of the tip of the nose with respect to the central section of the wing. This nose was combined with the final version of the front wing, inspired by the Mercedes design, introduced in China and then developed in Bahrain. It should be noted that the 2015 season was the first of the era post-Peter Prodromou, Newey's right-hand man as far as aerodynamics were concerned for the previous Red Bulls, who had moved to McLaren.

On its presentation the RB11 had caused a sensation with its remarkable camouflage livery, as had been the case in 2010 when a fake exhaust was painted on the end part of the sidepods to divert attention from the exact position of the exhaust blowing towards the diffuser.

The initial difficulties did not however overshadow the technical value of the RB11 project.

The sidepods presented an even greater undercut with respect to the 2014 car, which benefitted the air flow feeding the much more tapered Coke bottle area at the rear. The S-Duct at the front was retained and further devel-

Red Bull RB10
Budapest

Red Bull RB11
Melbourne

Red Bull RB11
Monza

Red Bull RB11
Sao Paolo

oped, as were the four-pot rear brake calipers, abandoned instead by Mercedes after the problems suffered at the Canadian GP in 2014. Also present were the blown hubs introduced by Red Bull but which were outlawed in 2012 because the holes were applied to the rotating hubs; they were then reintroduced in 2013 firstly by Williams and then by Red Bull again, this in line with the regulations as the blowing tube had been moved to the fixed part of the hub. However, the blown hubs seen at the presentation were used only on the slow circuits and in Singapore, together with the maximum rake setting. Aerodynamic development was continuous with novelties regarding the wings, the endplates and the turning vanes below the chassis at every race. Another important step in the RB11's development came at Silverstone with a new front wing that was even more similar to that of the Mercedes, in particular in the area close to the endplates.

RB11 EVOLUTION OVERHEAD VIEW

In this overhead view, the evolution of the RB11 can be seen only at the front with the new shorter nose (1) that appeared at the Spanish GP after having failed a number of homologation crash tests. The front wing (2) and the endplate were also new.

RENAULT POWER UNIT

This was Red Bull's true Achilles' heel and the cause of its lack of competitiveness with respect to its Mercedes and Ferrari rivals; it was certainly a determinant factor that prevented Red Bull from winning a single race in 2015. Only in extremis was a divorce from the French company avoided, in part due to Mercedes and Ferrari's refusal to supply Power Units.

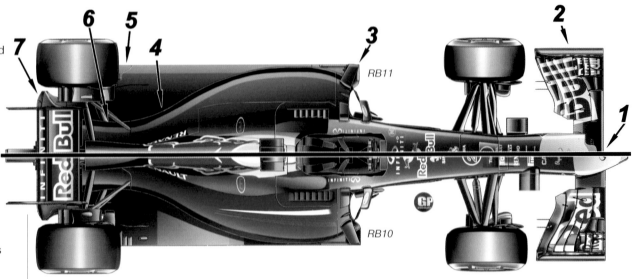

RB10/RB11 OVERHEAD VIEW

The RB11 represented a clear evolution with respect to the RB10, especially in terms of the front end aerodynamics where the long, innovative nose (1) with vertical slots was abandoned in favour of a much shorter nose with a kind of finger. On the car's presentation, the front wing (2) was the same, as was the initial part of the sidepods (3) and represented an evolution of the shapes of the RB10. There was a more accentuate pinch (4-6) in the so-called Coke bottle area and the hot air vent at the rear. There was a new L-shaped cut (5) in the area of the floor ahead of the rear wheels. The diffuser (7) was also new and designed to take full advantage of the rake adjustment.

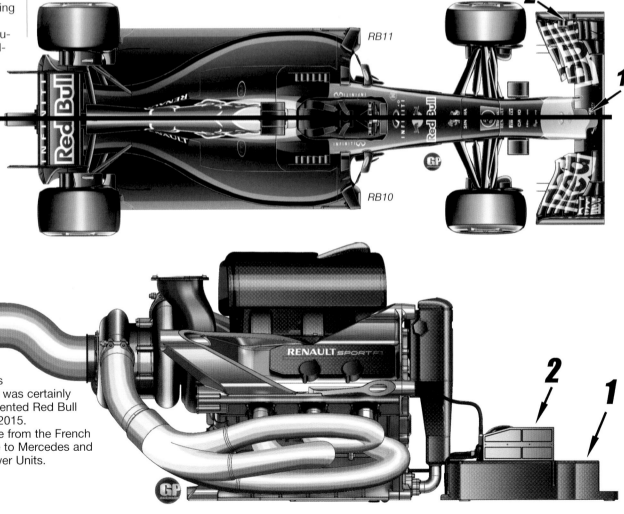

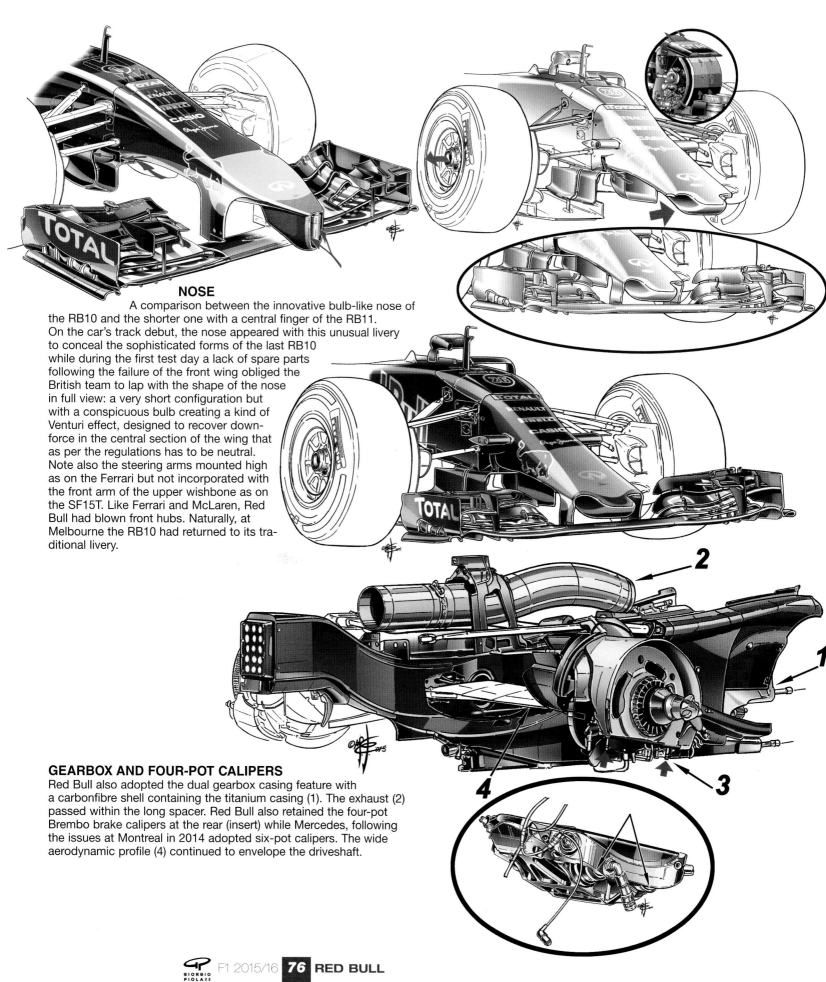

NOSE

A comparison between the innovative bulb-like nose of the RB10 and the shorter one with a central finger of the RB11. On the car's track debut, the nose appeared with this unusual livery to conceal the sophisticated forms of the last RB10 while during the first test day a lack of spare parts following the failure of the front wing obliged the British team to lap with the shape of the nose in full view: a very short configuration but with a conspicuous bulb creating a kind of Venturi effect, designed to recover down-force in the central section of the wing that as per the regulations has to be neutral. Note also the steering arms mounted high as on the Ferrari but not incorporated with the front arm of the upper wishbone as on the SF15T. Like Ferrari and McLaren, Red Bull had blown front hubs. Naturally, at Melbourne the RB10 had returned to its traditional livery.

GEARBOX AND FOUR-POT CALIPERS

Red Bull also adopted the dual gearbox casing feature with a carbonfibre shell containing the titanium casing (1). The exhaust (2) passed within the long spacer. Red Bull also retained the four-pot Brembo brake calipers at the rear (insert) while Mercedes, following the issues at Montreal in 2014 adopted six-pot calipers. The wide aerodynamic profile (4) continued to envelope the driveshaft.

REAR SUSPENSION

The elements making up the suspension have increasingly become aerodynamic devices integrated with the rest of the car.
One example is this upper rear wishbone mount on the Red Bull with a wing profile. Its function is to assist in extracting air in synergy with the brake ducts. Note instead how the hot air is expelled from the brakes via two small chimneys inside the rear wheels.

FRONT SUSPENSION

The third transverse element of the front suspension on the RB10 was easily accessible and had the task of controlling ride height and roll; it was fitted with disc springs.

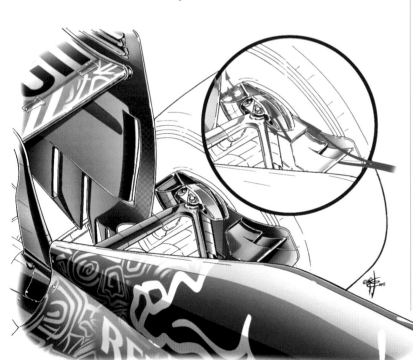

S-DUCT

This feature, debuted by Sauber in 2012 was immediately copied by Red Bull and retained in 2015. Compared with the 2014 version (insert) the ramp channelling air from the lower to the upper section was sharper. In the lower lateral area of the chassis, the ducts carried air to the electronic control units. In 2015 Force India and McLaren also used the S-Duct.

MELBOURNE

New rear wing endplates, principally characterised by the novelty of the vertical slot forming a single major vent with the first horizontal slot at the top. The endplates were introduced in the last test at Barcelona. However, on the Saturday morning the team had gone back to the version without the new vertical slot.

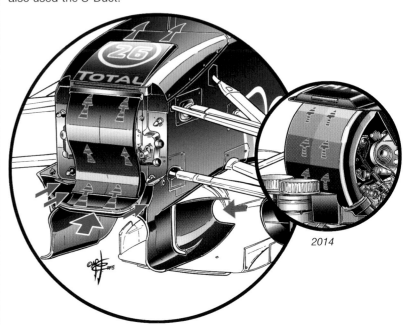

2014

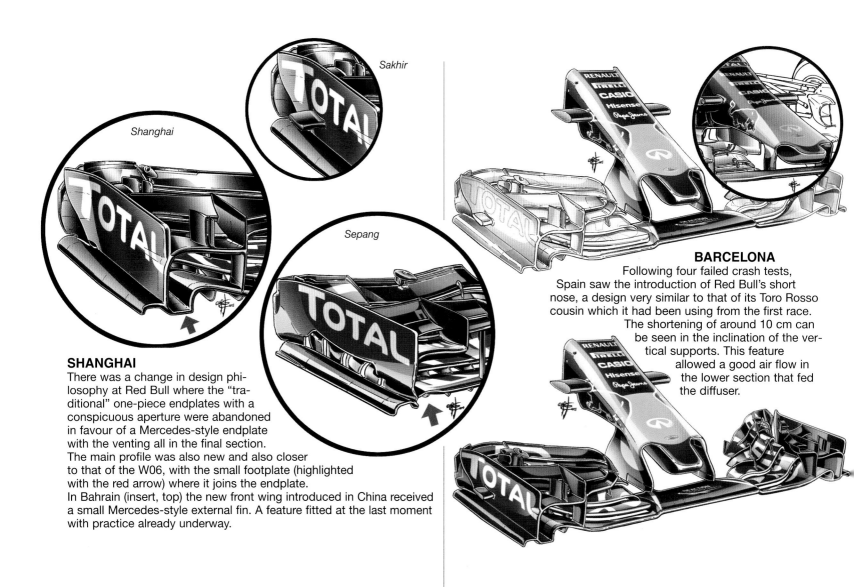

Shanghai

Sakhir

Sepang

SHANGHAI

There was a change in design philosophy at Red Bull where the "traditional" one-piece endplates with a conspicuous aperture were abandoned in favour of a Mercedes-style endplate with the venting all in the final section.
The main profile was also new and also closer to that of the W06, with the small footplate (highlighted with the red arrow) where it joins the endplate.
In Bahrain (insert, top) the new front wing introduced in China received a small Mercedes-style external fin. A feature fitted at the last moment with practice already underway.

BARCELONA

Following four failed crash tests, Spain saw the introduction of Red Bull's short nose, a design very similar to that of its Toro Rosso cousin which it had been using from the first race. The shortening of around 10 cm can be seen in the inclination of the vertical supports. This feature allowed a good air flow in the lower section that fed the diffuser.

MONACO

Red Bull raised the upper wishbone mounting point on the hub carrier so as to have a different camber recovery and improved traction; the insert shows the detail of the modified hub attachment plate.

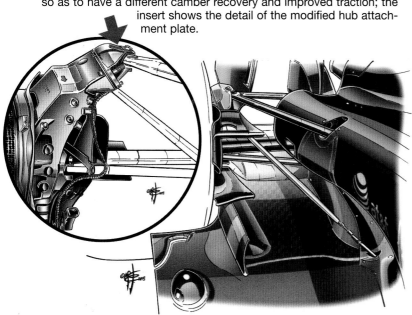

REAR SUSPENSION

Completely closed rear brake duct on the Red Bull, presenting a series of sophisticated aerodynamic appendages on the inside, both to seal the extractor profile and to create downforce.

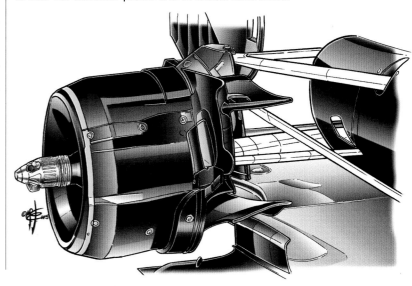

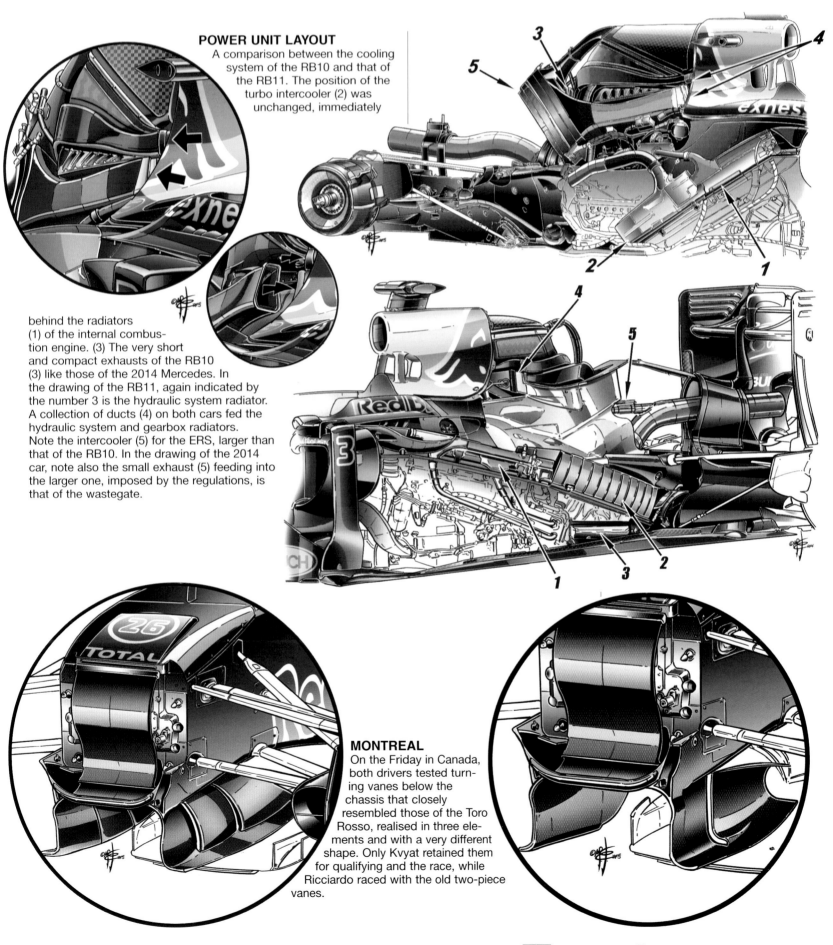

POWER UNIT LAYOUT

A comparison between the cooling system of the RB10 and that of the RB11. The position of the turbo intercooler (2) was unchanged, immediately

behind the radiators (1) of the internal combustion engine. (3) The very short and compact exhausts of the RB10 (3) like those of the 2014 Mercedes. In the drawing of the RB11, again indicated by the number 3 is the hydraulic system radiator. A collection of ducts (4) on both cars fed the hydraulic system and gearbox radiators. Note the intercooler (5) for the ERS, larger than that of the RB10. In the drawing of the 2014 car, note also the small exhaust (5) feeding into the larger one, imposed by the regulations, is that of the wastegate.

MONTREAL

On the Friday in Canada, both drivers tested turning vanes below the chassis that closely resembled those of the Toro Rosso, realised in three elements and with a very different shape. Only Kvyat retained them for qualifying and the race, while Ricciardo raced with the old two-piece vanes.

GIORGIO PIOLA

BRAKE SHROUDS

A comparison between the standard version of the brake shrouds (in the complete front end view) used through to the Spanish GP and the version introduced at Monaco with a small duct dedicated to cooling the underslung caliper, with the addition of a Mercedes-style sharply curving vane in the lower section, introduced to increase the flow of air towards the braking system.

BLOWN HUBS

After having first introduced the feature in 2012 in a configuration held to be illegal because the blowing was determined by holes in the rotating section, Red Bull then copied the Williams blown hubs with the blowing provided by a channel inside the hub (and as such fixed). It did so in 2014, with the feature being retained in 2015 on the medium-high downforce tracks but not on the low downforce circuits. Note that in 2015 blown hubs were also used by Ferrari and McLaren.

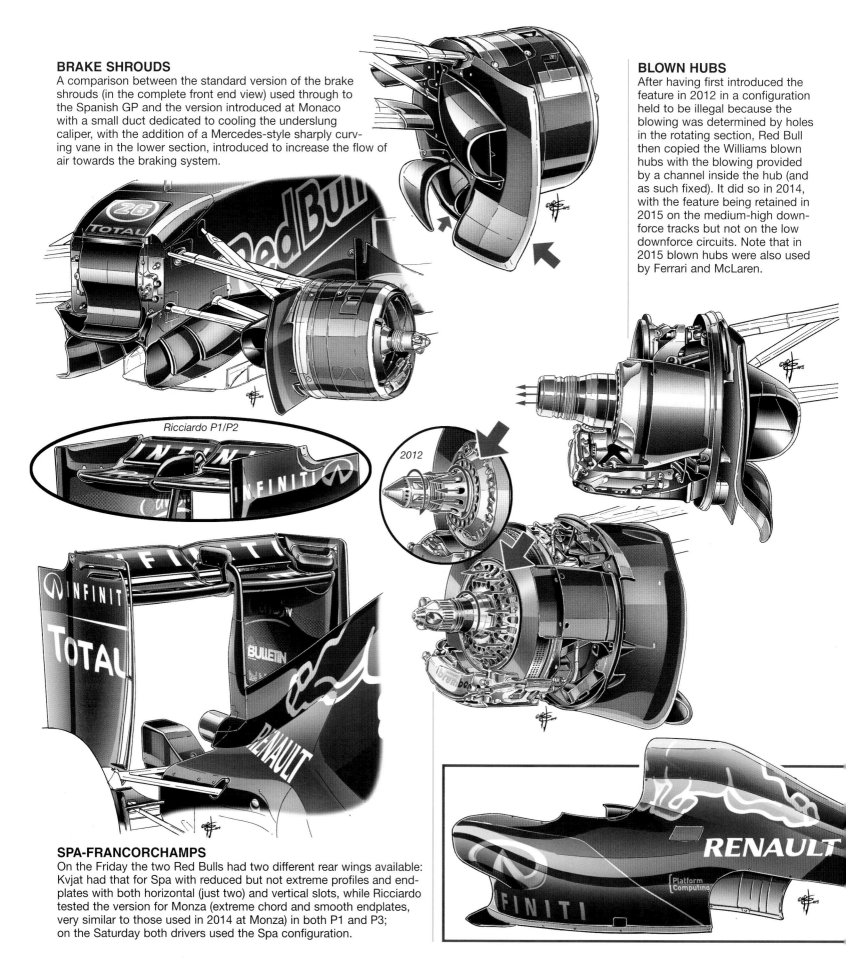

Ricciardo P1/P2

2012

SPA-FRANCORCHAMPS

On the Friday the two Red Bulls had two different rear wings available: Kvjat had that for Spa with reduced but not extreme profiles and endplates with both horizontal (just two) and vertical slots, while Ricciardo tested the version for Monza (extreme chord and smooth endplates, very similar to those used in 2014 at Monza) in both P1 and P3; on the Saturday both drivers used the Spa configuration.

SUZUKA

In practice and the race, both drivers used the new turning vanes under the chassis which in Singapore had been fitted for the race only to Kvyat's car. Red Bull also modified the mini-profile (now arched) linking the two vanes.

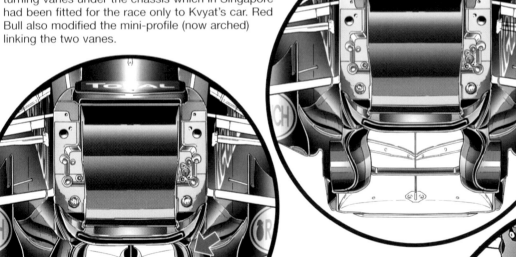

COOLING

The removal of the turning vanes below the chassis allows us to see the ducting (highlighted by the blue arrows) in the lower lateral part of the chassis channelling air to the electronic control units at the front of the sidepods.

AUSTIN

It was only at Austin that Red Bull copied, along with McLaren, the wide footplate in proximity to the endplates of the Mercedes front wing, clearly to better direct the air towards the outside of the front wheels.

BODYWORK

Red Bull was the only team to adopt one-piece bodywork, while all the others preferred a three-piece design: centre section (engine cover) and two lateral half-shells (sidepods).

MEXICO

In order to overcome the altitude issues, Red Bull completely opened the end part of the engine cover/sidepods with a configuration very similar to that adopted by Toro Rosso for the hot tracks. Note the small vortex generators in the central part of the diffuser.

FORCE INDIA

CONSTRUCTORS' CLASSIFICATION			
	2014	2015	
Position	6°	5°	+1▲
Points	155	136	-19▼

Force India VJM07
Hockenheim

Force India VJM08
Melbourne

Force India VJM08
Monza

Force India VJM08
Sao Paolo

Despite a restricted budget, Force India managed to optimize its investments and achieve excellent results, reinforcing its success in the Constructors' Championship: the team in fact climbed a place in the standings from 6th to 5th, on the shoulder of the top teams (Mercedes, Ferrari and Red Bull Racing) and Williams, even though it collected 136 points against the 155 of 2014. Perez's 3rd place in Russia was the best result of the season, with the South American driver also qualifying the VJM08 on the second row for the Belgian GP. The early part of 2015 was particularly difficult for Force India due to its well-known economic problems. The first two winter testing sessions were therefore conducted with the 2014 car because the new one could not be finished in the absence of the necessary finds to pay certain suppliers (including that of the fuel tanks...). The VJM08 was therefore simply a revised version of the previous car with the lower nose to respect the new regulations, while at the rear the bodywork was more tapering with the gearbox significantly lower, obliging the introduction of a long supporting arch for the rear wing mono-pylon. The radiator mouths in the sidepods cooling the more powerful Mercedes Power Unit were larger and more square-cut. Andy Green developed the sus-pension with the hydraulic control system that was useful in preserving the Pirelli tyres and frequently permitted one less pit stop. Despite the clear derivation from the 2014 car, of which it initially retained the chassis, the VJM08 did present some important novelties. It adopted the S-Duct, joining the ranks formed in 2015 by Red Bull and McLaren, together with Ferrari which in its turn used the narrow base lower wishbone in the front suspension introduced the previous season by Mercedes. Australia saw the first appearance of the digital display (of the old type) integrated into the steering wheel, while in Malaysia there were modifications to the rear wing endplates.

At the Monaco GP, the previously mentioned lack of funds obliged Force India to forego the front brake calipers mounted ahead of the axle. Thus after six seasons, the team adopted the more traditional layout used by everyone except Red Bull and Ferrari which went with underslung calipers. Again talking about brakes, in Canada the drivers decided to adopt Carbon Industrie discs, while in the meantime the factory was preparing the VJM08 Spec B that was due to debut in the Austrian GP but which was instead seen for the first time only in the post-race tests before officially appearing at the British GP. The delay was due to a failed crash test at Cranfield required to homologate the new short nose characterised by two "nostrils" that allowed the flow of air to be increased, with a configuration destined to guarantee increased downforce on the front end and a well balanced rear, combining the advantages of the short nose with those of the long version. In order to exploit this novelty, the front part of the monocoque was modified, while the central and rear sections of the car were thoroughly revised with the objective of creating significantly

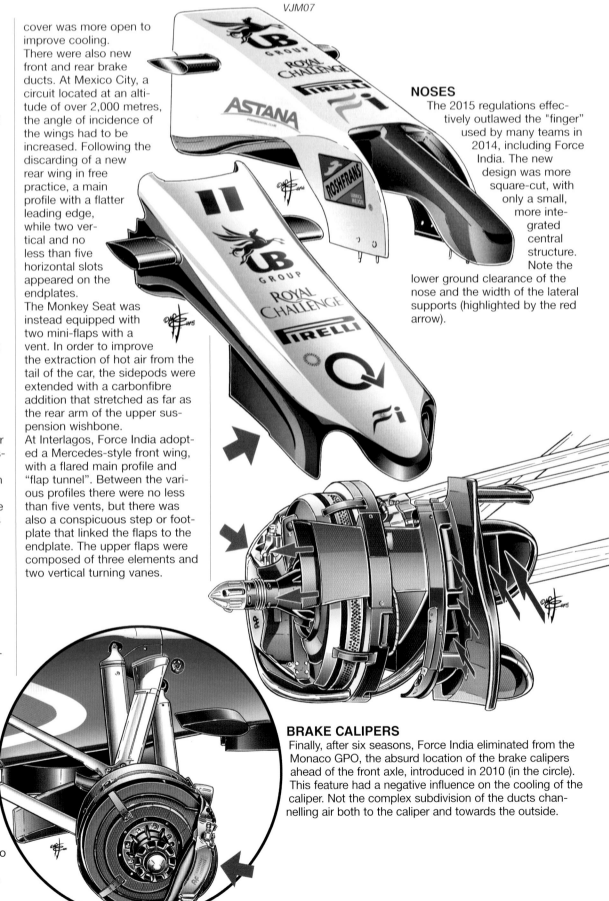

VJM07

reduced sections. The shifting of the gearbox oil cooler to the sidepods permitted the creation of a much sleeker engine cover equipped with a conspicuous dorsal fin at the top.

The rear suspension geometry was modified at the hub carrier mount given the impossibility of working on the one on the gearbox supplied by Mercedes.

The exhaust and the rear wing support were also different, as were the rear brake ducts and the wheel rims. In order to respect the weight distribution imposed by the regulations, Green's engineers placed ballast below the gearbox.

The new version of the VJM08 immediately showed considerable potential event though in Hungary it revealed a surprising fragility: Perez rolled his car violently on the Friday morning after a lower wishbone of the rear suspension broke. The team had to reinforce the component on both cars given that loadings 50% higher than those predicted were recorded following modifications that had not been agreed with the FIA to a kerb on the track. In the crash the Mexican destroyed the sole example of the new rear wing and both drivers thus had to race with the usual configuration.

At Spa, a shaped rear suspension wishbone was introduced, equipped with a carbonfibre fairing. Again in Belgium, a lower downforce rear wing was seen that was then successfully employed at Monza too.

In Singapore instead the team introduced a new aerodynamic package designed for the street circuit requiring high downforce: as well as the rear wing with larger profiles, a Monkey Seat was introduced with the flap equipped with three profiles cantilevered with respect to the mono-pylon supporting the wing. There were also interesting modifications to the central part of the diffuser, while the end section of the engine

cover was more open to improve cooling.

There were also new front and rear brake ducts. At Mexico City, a circuit located at an altitude of over 2,000 metres, the angle of incidence of the wings had to be increased. Following the discarding of a new rear wing in free practice, a main profile with a flatter leading edge, while two vertical and no less than five horizontal slots appeared on the endplates.

The Monkey Seat was instead equipped with two mini-flaps with a vent. In order to improve the extraction of hot air from the tail of the car, the sidepods were extended with a carbonfibre addition that stretched as far as the rear arm of the upper suspension wishbone.

At Interlagos, Force India adopted a Mercedes-style front wing, with a flared main profile and "flap tunnel". Between the various profiles there were no less than five vents, but there was also a conspicuous step or footplate that linked the flaps to the endplate. The upper flaps were composed of three elements and two vertical turning vanes.

NOSES

The 2015 regulations effectively outlawed the "finger" used by many teams in 2014, including Force India. The new design was more square-cut, with only a small, more integrated central structure. Note the lower ground clearance of the nose and the width of the lateral supports (highlighted by the red arrow).

BRAKE CALIPERS

Finally, after six seasons, Force India eliminated from the Monaco GPO, the absurd location of the brake calipers ahead of the front axle, introduced in 2010 (in the circle). This feature had a negative influence on the cooling of the caliper. Not the complex subdivision of the ducts channelling air both to the caliper and towards the outside.

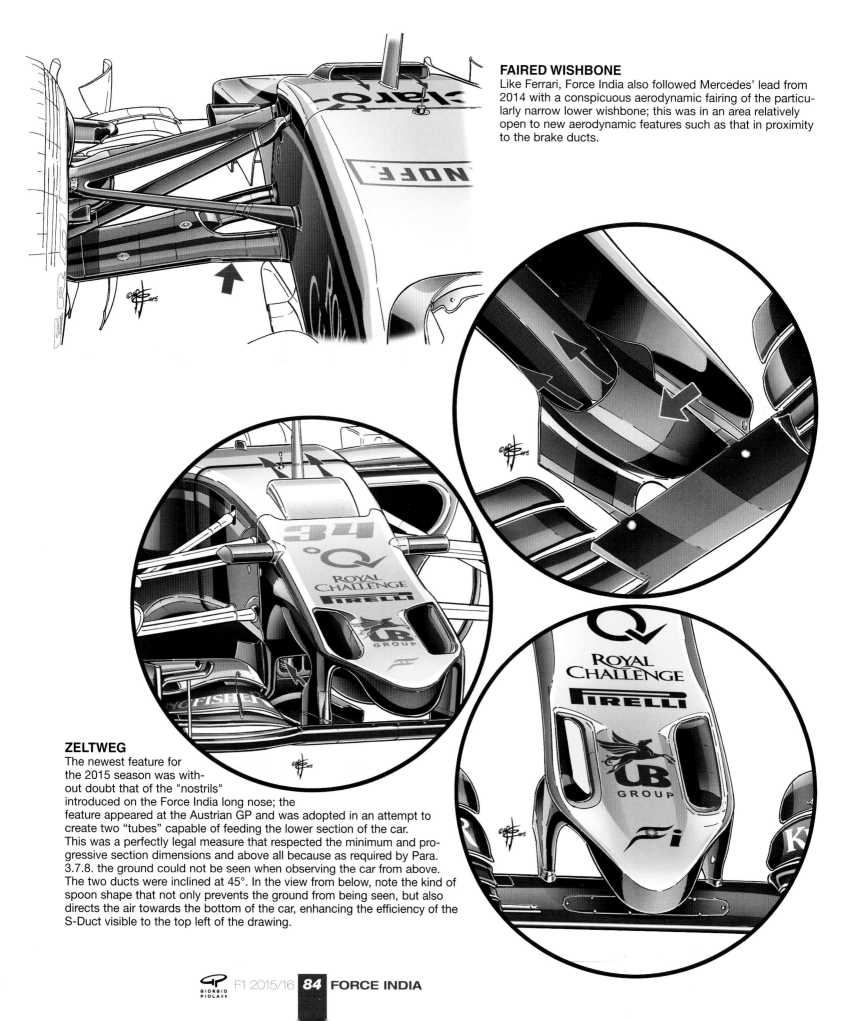

FAIRED WISHBONE

Like Ferrari, Force India also followed Mercedes' lead from 2014 with a conspicuous aerodynamic fairing of the particularly narrow lower wishbone; this was in an area relatively open to new aerodynamic features such as that in proximity to the brake ducts.

ZELTWEG

The newest feature for the 2015 season was without doubt that of the "nostrils" introduced on the Force India long nose; the feature appeared at the Austrian GP and was adopted in an attempt to create two "tubes" capable of feeding the lower section of the car. This was a perfectly legal measure that respected the minimum and progressive section dimensions and above all because as required by Para. 3.7.8. the ground could not be seen when observing the car from above. The two ducts were inclined at 45°. In the view from below, note the kind of spoon shape that not only prevents the ground from being seen, but also directs the air towards the bottom of the car, enhancing the efficiency of the S-Duct visible to the top left of the drawing.

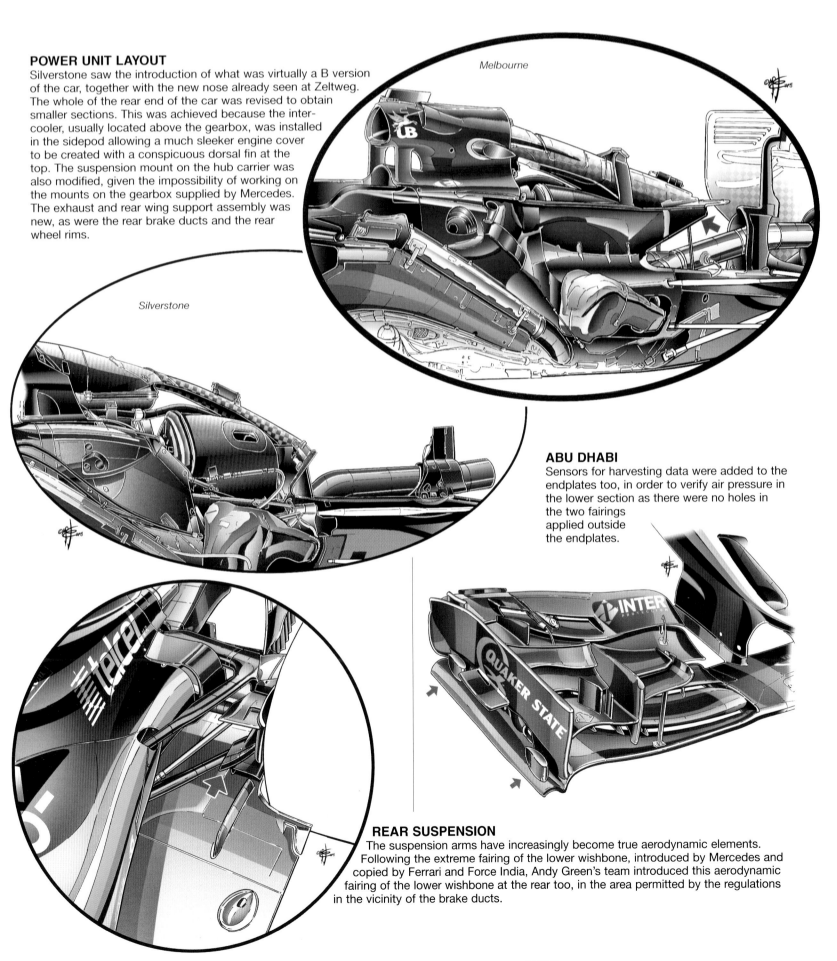

POWER UNIT LAYOUT

Silverstone saw the introduction of what was virtually a B version of the car, together with the new nose already seen at Zeltweg. The whole of the rear end of the car was revised to obtain smaller sections. This was achieved because the inter-cooler, usually located above the gearbox, was installed in the sidepod allowing a much sleeker engine cover to be created with a conspicuous dorsal fin at the top. The suspension mount on the hub carrier was also modified, given the impossibility of working on the mounts on the gearbox supplied by Mercedes. The exhaust and rear wing support assembly was new, as were the rear brake ducts and the rear wheel rims.

Melbourne

Silverstone

ABU DHABI

Sensors for harvesting data were added to the endplates too, in order to verify air pressure in the lower section as there were no holes in the two fairings applied outside the endplates.

REAR SUSPENSION

The suspension arms have increasingly become true aerodynamic elements. Following the extreme fairing of the lower wishbone, introduced by Mercedes and copied by Ferrari and Force India, Andy Green's team introduced this aerodynamic fairing of the lower wishbone at the rear too, in the area permitted by the regulations in the vicinity of the brake ducts.

GIORGIO PIOLA

LOTUS

CONSTRUCTORS' CLASSIFICATION			
	2014	2015	
Position	8°	6°	+2▲
Points	10	78	+68▲

2015 was a season of alternating fortunes for Lotus. The Enstone team in fact managed make considerable progress with respect to the previous year's disaster when it obtained just 10 points in the Constructor's championship, slipping back to 8th place in the final standings. With the E23 Hybrid, the team led by the technical director Nick Chester climbed up to sixth place with a total of no less than 78 points. Grosjean also managed a surprising podium finish at Spa when the team was already mired in the financial crisis that led after long and gruelling negotiations to its sale to Renault. The E23 Hybrid was a more conventional car that the one with the walrus nose and numerous asymmetrical features that had generated an ungovernable chronic understeer.

The short nose was not as extreme as that of other designs and it was slightly higher than the one tested at Austin late in 2014. However, the great step forwards came with when the team swapped the Renault Power Unit for the Mercedes version. As well as benefitting from a significant increase in power, the Brixworth Power Unit permitted a more efficient installation with a reduction in dimensions that benefitted aerodynamic efficiency. The gearbox casing in cast titanium was redesigned to allow the single exhaust to pass through it, as was the case with all the cars powered by the Mercedes engine. The hydraulic suspension connecting the wheels on each axle was abandoned in favour of a configuration equipped with traditional springing.

The layout of the front suspension was moreover changed by lowering the mounting point of the strut on the monocoque. Also of note was the new design of the ogival air intake for the Mercedes engine, around which appeared a further three apertures in an area almost totally covered by the driver's helmet. The Enstone engineers lowered the ears that could be seen on the engine cover in 2014, changing their function. In the roll-bar area, the air speed was very high and so the two lateral "gills" and the central hole could be exploited to obtain good cooling with a smaller and lighter radiator array. The rear wing was instead supported on a mono-pylon that was fairly steeply inclined towards the rear: in this area Lotus refined the concept seen in 2014, seeking a programmed flexion that would allow the wing to be stalled at the highest speeds, while respecting the FIA's static tests. The E23 Hybrid displayed a certain lack of downforce in fast corners, with a tendency towards oversteer, together with instability under braking due to a brake-by-wire system less efficient than others. In Malaysia, Lotus introduced larger new brake ducts, while in China much shorter pylons appeared supporting the front wing equipped with new flaps. In Bahrain instead, there were different front wing endplates and brake ducts. For the European season debut at Barcelona, Lotus introduced a steering wheel-cum-computer equipped with a large digital display: in reality, this new feature had been available for the last

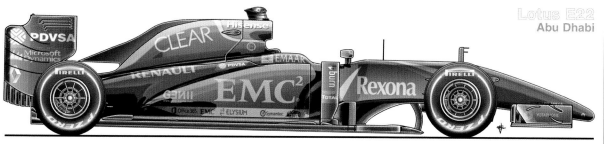

Lotus E22
Abu Dhabi

Lotus E23
Melbourne

Lotus E23
Monza

Lotus E23
Sao Paolo

RENAULT ENGINE

In the second season of the Power Units Renault again disappointed to the extent that such was the discontent among the powers that be at Red Bull that there was almost a dramatic divorce. In the drawing based on a rendering by the French company you can see the large battery pack and the electronic control units in the area of the fuel tank, while the turbine-compressor assembly is mounted at the back of the engine.

few races, but the team decided to keep it back until both drivers were able to use it.

In order to increase downforce, a new rear wing was introduced, while Monaco saw the fitting of maximum downforce profiles. Canada saw the adoption of Hitco brake discs, while the pre-announced short nose failed to appear but the wings were adapted to the medium-low downforce circuit; moreover, a curious double flared profile appeared below from the front wing flaps that functioned as a splitter. The brake ducts and the rear bodywork were revised with a wider hot air vent from the radiators on the left-hand side and smaller on the right. At this point development of the car practically ceased due to the cash-flow crisis: many components that had been designed were never realised and the potential of the car that had started the season ahead of the Force India gradually faded.

In free practice on the Friday at Spa, the third driver, Jolyon Palmer, tested a front wing with five elements instead of four, but the feature was not used in the race. At Monza, the team adapted the wing profiles to the low downforce track while at Austin there was an additional inclined flap on the external part of the endplate, which became a kind of extension of the upper flaps. At the bottom, instead, a number of slots were added ahead of the rear wheels. The dual Monkey Seat appeared in Mexico after having been tested at Montmelò following the Spanish GP and at Monaco. The front wing that had been taken to Singapore but not used finally appeared in Brazil, while the team sprung a surprise at the last race in Abu Dhabi with a new nose on Grosjean's car that prefigured the 2016 design: shorter, taller at the front, equipped with a central hump and a conspicuous pelican's craw in the lower part to increase downforce on the front axle.

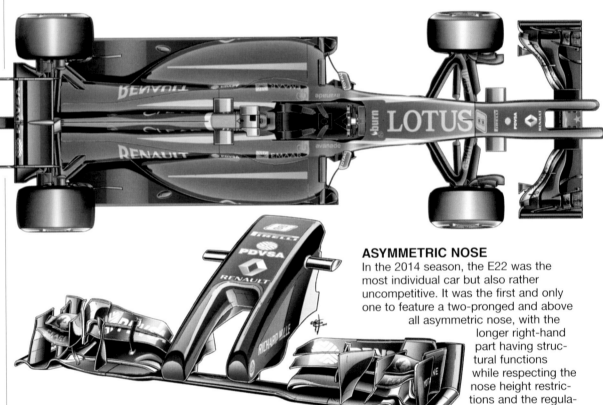

ASYMMETRIC NOSE

In the 2014 season, the E22 was the most individual car but also rather uncompetitive. It was the first and only one to feature a two-pronged and above all asymmetric nose, with the longer right-hand part having structural functions while respecting the nose height restrictions and the regulations relating to the frontal crash test.

E22 ASYMMETRIC EXHAUST

The vent in the end part of the sidepod was also wider on the left-hand side (in correspondence with the intercooler). Above all, the exhaust which was centrally located on all the other cars, was set to the right of the rear wing pylon.

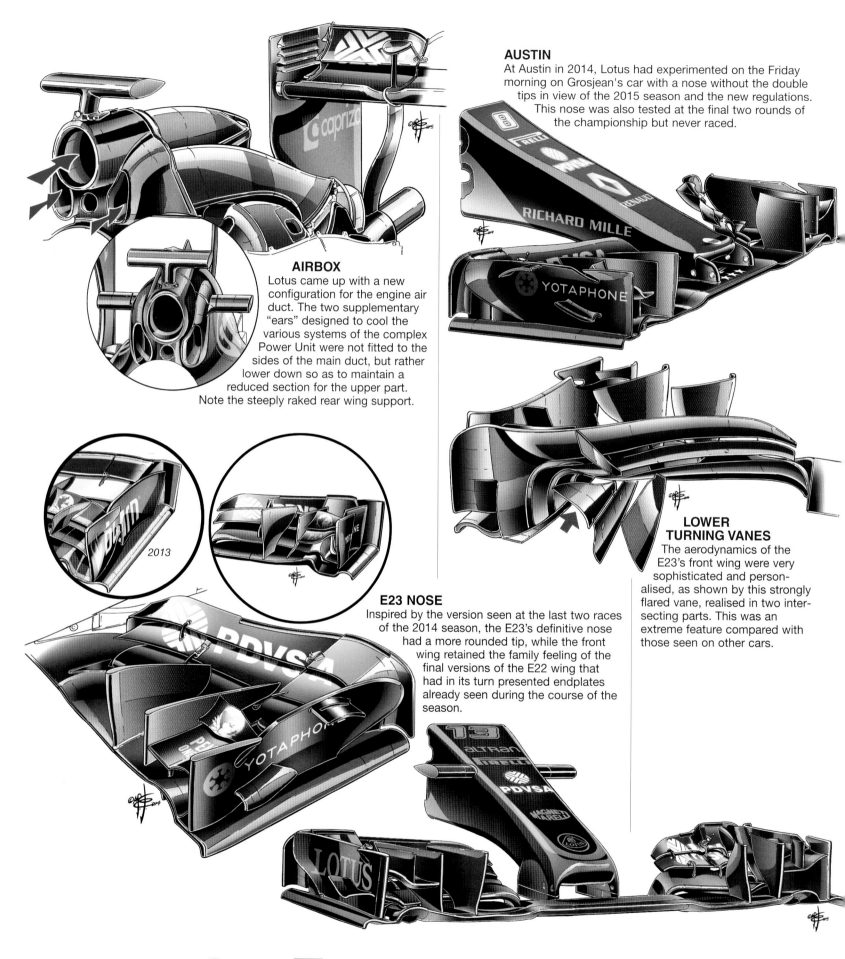

AUSTIN

At Austin in 2014, Lotus had experimented on the Friday morning on Grosjean's car with a nose without the double tips in view of the 2015 season and the new regulations. This nose was also tested at the final two rounds of the championship but never raced.

AIRBOX

Lotus came up with a new configuration for the engine air duct. The two supplementary "ears" designed to cool the various systems of the complex Power Unit were not fitted to the sides of the main duct, but rather lower down so as to maintain a reduced section for the upper part. Note the steeply raked rear wing support.

2013

LOWER TURNING VANES

The aerodynamics of the E23's front wing were very sophisticated and personalised, as shown by this strongly flared vane, realised in two intersecting parts. This was an extreme feature compared with those seen on other cars.

E23 NOSE

Inspired by the version seen at the last two races of the 2014 season, the E23's definitive nose had a more rounded tip, while the front wing retained the family feeling of the final versions of the E22 wing that had in its turn presented endplates already seen during the course of the season.

GIORGIO PIOLA

TORO ROSSO

CONSTRUCTORS' CLASSIFICATION			
	2014	2015	
Position	7°	7°	=
Points	30	67	+37▲

For Toro Rosso the 2015 season was important as the Faenza-based team was celebrating its 10th year in F1. It was unable to improve on its 7th place in the Constructors' Championship from 2014, but did give debuts to two very young drivers: Max Verstappen, who began the World Championship at just 17 years of age, and Carlos Sainz, two years "older"... Despite their lack of experience, the two rookies harvested 67 points, 37 more than the previous season, despite racing with the Renault Energy Power Unit of the STR10 that suffered serious reliability issues (Verstappen used eight internal combustion engines over the course of the season against the four allowed by the regulations, while Sainz used seven) that frequently sidelined the two "kids" when they were challenging for very respectable positions.

On a number of occasions Toro Rosso, sharing the same Renault power units, appeared to be more competitive than its Red Bull "cousin" designed and constructed with the resources of a top team. It is right to say that the STR10 was born thanks to closer synergy with Red Bull Technology.

The technical director, James Key, focused more on a search for downforce than aerodynamic efficiency, adopting the classic Milton Keynes philosophy and turning the page with respect to the SRT9.

The English engineer was flanked by the aerodynamicist Brendan Gilholme, Paolo Marabini (head of composites) and Matteo Piraccini (head of the technical department) with the assistance of Ben Waterhouse (ex-Sauber), Key's deputy technical director.

The STR10 retained the push-rod front suspension configuration with the steering arm aligned with that of the upper wishbone. The triangular radiator mouths reached almost the maximum permitted width, despite being strongly undercut at the bottom in order to favour the flows towards the rear of the car, to the point that a rather pronounced step appeared on the floor.

The sidepods tapered very early, following a concept already seen on the RB10.

Despite the Renault Energy V6 turbo being set around 100 mm further forwards, the wheelbase was long: the rear wheels were distanced from the sidepods, thus creating a particularly tapered Coke bottle area

Toro Rosso STR10
Sao Paolo

Toro Rosso STR10
Launch

Toro Rosso STR10
Melbourne

Toro Rosso STR10
Monza

Toro Rosso STR10
Sao Paolo

facilitating flows towards the rear diffuser.

The installation of the Power Unit remained identical to that of the Red Bull: the ERS control units, which on the STR9 were located close to the battery pack were moved to the sidepods.

The majority of the rear end components were developed at Milton Keynes, including the gearbox and the hydraulic system. The Brake-by-Wire control system was transferred to the sidepods in the area freed-up by the abolition of FRIC.

The rear suspension retained the pull-rod configuration while the rear wing was mounted on a mono-pylon.

The aluminium gearbox had a more tapered casing that favoured aerodynamics.

The roll hoop area of the STR10 was very striking: Key retained the dual air intake with the upper part feeding the V6 Turbo engine and two small external ears for the gearbox radiator, with the lower section instead devoted to the ERS radiator pack.

The sidepods were slimmer, albeit particularly voluminous behind the driver.

The STR10 debuted with the long nose, but was actually conceived for the short nose configuration seen in the second winter test at Barcelona, together with different wings, Monkey Seat, engine cover and floor.

The sidepods were sharply tapered and undercut in the lower section.

In Australia the mono-pylon was developed: the unusual feature was that the rear wing support passed through the central exhaust favouring a light design (lacking the external arch) and also useful in "laminating" the exhaust gases.

This was a new feature that was to be widely copied.

At Sakhir Toro Rosso was obliged to open the sidepods to improve the durability of the Renault Power Units that were struggling with reliability issues: we were therefore able to see the large megaphone air vents on the STR10.

In order to find a solution ahead of the Spanish GP, the opening race of the European season, one of the Faenza cars was taken to the AVL dynamic test bench with the Renault Sport F1 engineers also present.

At Monaco the aerodynamicists at Bicester (home of the Toro Rosso wind tunnel) introduced a modified T-Tray: three small flaps with two vents in the outermost edge appeared in order to increase the STR10's already healthy downforce.

The Canadian GP saw the debut of the low downforce rear wing designed specifically for the circuit's long straights: the main profile showed a raised leading edge, while the endplates were characterised by two horizontal slots and the absence of the Monkey Seat.

In Austria, on the track owned by the Red Bull patron Dietrich Mateschitz, James Key introduced a new rear suspension configuration: the lower wishbone was partially faired on the side of the wheel, similar to the front "tuning fork" with the arms closer together than usual and helping create a wing profile.

The upper wishbone was raised with a shaped plate inserted between the stub axle and the arms, creating more space in which to exploit the aerodynamics of the carbonfibre brake duct, characterised by a dual vent in the upper part.

At the front instead, we noted a new brake duct in Austria, similar to the McLaren design which used the tyre as the external wall, together with the S-shaped carbonfibre brow in the centre, where the majority of the flow for cooling the brakes is drawn.

After Max Verstappen's 4th place at the Hungaroring, the Faenza team adopted a defensive strategy at Spa: Key's engineers tried to reduce drag by working on the final front wing flap which was trimmed and reshaped.

This modification was accompanied by a very low downforce rear wing: the short chord main profile was paired with a flap with a lower surface area but equipped with a small Gurney flap.

The concepts from Belgium were then taken to extremes at Monza where the mobile flap of the rear wing was trimmed: the engineers removed around a centimetre to reduce drag, while the third flap on the front wing was eliminated. During the night at Singapore, Toro Rosso presented a new front wing characterised by a main profile with a dual flap and three additional profiles, while the upper flaps featured a turning vane in the centre to which were added a further two mini-flaps that curved upwards.

At Suzuka the dual turning vane that had already been seen at Marina Bay reappeared.

In Japan, the traditional bargeboard was joined by a second profile in search of the high downforce required by the Honda circuit.

At Sochi, the two ears on the engine cover reappeared to improve cooling of the mechanical organs and the reliability of the Renault Power Unit, while at Austin the idea was reprised on Verstappen's car only, with Sainz running with the standard configuration.

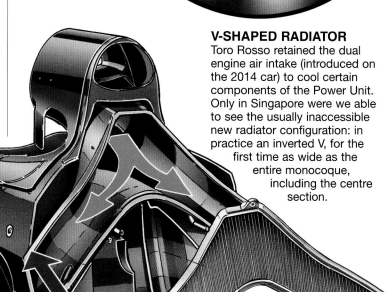

V-SHAPED RADIATOR

Toro Rosso retained the dual engine air intake (introduced on the 2014 car) to cool certain components of the Power Unit. Only in Singapore were we able to see the usually inaccessible new radiator configuration: in practice an inverted V, for the first time as wide as the entire monocoque, including the centre section.

LONG NOSE/SHORT NOSE

At its launch the STR10 had a very long nose (like that of the Ferrari), with a flat, pointed shape, but by the second pre-season test session a short version had been adopted that was then retained for the rest of the season, mated to the main profile close to its trailing edge. This new version not only permitted a more efficient front wing, but also optimised the flow towards the rear of the car and the diffuser, guaranteeing improved aerodynamic balance.

Jerez

Barcelona

Melbourne

SEPANG
Sepang saw the debut of this rear bodywork section with a huge megaphone vent, then used at all the circuits that demanded particularly efficient cooling.

REAR WING AND MONKEY SEAT

Again in pre-season testing, Toro Rosso introduced two versions of the Monkey Seat: in the circle the new version that debuted in the second test session: different in all its components (endplates with dual slots, vertical support) and combined with the new wing, it guaranteed increased downforce. The engine cover was also new: in the main drawing you can see that the Monkey Seat was less complex, designed for low-medium downforce tracks, while the Barcelona circuit required a medium-high configuration. At the first race of the season we saw a further refinement of the end part of the engine cover and the vertical rear wing support. In practice, this was the third version of this particular area, with the modification of the central pylon mounting with respect to what had been seen in the second test session at Barcelona. However, the most interesting feature concerned the pylon that like a kind of blade, traversed the exhaust and attached to the deformable structure in an inverted T. This last feature, which was widely copied, influenced the quality of the exhaust gas flow.

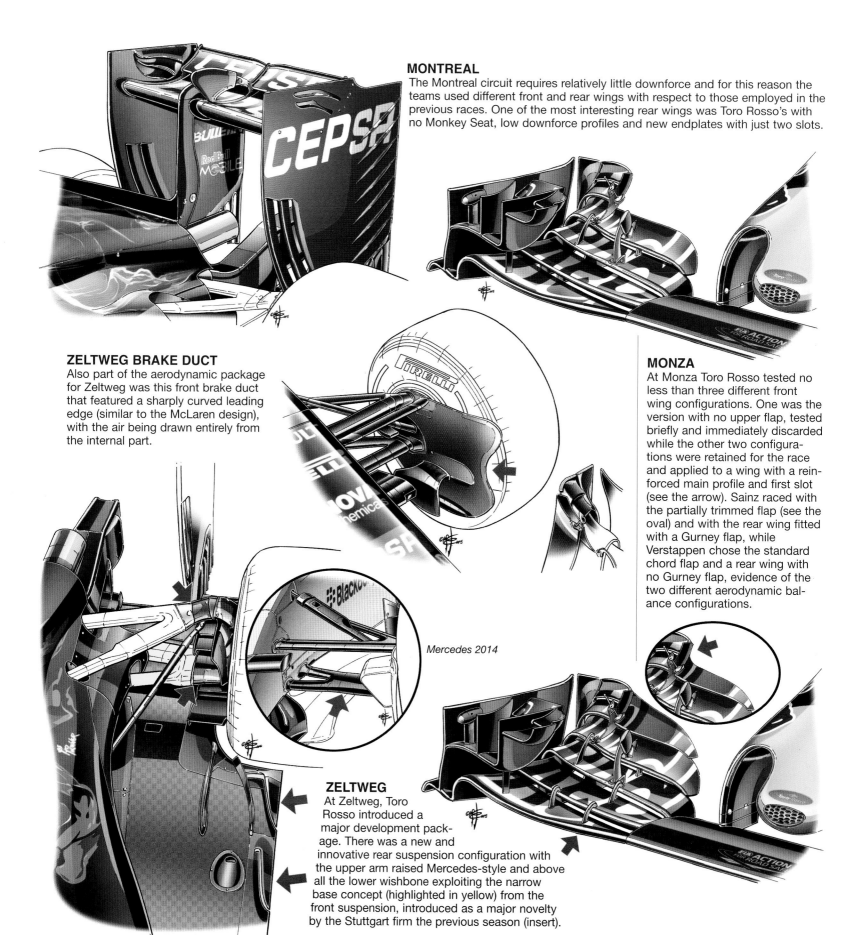

MONTREAL

The Montreal circuit requires relatively little downforce and for this reason the teams used different front and rear wings with respect to those employed in the previous races. One of the most interesting rear wings was Toro Rosso's with no Monkey Seat, low downforce profiles and new endplates with just two slots.

ZELTWEG BRAKE DUCT

Also part of the aerodynamic package for Zeltweg was this front brake duct that featured a sharply curved leading edge (similar to the McLaren design), with the air being drawn entirely from the internal part.

Mercedes 2014

MONZA

At Monza Toro Rosso tested no less than three different front wing configurations. One was the version with no upper flap, tested briefly and immediately discarded while the other two configurations were retained for the race and applied to a wing with a reinforced main profile and first slot (see the arrow). Sainz raced with the partially trimmed flap (see the oval) and with the rear wing fitted with a Gurney flap, while Verstappen chose the standard chord flap and a rear wing with no Gurney flap, evidence of the two different aerodynamic balance configurations.

ZELTWEG

At Zeltweg, Toro Rosso introduced a major development package. There was a new and innovative rear suspension configuration with the upper arm raised Mercedes-style and above all the lower wishbone exploiting the narrow base concept (highlighted in yellow) from the front suspension, introduced as a major novelty by the Stuttgart firm the previous season (insert).

SAUBER

CONSTRUCTORS' CLASSIFICATION			
	2014	2015	
Position	10°	8°	+2▲
Points	0	36	+36▲

Sauber emerged from its nightmare in 2015: with 8th place in the Constructors' Championship and 36 points conquered the Swiss team in fact succeeded in erasing memories of the previous season when it had finished the season in 10th place, failing to secure a single point. After having sunk to the lowest level in its history, the Hinwil-based team slowly began to climb back up, despite being hampered by economic difficul-

ties. Both drivers brought signifi-cant investment that permitted Eric Gandelin to complete the C34. The chassis was revised, in particular at the rear with the new installation of the Ferrari 059/3 Power Unit that entailed moving the oil tank to a location between engine and chassis.
The long, voluminous nose did not allow much passage of air between the principal profile and the support pylons of the front wing. The sidepods were com-

pletely different: the triangular intake mouths cooling the engine were small while the radiators were mounted almost horizontal-ly, similar to the configuration adopted on the Red Bull RB10. The roll-up was cut away sharply, with the body of the roll bar detached from the engine's dynamic air intake. Set either side of the triangular airbox were two ears for cooling the gearbox radiator, while a conspicuous fin stood on the engine cover.

At the rear there was new pull-rod rear suspension configura-tion: in particular, the lower wish-bone feature separate arms, while the dual rear wing pylon was anchored directly to the deformable structure of the gear-box.
As early as the Australian GP, Felipe Nasr drew on the full potential of the C34 to finish in an unexpected 5th place.
In Malaysia where it was instead disappointing, the blue and yel-low car presented larger front brake ducts and air intakes, while in China the team used the first example of the new Mercedes-style front wing, entrusted to Nasr in the hope of creating more downforce on the front axle.
The C34 proved to be fairly com-petitive on fast circuits, while it suffered on the slower tracks.
In Bahrain Ericsson also used the new configuration, but both dri-vers complained about the car's instability and in Spain the origi-nal feature returned. New vertical turning vanes ahead of the side-pods were seen in Barcelona.
A certain degree of curiosity was aroused by the fact that in Canada Sauber retained the Monkey Seat from Monaco, albeit with a single almost neutral profile working in synergy with the rear wing. The brake ducts were new, while at the rear Brembo discs were used.
Development was all but frozen through to the Italian GP where a rear wing was introduced with a flat central section to the profile that then dipped towards the endplates. The Swiss team fitted lateral vanes with no less than six horizontal slots and a mobile flap with a fairly wide chord, unusual for the "Temple of Speed".
An aerodynamic package arrived in Singapore that effectively cre-ated a B version of the C34: the most eye-catching novelty was the short nose combined with the revised wing from China, while the sidepods were redesigned, proving to be sleeker behind the radiators and with a hot air vent

Sauber C34
Abu Dhabi

Sauber C34
Melbourne

Sauber C34
Monza

Sauber C34
Singapore

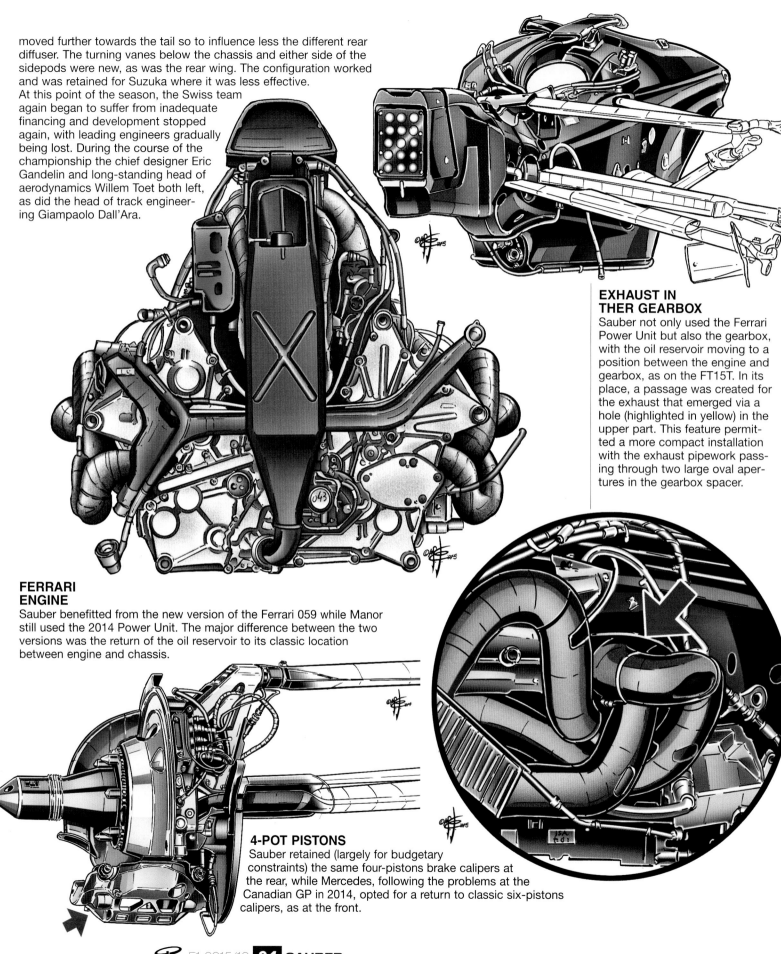

moved further towards the tail so to influence less the different rear diffuser. The turning vanes below the chassis and either side of the sidepods were new, as was the rear wing. The configuration worked and was retained for Suzuka where it was less effective.

At this point of the season, the Swiss team again began to suffer from inadequate financing and development stopped again, with leading engineers gradually being lost. During the course of the championship the chief designer Eric Gandelin and long-standing head of aerodynamics Willem Toet both left, as did the head of track engineering Giampaolo Dall'Ara.

EXHAUST IN THER GEARBOX

Sauber not only used the Ferrari Power Unit but also the gearbox, with the oil reservoir moving to a position between the engine and gearbox, as on the FT15T. In its place, a passage was created for the exhaust that emerged via a hole (highlighted in yellow) in the upper part. This feature permitted a more compact installation with the exhaust pipework passing through two large oval apertures in the gearbox spacer.

FERRARI ENGINE

Sauber benefitted from the new version of the Ferrari 059 while Manor still used the 2014 Power Unit. The major difference between the two versions was the return of the oil reservoir to its classic location between engine and chassis.

4-POT PISTONS

Sauber retained (largely for budgetary constraints) the same four-pistons brake calipers at the rear, while Mercedes, following the problems at the Canadian GP in 2014, opted for a return to classic six-pistons calipers, as at the front.

DYNAMIC AIR INTAKE

The C34 was characterised by a Power Unit air intake with a triangular section, distinctly separate from the body of the car and equipped with slim "ears" either side, leading to the various radiators. There was a conspicuous dorsal fin over the engine cover.

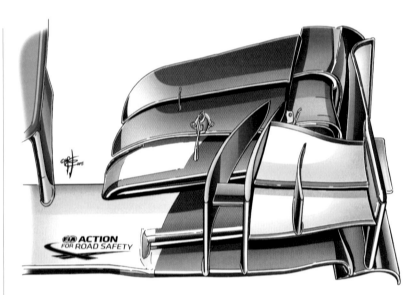

SHANGHAI

Shanghai saw the debut of a new front wing, but only for Nasr. Clearly of the Mercedes school, every element of the wing was new. Alongside the raised flaps was a single vertical fin, as on the Ferraris. The small fin outside the endplate was different and shorter.

SINGAPORE

At Singapore Sauber introduced the final iteration of the season, with the principal novelties being in the nose and the front wing. This drawing highlights the differences between the long nose (left) and the new short version (right). (1) The short nose has the McLaren-type finger with an arch (2) formed by the pylons. (3) The main profile is also completely new with a broader flat area (3) in the zone close to the endplates. (4) The blown flap curving towards the centre is also new. The Ferrari-style vertical fin sharply curves towards the outside (5) while the peripheral area (6) has McLaren type slots.

NOSES COMPARISON

Compared from the same angle and without the front wing, the new nose is equipped with a keel (red arrow) in the lower section. The new version closely resembles the nose introduced by McLaren at the Austrian GP. In practice Sauber was the last car to adopt the short nose configuration, leaving only Ferrari with the long nose on the SF15T.

SAUBER **95** F1 2015/16 GIORGIO PIOLA

McLAREN

The eagerly awaited World Championship return of Honda, absent since 2008, proved to be the biggest flop in modern F1. The major Japanese manufacturer clearly failed to repeat the feats of the McLaren-Honda combination that in five years together from 1988 to 1992 brought the Woking-based team no less than four Drivers' titles, four Constructors' titles, 39 victories in 65 races with total domination in the 1988 debut season that saw McLaren win 15 of the 16 scheduled races.

The experience McLaren had gained with the Mercedes Power Unit in 2014 proved to be in vain, as did the repetition of the winning strategy employed by John Barnard when he imposed dimensional constraints on Porsche with regard to the design of the six-cylinder turbo engine way back inn 1983, inaugurating a period of success for McLaren that was to last through to 1987.

During the definition of the MP4-30 project, the engineers led by Tim Goss bet heavily on the maximum reduction of the dimensions of the rear end to the point that they defined the entire operation "size zero", giving rise to a kind of scaled-down version of the 2014 car. This conditioned the Power Unit as it had to be configured to fit within the space established in Woking.

Therefore, in contrast with Mercedes, which had chosen a large turbo so as to guarantee the hybrid system sufficient recharging energy, at Honda's Tochigi Research Centre, the engineers opted for a very small turbo compressor assembly that could fit in the V of the engine. The idea was to produce energy that would obtain the same power output as the Mercedes but with a turbocharger spinning at 125,000 rpm rather than the usual 80,000/100,000 rpm of the larger compressors.

Problems arose during the first laps of the track in winter testing, with a chronic lack of reliability associated with a lower power output from the electrical component of the hybrid system. However, from its launch the MP4-30 had a stunning aerodynamic package. Beautifully detailed, it was born with a relatively long, low nose, combined with the wing that had in part been seen in Abu Dhabi and which reprised those designed by Prodromou for Red Bull. The form of the brake ducts was very unusual and drew air from between the tyre and the brake shroud that had an indent in the central section where there was a greater supply of air towards the inside of the wheel. It should be noted that the MP4-30 presented blowing front hubs, a legacy of the configuration established by the former aerodynamics chief

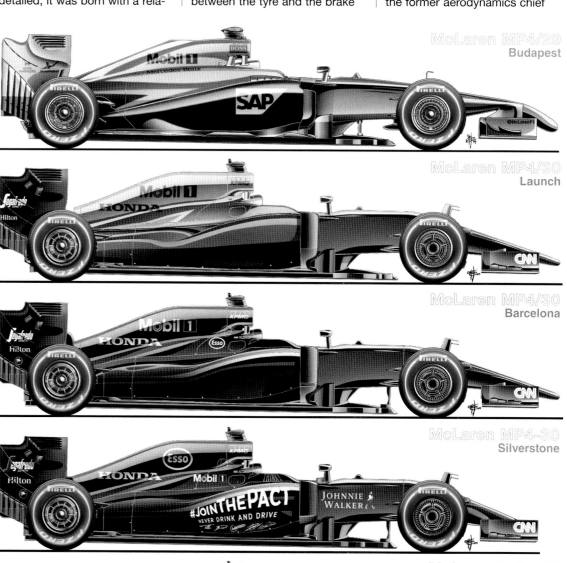

McLaren MP4/29
Budapest

McLaren MP4/30
Launch

McLaren MP4/30
Barcelona

McLaren MP4-30
Silverstone

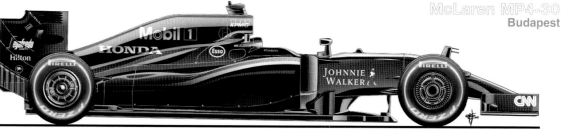

McLaren MP4-30
Budapest

Newey. The sidepods were very tall at the front but very low and narrow at the rear, with a new and sophisticated radiator configuration that gave encouraging results. Great attention was focussed on the installation of the Power Unit, with a particular compressor configuration: it was detached from the turbo and located almost centrally.

Another new feature was that of the rear suspension: after the faired double wishbones of the MP4-29 of 2014, a more extreme example of how aerodynamics have prevailed in this sector too, on the MP4-30 the lower wishbone was retracted as far as possible behind the front axle so as to allow the rear arm to work in synergy with the diffuser.

For the first time, its rear mounting point was no longer on the gearbox casing but on the deformable structure.

Despite the disappointing results, the MP4-30 was subjected to almost constant evolutions at every race, thanks in part to the dynamic support of Peter Prodromou. An initial major step came in Malaysia with a new front wing but above all with the introduction of the S-Duct, used n a slightly different way to preceding examples (Sauber and Red Bull). In Bahrain there was a further major step with the introduction of a sophisticated diffuser mounted on both cars rather than just one (Button's) as had been the case in Shanghai; also new was the rear wing without the sawtooth trailing edge on the main profile and the leading edge of the flap. Yet another fundamental step came in Austria with the arrival of the short nose on Alonso's car only and only in the afternoon while awaiting definitive approval from the FIA. This nose was due to have been combined with the new lighter chassis that was to appear at the following British GP.

The regulations in fact stated that the crash test had to be done with the car being used on track and the lighter chassis was obviously not identical to those taken to Zeltweg. In the end, logic prevailed in the sense that the crash test would be even easier to pass with the heavier, stronger chassis.

The final major step came in the USA: a new Mercedes-style front wing, new endplates, modifications to the turning vanes at the sides of the front of the sidepods (both the low front ones and the vertical lateral ones) and to the diffuser. There was surprise at the abandoning of the complicated blowing in the area ahead of the front wheels in favour of copying the configuration introduced by Ferrari in Singapore, with 11 slots in place of the 9 on the SF15T.

In terms of the Power Unit it should be noted that Honda was allowed to use no less than nine tokens and an extra unit with respect to the four allowed for the other manufacturers in 2015. Moreover, the Japanese firm homologated a new unit in February following the one tested in November 2014 at Abu Dhabi. The total lack of reliability then obliged Alonso to use no less than 12 units against the four used by Mercedes and its client teams. This more than anything else gives a measure of the failure of the Japanese manufacturer's return to F1. Nonetheless, Honda did not give up on development of the RA615 H, spending two tokens in Canada, three at Spa for new injectors and camshafts and four in Sochi where it introduced a version of the engine with a new combustion chamber design and different exhausts. As if this were not enough, the battery pack produced by McLaren also suffered significant overheating problems.

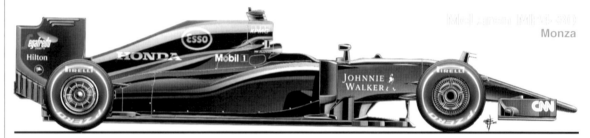

McLaren MP4-30
Monza

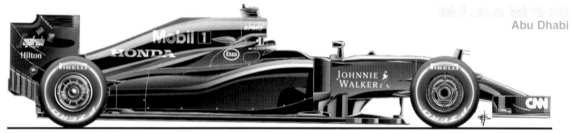

McLaren MP4-30
Abu Dhabi

OVERHEAD COMPARISON MP4-29/MP4-30

The overhead comparison of the MP4-29 from 2014 and the MP4-30 from 2015 illustrates the "Size Zero" concept at the rear of the car in the so-called Coke bottle area highlighted with the yellow bar that was much narrower. (1) The MP4-30 was introduced with a very flat, wide and long nose but with the Red Bull-style front wing (2) introduced in the last race at Abu Dhabi. (3) The steering arm was at the same height as the upper wishbone while the brake ducts were new. (4) The sidepods were shorter and therefore further from the turbulence of the front wheels and were also slightly narrower which meant that the protection structures were revealed as their dimensions were imposed by the regulations. (5) New bargeboards. (6) The tapering of the rear end without the large vents (7) was much more pronounced. (8) New rear suspension with the rear arm of the lower wishbone pivoting on the deformable structure rather than the gearbox casing for the first time. (9) In order to render the mechanicals more compact the wheelbase was lengthened (the difference is highlighted in yellow). (19) The diffuser designed by Prodromou was also new.

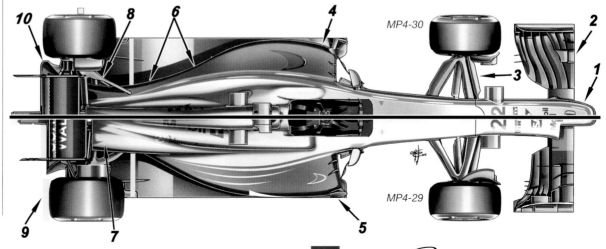

OVERHEAD COMPARISON MELBOURNE-BUDAPEST

The short nose (1) made its debut at the Austrian GP with a very square-cut shape, but it was in Budapest that further new features arrived, while the livery was modified for the Spanish GP. (2-3) Refinements were introduced to the front wing at virtually every race. (4) The S-Duct arrived at the second race of the season in Sepang. (5) There were now three fins at the front of the sidepods. (6) Vents for the hot air from the sidepods. (7) New slots ahead of the rear wheels introduced in Austria. (8) The diffuser was subjected to constant development.

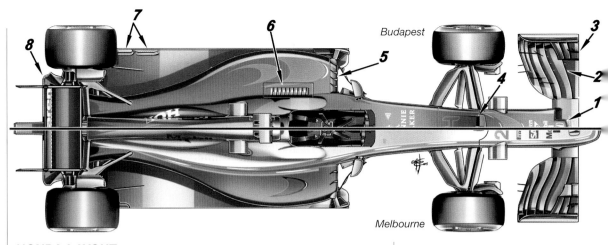

Budapest

Melbourne

HONDA LAYOUT

Honda used a different configuration for the layout of the Power Unit components. The MGU-H continued to be located between compressor and turbine as on the Mercedes, but while the compressor on the Stuttgart V6 was at the front of the engine, therefore some distance from the turbine set at the other end, on the Honda the three components were brought closer with the compressor in the V of the engine; this feature proved to be less than optimal for the cooling of the MGU-H and above all detrimental due to the reduced dimensions of the compressor. Note the rather unsuccessful location of the intercooler above the airbox. The new combustion chamber design is of course concealed.

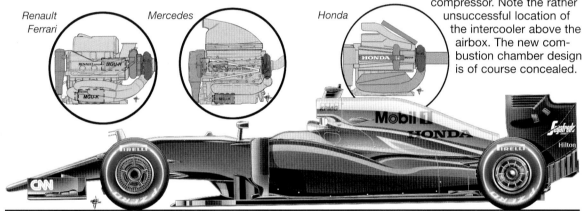

Renault
Ferrari

Mercedes

Honda

BATTERY PACK

The lithium battery pack produced by McLaren itself also suffered problems. Of notable dimensions and weight, the batteries proved to be unreliable with drops in efficiency. This was in part due to a usage window that was very restricted in terms of operating temperatures.

HONDA ENGINE

A comparison between the Honda RA615 H six-cylinder turbo and the second version introduced at Sochi. From the outside, the most obvious modification concerned the exhausts with very short manifolds enclosed in a kind of lung as with the Mercedes engines in 2014. In the second version, the manifolds had a more traditional configuration.

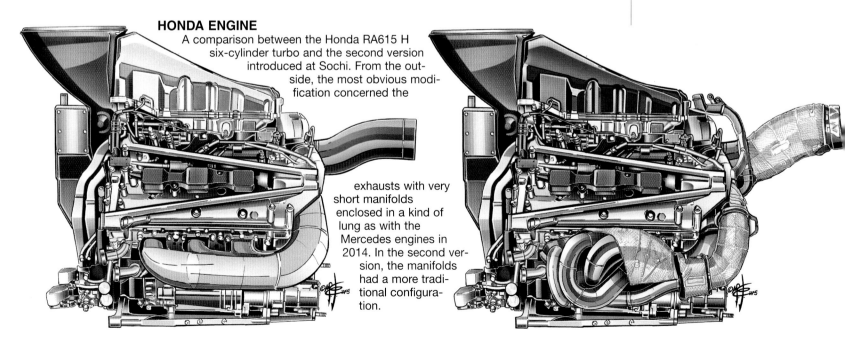

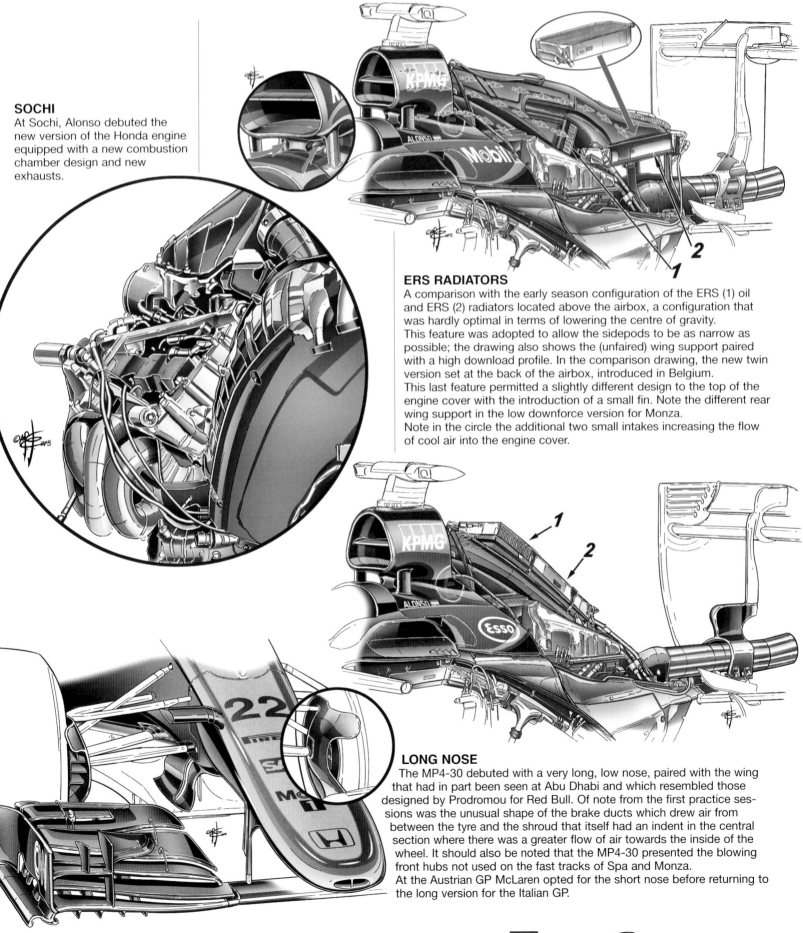

SOCHI

At Sochi, Alonso debuted the new version of the Honda engine equipped with a new combustion chamber design and new exhausts.

ERS RADIATORS

A comparison with the early season configuration of the ERS (1) oil and ERS (2) radiators located above the airbox, a configuration that was hardly optimal in terms of lowering the centre of gravity.

This feature was adopted to allow the sidepods to be as narrow as possible; the drawing also shows the (unfaired) wing support paired with a high download profile. In the comparison drawing, the new twin version set at the back of the airbox, introduced in Belgium.

This last feature permitted a slightly different design to the top of the engine cover with the introduction of a small fin. Note the different rear wing support in the low downforce version for Monza.

Note in the circle the additional two small intakes increasing the flow of cool air into the engine cover.

LONG NOSE

The MP4-30 debuted with a very long, low nose, paired with the wing that had in part been seen at Abu Dhabi and which resembled those designed by Prodromou for Red Bull. Of note from the first practice sessions was the unusual shape of the brake ducts which drew air from between the tyre and the shroud that itself had an indent in the central section where there was a greater flow of air towards the inside of the wheel. It should also be noted that the MP4-30 presented the blowing front hubs not used on the fast tracks of Spa and Monza.

At the Austrian GP McLaren opted for the short nose before returning to the long version for the Italian GP.

GIORGIO PIOLA

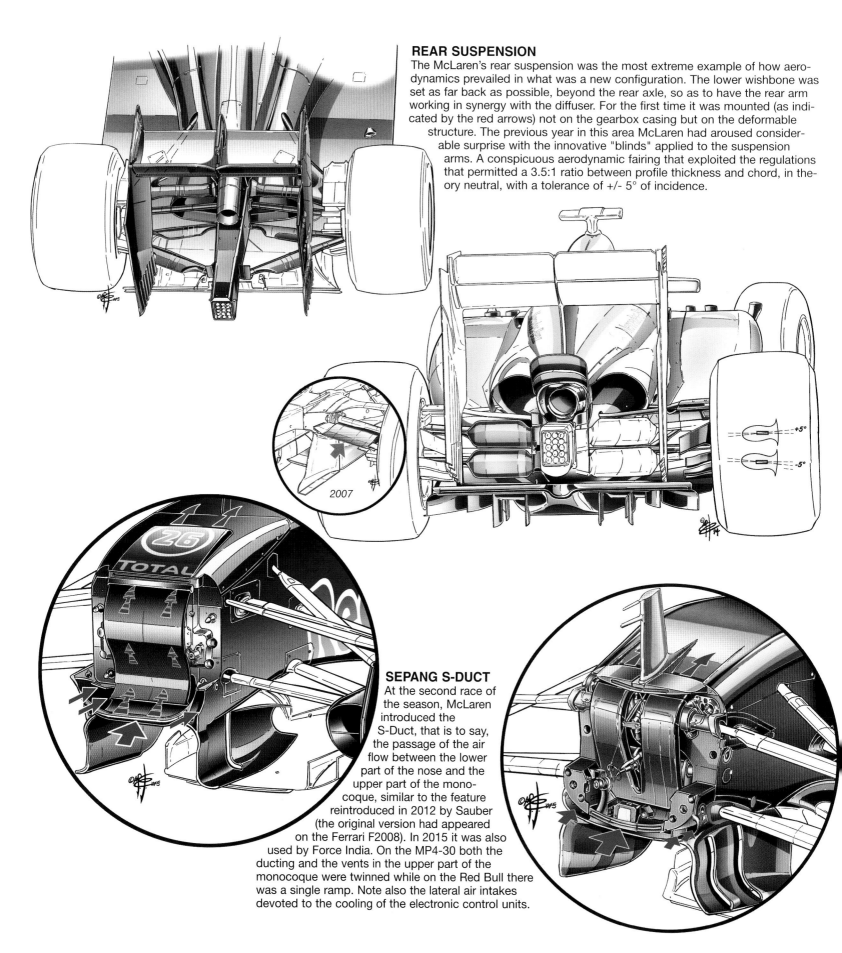

REAR SUSPENSION

The McLaren's rear suspension was the most extreme example of how aerodynamics prevailed in what was a new configuration. The lower wishbone was set as far back as possible, beyond the rear axle, so as to have the rear arm working in synergy with the diffuser. For the first time it was mounted (as indicated by the red arrows) not on the gearbox casing but on the deformable structure. The previous year in this area McLaren had aroused considerable surprise with the innovative "blinds" applied to the suspension arms. A conspicuous aerodynamic fairing that exploited the regulations that permitted a 3.5:1 ratio between profile thickness and chord, in theory neutral, with a tolerance of +/- 5° of incidence.

2007

+5°

-5°

SEPANG S-DUCT

At the second race of the season, McLaren introduced the S-Duct, that is to say, the passage of the air flow between the lower part of the nose and the upper part of the monocoque, similar to the feature reintroduced in 2012 by Sauber (the original version had appeared on the Ferrari F2008). In 2015 it was also used by Force India. On the MP4-30 both the ducting and the vents in the upper part of the monocoque were twinned while on the Red Bull there was a single ramp. Note also the lateral air intakes devoted to the cooling of the electronic control units.

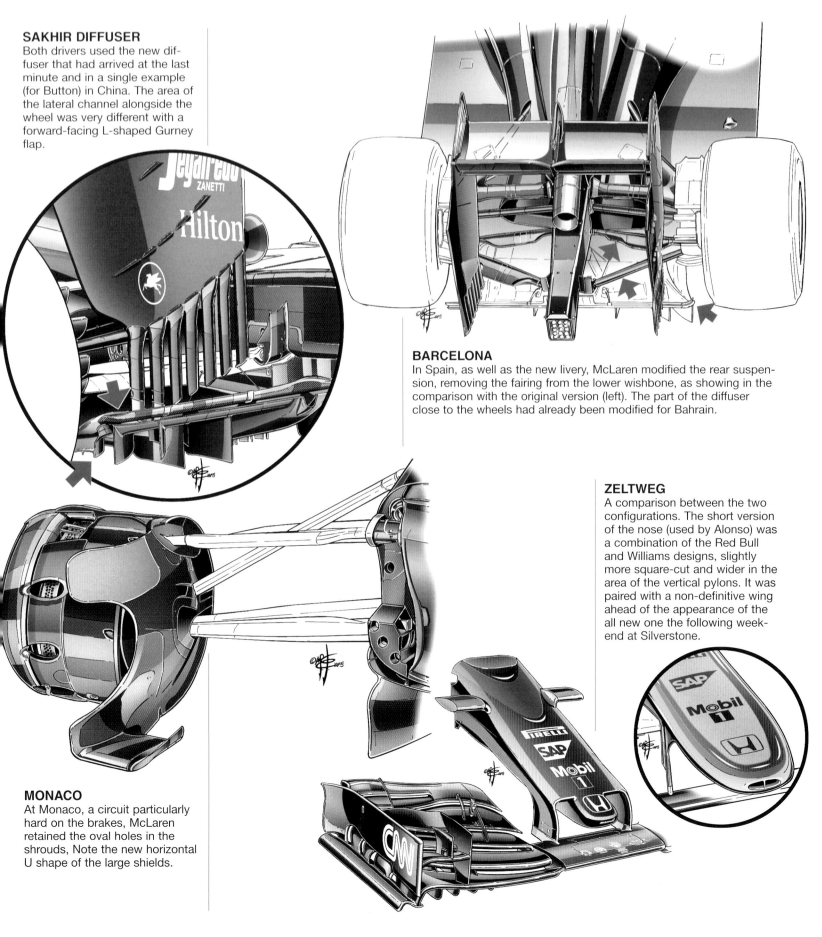

SAKHIR DIFFUSER

Both drivers used the new diffuser that had arrived at the last minute and in a single example (for Button) in China. The area of the lateral channel alongside the wheel was very different with a forward-facing L-shaped Gurney flap.

BARCELONA

In Spain, as well as the new livery, McLaren modified the rear suspension, removing the fairing from the lower wishbone, as showing in the comparison with the original version (left). The part of the diffuser close to the wheels had already been modified for Bahrain.

ZELTWEG

A comparison between the two configurations. The short version of the nose (used by Alonso) was a combination of the Red Bull and Williams designs, slightly more square-cut and wider in the area of the vertical pylons. It was paired with a non-definitive wing ahead of the appearance of the all new one the following weekend at Silverstone.

MONACO

At Monaco, a circuit particularly hard on the brakes, McLaren retained the oval holes in the shrouds, Note the new horizontal U shape of the large shields.

GIORGIO PIOLA

ZELTWEG

Again at Zeltweg, there was a significant and previously unseen modification in the high pressure area ahead of the front wheels which had increasingly become a location for new features.

Following the L-shaped longitudinal cuts of the Toro Rosso, on Alonso's car McLaren presented four longitudinal and two transverse slots in line with the rear wheel. The aim was to reduced the lift generated at this point by the rotation of the rear tyres.

SILVERSTONE

The final piece in the "B" version jigsaw introduced between Austria and Great Britain saw the arrival of these L-shaped winglets below the mirrors in place of the triangular arrow-head ones. They were fitted to the new lightened chassis.

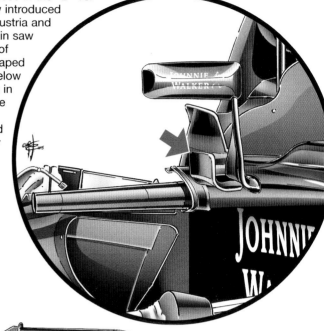

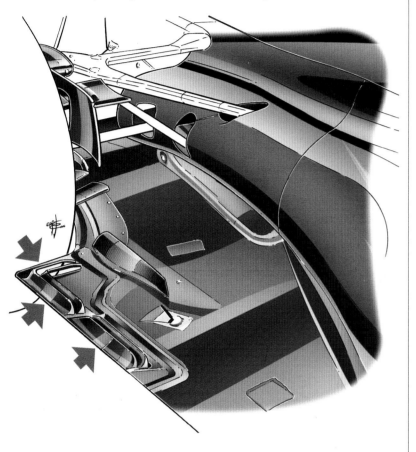

SINGAPORE

In order to guarantee greater downforce on the rear end, in Singapore McLaren introduced a new Monkey Seat based on the rear wing from Budapest.

SPA-FRANCORCHAMPS

For the fast track at Spa, McLaren modified the T-Tray area with two vents in the bargeboards of the MP4-30, together with numerous other modifications (ERS radiators, engine cover and sidepods).

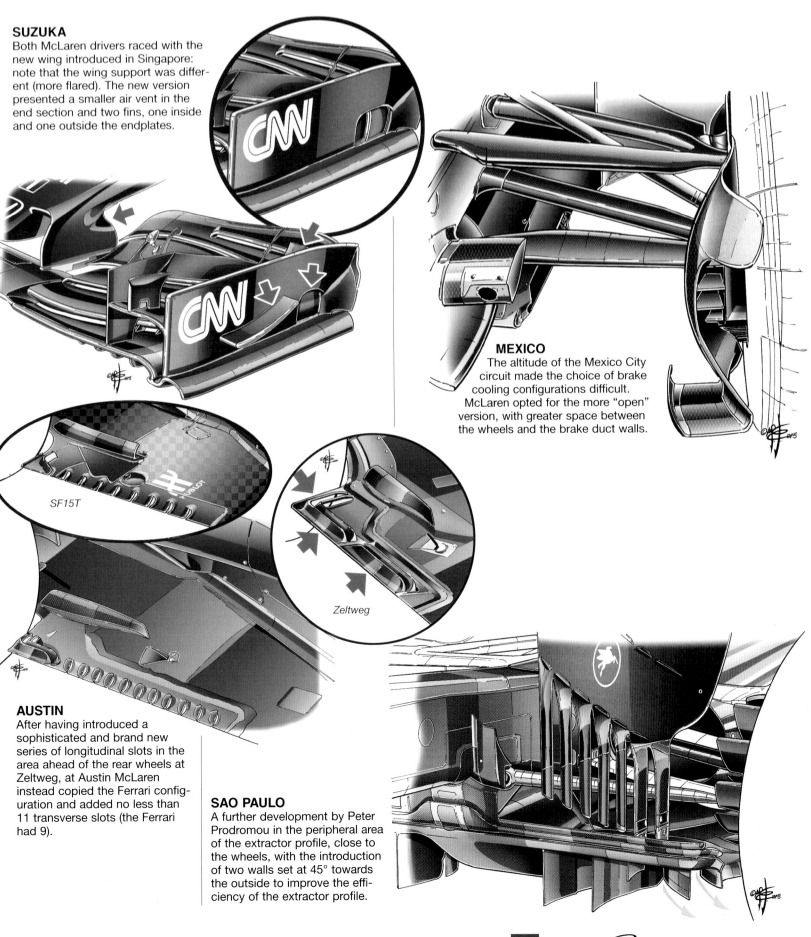

SUZUKA
Both McLaren drivers raced with the new wing introduced in Singapore: note that the wing support was different (more flared). The new version presented a smaller air vent in the end section and two fins, one inside and one outside the endplates.

SF15T

Zeltweg

MEXICO
The altitude of the Mexico City circuit made the choice of brake cooling configurations difficult. McLaren opted for the more "open" version, with greater space between the wheels and the brake duct walls.

AUSTIN
After having introduced a sophisticated and brand new series of longitudinal slots in the area ahead of the rear wheels at Zeltweg, at Austin McLaren instead copied the Ferrari configuration and added no less than 11 transverse slots (the Ferrari had 9).

SAO PAULO
A further development by Peter Prodromou in the peripheral area of the extractor profile, close to the wheels, with the introduction of two walls set at 45° towards the outside to improve the efficiency of the extractor profile.

MANOR

2015 was a difficult season for Manor following the tragedy of Jules Bianchi and the impossibility of building a new chassis that respected the modifications made to the regulations regarding the lateral protection structures, as well as the new restrictions on the noses and the consequent frontal crash test. The solution that was found was to attach an extension to the monocoque, effectively an addition to the front bulkhead, permitted by the regulations that did not impose a single chassis structure. The roll safety bar was not an integral part of the monocoque design, but was applied to the same. With this expedient, Manor in practice fielded the 2014 car equipped with the same Ferrari Power Unit with the revolutionary, but rather inefficient oil reservoir located in the gearbox spacer. Hence the decision to dispute the 2015 championship as if it was a proving ground for the following season when the team would be using new Mercedes power units.

The MR03B was never even wind tunnel tested, with all efforts being focussed on the future MR04. In effect the wind tunnel development of the 2016 car began in late June, with the first drawings having been prepared as early as May and with a staff reduced to the bare minimum (around a 100 employees against the 200 of the previous year).

John McQuilliam was appointed as technical director, while Tim Milner took on responsibility for aerodynamics. Luca Furbatto (ex-Toro Rosso) joined the group in May as designer.

The price was paid in terms of development, with a single major step being introduced with a B-version at Silverstone. This was equipped with a new front wing with a "marsupial" nose, different turning vanes beneath the chassis, new sidepods and bargeboards with a new diffuser in the upper section and new rear wing endplates. There was little development of the engine given that Ferrari and Sauber were using the 2015 version of the Maranello Power Unit. Only at Spa did a software evolution appear together with a new lubricant that permitted a gain of 15 hp.

Marussia MVR02
Sao Paolo

Manor MR03B
Sepang

Manor MR03B
Monza

Manor MR03B
Sao Paolo

FERRARI ENGINE
Manor ran the risk of not participating in the 2015 season and raced with the 2014 version of the Ferrari engine and gearbox, with the ineffective feature of the oil tank (highlighted in green) in the gearbox spacer, and therefore with a very restricted development of the Power Unit that was instead significantly modified at Maranello for Ferrari itself and Sauber. The insert shows the exhaust which were naturally the same as in 2014.

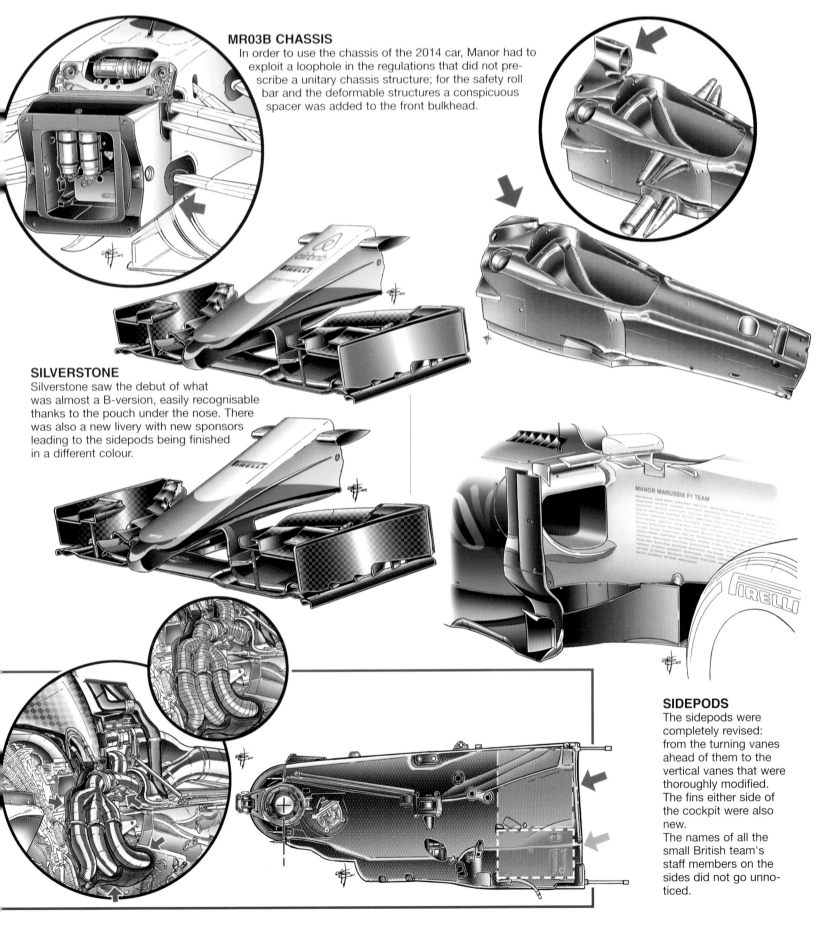

MR03B CHASSIS
In order to use the chassis of the 2014 car, Manor had to exploit a loophole in the regulations that did not prescribe a unitary chassis structure; for the safety roll bar and the deformable structures a conspicuous spacer was added to the front bulkhead.

SILVERSTONE
Silverstone saw the debut of what was almost a B-version, easily recognisable thanks to the pouch under the nose. There was also a new livery with new sponsors leading to the sidepods being finished in a different colour.

SIDEPODS
The sidepods were completely revised: from the turning vanes ahead of them to the vertical vanes that were thoroughly modified. The fins either side of the cockpit were also new.
The names of all the small British team's staff members on the sides did not go unnoticed.

2016 REGULATIONS

The 2016 season opened in a climate of technical stability, with just a few modifications being made in the interests of safety, the sound of the power unit and a drastic reduction in electronic driving aids at the start. In particular, the changes eliminated the electronic devices governing the clutch that had come to replace the traction control that had been outlawed from 2008 after having been reintroduced in 2001 for the start only. Lastly, Pirelli introduced a new Ultrasoft compound, distinguished by a purple band so as to guarantee greater strategic freedom with the possibility of having not two but three compounds available to the teams at every race, while respecting the limit of 13 sets assigned for the race weekend.

In order to enhance protection of the drivers' head, as well as commissioning Mercedes to work on the Halo project for a kind of extended roll-bar (see the 2015 Regulations chapter), the Federation introduced for the 2016 season an increase of 20 mm in the lateral protections either side of the driver's head and more importantly radically increased the severity of the mandatory crash test. The value in fact more than tripled from 15 N to 50 N, applied for three seconds. A test that was therefore even more difficult to pass than the frontal impact test applied to the nose.

In order to improve the sound of the power unit, the exhaust of the wastegate could no longer flow into the principal exhaust but had to take a separate route. There could actually be two small terminals, something that opened the way for diverse configurations, as in part illustrated. However, these terminals had to be symmet-

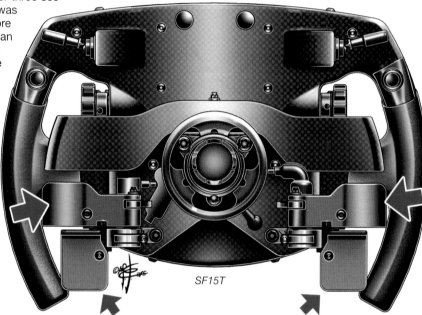

SF15T

FERRARI STEERING WHEEL

From the very first race we were able to reveal one of the SF16H's secrets: the long paddle in place of the dual clutch levers controlling the clutch, which for the 2016 season had to be governed by just one of the driver's hands. The most important thing, however, is that the paddle is hinged at one aide rather than in the middle. On the SF15T's steering wheel in 2015 there were no less than six levers.

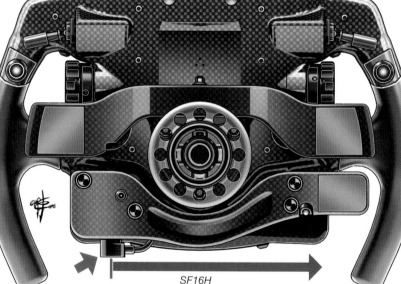

SF16H

OFFSET PADDLE

The offset pivot of the long clutch lever on the Ferrari steering wheel can be clearly be seen; it allows greater modulation of the clutch handling during the start phase. Consequently the Ferrari camera was the one subjected to the closest scrutiny by its rival teams at the start of the season.

GIORGIO PIOLA

rical and set within 10 mm from the principal exhaust. From the launch of the new cars, the generalised tendency has been to adopt two small symmetrical exhausts placed lower than the principal one. The only example of single wastegate exhaust is found on the power unit used by Renault, while the one employed by Red Bull falls in line with the twin-terminal configuration.

The total of five power units available over the course of the season remains unchanged, despite the intention to reduce the number to four units; the increased number races led to a postponement of this decision.

The number of development tokens also remains unchanged at 32 (they had been due to be reduced to just 25) for each manufacturer, with the possibility of homologating a unit from the 2015 season for a client team (as in the case of Toro Rosso with Ferrari). Lastly, the limitation of a single clutch lever at the start of the race and a drastic restriction on radio communications with the team has meant a return of the driver as the protagonist when the lights change.

Actuated together with the first lever, the second in fact allowed the driver, once the gear had been engaged, to modulate power handling according to the bite point of the clutch, effectively creating a form of manual traction control. It should be remembered that the dual clutch was initially introduced so as to be able to intervene promptly with either hand in the case of an incident.

However, from 2001 when traction control was still tolerated, the second lever lost its "recovery" function in the case of a spin and instead became a kind of manual traction control, with the driver able to jockey the lever to avoid wheelspin.

As seen in the drawings of the Mercedes and Red Bull steering wheels, all the teams left the arrangement of the levers unchanged, while Ferrari revolutionised the rear part of the SF16H's steering wheel.

In place of the dual levers, there is a long paddle hinged at one side rather than in the centre, which means a much longer range of movement for just one of the driver's hands.

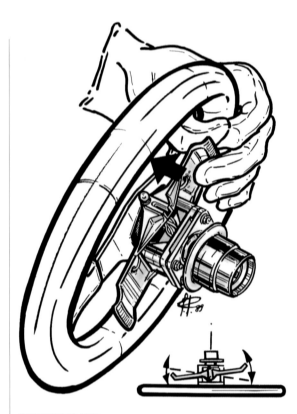

FERRARI 640

The merit for the introduction of gear changing via a rocker set behind the steering wheel goes to John Barnard, not only for having reprised Mauro Forghieri's idea from the late Seventies but above all for the daring decision to design the 640 monocoque in such a way that there was no room for a classic gear lever. With this move Barnard succeeded in overcoming the resistance of the race management (Cesare Fiorio) who would have preferred to abandon the feature after repeated retirements that afflicted Berger and Mansell in the first half of the '89 championship. The English driver had of course pulled off a surprise victory in the first race of the season in Brazil.

On the 640 the clutch was still controlled by a pedal.

MERCEDES AND RED BULL

Both Mercedes and Red Bull effectively retained the same steering wheel architecture as in 2015. See Rosberg's wheel with the levers slightly modified in terms of their ergonomic functionality. The RB12 also retained the two supplementary levers at the bottom that never appeared on the Mercedes steering wheels.

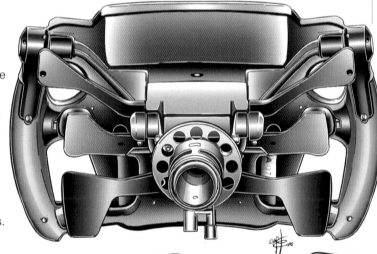

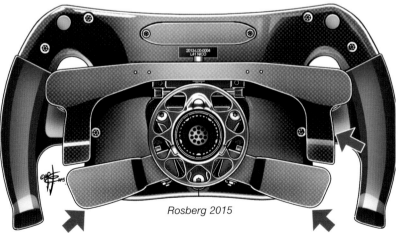

Rosberg 2015

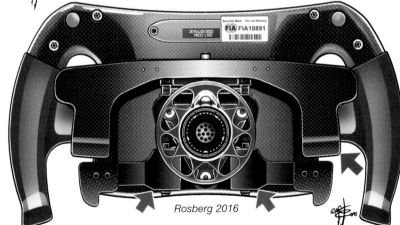

Rosberg 2016

McLAREN 1994

It was McLaren that in 1994 transferred the clutch control to the steering wheel too, eliminating the clutch pedal on Häkkinen's car. Brundle retained the pedal as after his accident in 1984 with the Tyrrell he no longer had the necessary strength to brake with his badly fractured left foot.

FERRARI 1995

From the 1995 season Ferrari, like the other teams, adopted clutch control at the steering wheel with dual levers guaranteeing immediate actuation in the event of a spin via the hand best placed to control the car.
Only from 2001 was the lever utilised with a manual traction control function.

Häkkinen

Brundle

JACQUES VILLENEUVE

Jacques Villeneuve warrants particular mention. The Canadian actuated the gearbox with a single lever, using the right hand only to pull it towards him to change down and pushing it away to change up. He also had a single lever for the clutch.

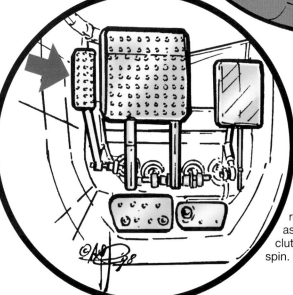

COULTHARD

Another curiosity concerns David Coulthard. Even though he had very long levers (indicated by the red arrows), he also wanted a small recovery pedal (yellow) to as to be able to actuate the clutch instantly the case of a spin.

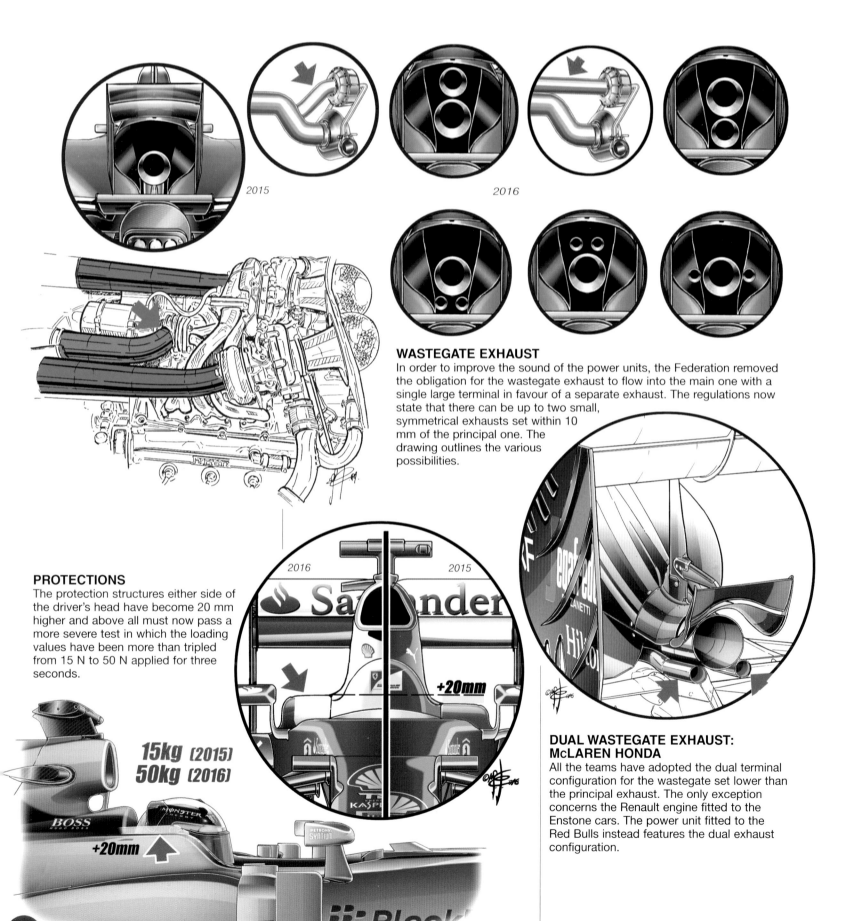

WASTEGATE EXHAUST

In order to improve the sound of the power units, the Federation removed the obligation for the wastegate exhaust to flow into the main one with a single large terminal in favour of a separate exhaust. The regulations now state that there can be up to two small, symmetrical exhausts set within 10 mm of the principal one. The drawing outlines the various possibilities.

PROTECTIONS

The protection structures either side of the driver's head have become 20 mm higher and above all must now pass a more severe test in which the loading values have been more than tripled from 15 N to 50 N applied for three seconds.

15kg (2015)
50kg (2016)

+20mm

DUAL WASTEGATE EXHAUST: McLAREN HONDA

All the teams have adopted the dual terminal configuration for the wastegate set lower than the principal exhaust. The only exception concerns the Renault engine fitted to the Enstone cars. The power unit fitted to the Red Bulls instead features the dual exhaust configuration.

GIORGIO PIOLA

PROPOSALS 2017

The Federation has already confirmed the regulations that will come into force from 2017 through to 2020, effectively adopting the project presented by McLaren that compared to the 2016 car provides a 25% increase in downforce.The Red Bull proposal, felt to be more extreme as it provided for an even more downforce.

2017

800mm

175mm

2016

950mm

125mm

With respect to the Red Bull version, a number of differences emerged in the car seen at the last race of the 2015 season in Abu Dhabi. In particular, the greater distance of the front wheel from the endplates and the maximum width of the bodywork and therefore the bottom of the car, fixed at 1,600 mm.

Similarly, the extractor profile width was fixed at 175 mm against the previous 330 mm. The braking systems will be able to fitted with discs that are 32 mm thick against the current 28 mm, improving braking force by an estimated 30%.

This will require the creation of slightly more rigid, larger and heavier calipers.

The hub carriers will also have to be reinforced.

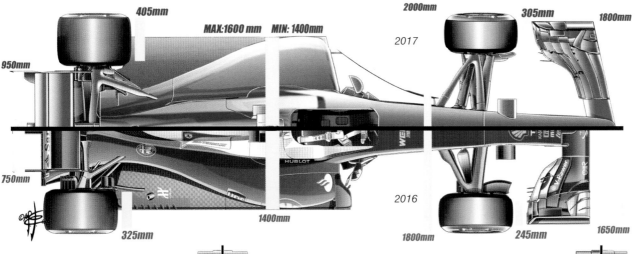

405mm

2000mm   305mm

MAX:1600 mm   MIN: 1400 mm

1800mm

950mm

2017

750mm

2016

325mm   1400mm   1800mm   245mm   1650mm

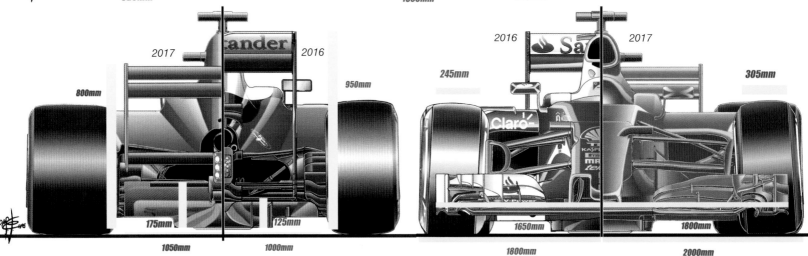

2017   *2016*   *2016*   *2017*

800mm   950mm   245mm   305mm

175mm   125mm   1650mm   1800mm

1050mm   1000mm   1800mm   2000mm

HALO

The Federation has chosen the Halo system for protecting the driver's head, conceived by Mercedes, revealed for the first time at the Malaysian Grand Prix and tested on track in revised form by Ferrari in pre-season testing at Barcelona. It is a kind of open ring in carbonfibre with a single vertical support in the centre. Compared with the version illustrated in these two drawings, the definitive Halo is to be made in titanium rather than carbonfibre and it will be extractable. Better visibility and greater safety in the case of impact favoured this design rather than the aeroscreen proposed by Red Bull. However, the Halo does have the disadvantage that it cannot prevent the passage of a small object such as, for example, the spring that struck Felipe Massa in the face at the Hungarian GP in 2009.

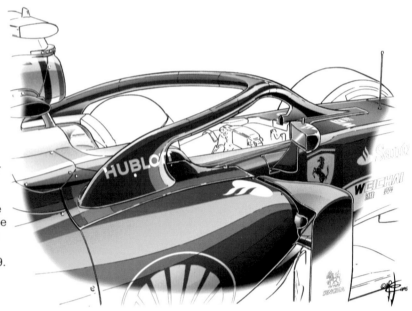

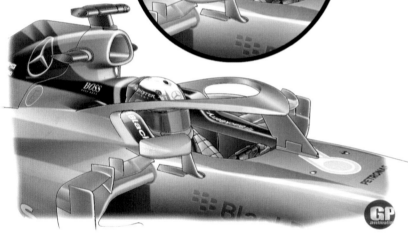

RED BULL AEROSCREEN

Red Bull has decided not to proceed with its protection device project known as the "aeroscreen" in order to concentrate on creating the car destined to be fitted with wider tyres from 2017. In total, €250,000 were devoted to this operation. However, it should be noted that the aeroscreen, tested on track at Sochi on the Friday by Ricciardo, had immediately aroused discordant opinions due both to the impaired visibility and the need for cleaning in the case of smearing of the screen.

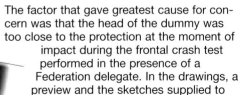

The factor that gave greatest cause for concern was that the head of the dummy was too close to the protection at the moment of impact during the frontal crash test performed in the presence of a Federation delegate. In the drawings, a preview and the sketches supplied to the press by Red Bull on the eve of the Sochi Grand Prix.

The 2016 **SEASON**

The 2016 season was characterised by the Ferrari-Mercedes duel with both teams creating radical cars, the SF16H to be considered as merely a point of departure for Maranello. The novelties and changes were numerous and included a return after four years to the push-rod front suspension layout. During the winter break, Mercedes made even greater progress than during the 2015 pre-season, laying claim to the 2016 championship from the very first test day. The W07 is in fact crammed with new and in some cases wholly unique features.

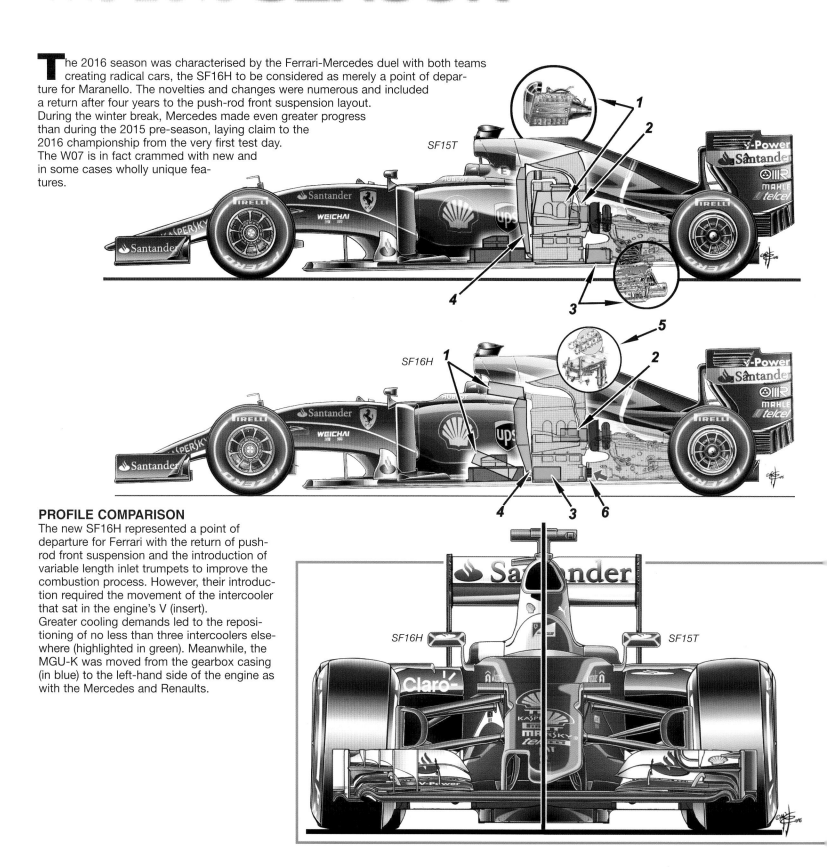

SF15T

SF16H

PROFILE COMPARISON

The new SF16H represented a point of departure for Ferrari with the return of push-rod front suspension and the introduction of variable length inlet trumpets to improve the combustion process. However, their introduction required the movement of the intercooler that sat in the engine's V (insert).
Greater cooling demands led to the repositioning of no less than three intercoolers elsewhere (highlighted in green). Meanwhile, the MGU-K was moved from the gearbox casing (in blue) to the left-hand side of the engine as with the Mercedes and Renaults.

SF16H

SF15T

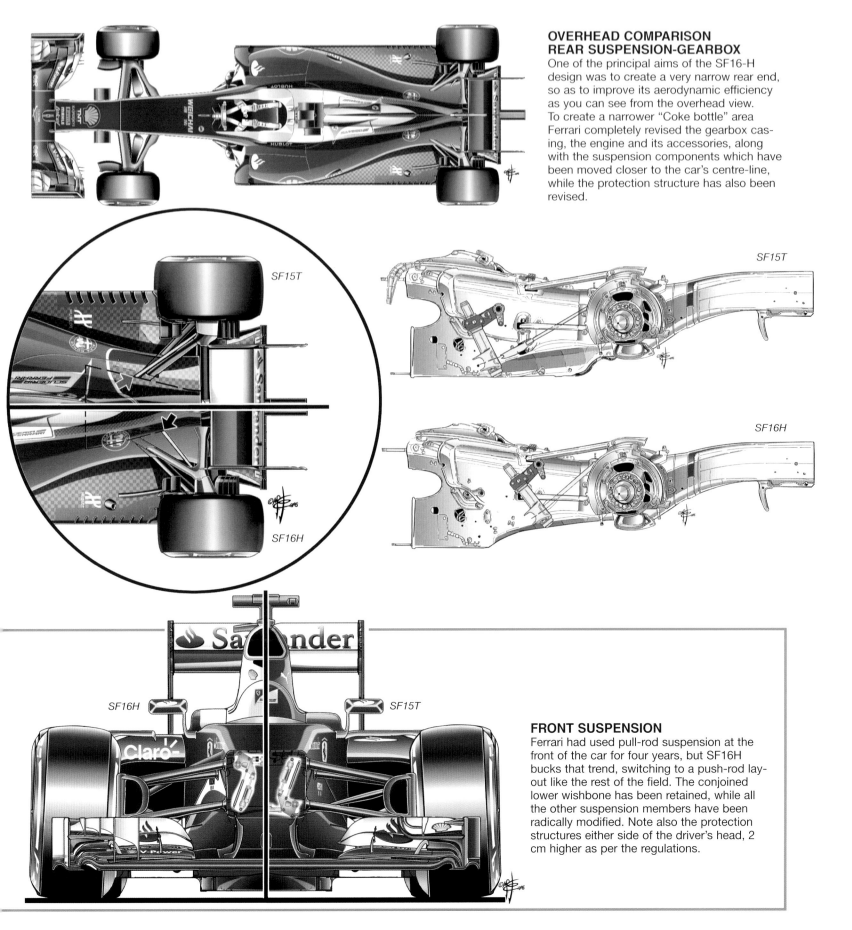

OVERHEAD COMPARISON REAR SUSPENSION-GEARBOX

One of the principal aims of the SF16-H design was to create a very narrow rear end, so as to improve its aerodynamic efficiency as you can see from the overhead view. To create a narrower "Coke bottle" area Ferrari completely revised the gearbox casing, the engine and its accessories, along with the suspension components which have been moved closer to the car's centre-line, while the protection structure has also been revised.

SF15T

SF16H

SF15T

SF16H

SF16H

SF15T

FRONT SUSPENSION

Ferrari had used pull-rod suspension at the front of the car for four years, but SF16H bucks that trend, switching to a push-rod layout like the rest of the field. The conjoined lower wishbone has been retained, while all the other suspension members have been radically modified. Note also the protection structures either side of the driver's head, 2 cm higher as per the regulations.

MERCEDES LAUNCH

Given their dominance over the last two seasons you would have expected Mercedes to retain a similar philosophy going into 2016. Instead, the W07 represents a radical evolution with the objective of increasing the gap to the rest of the field. An array of new and interesting features were introduced from the launch. Above all, the bargeboards featured innovative six vertical surfaces, with horizontal strakes at the bottom (highlighted in the oval) designed to manage the flow of air towards the lower area and the diffuser.

MERCEDES SECOND TEST

In the second week of pre-season testing, Mercedes introduced unique new vertical turning vanes ahead of the sidepods, divided into two parts.

The lower section is attached to the floor and is shaped to improve the direction of airflow around the sidepod the ear introduced by Sauber in 2013. The upper element is vertical with a part curving inwards to better control the airflow.

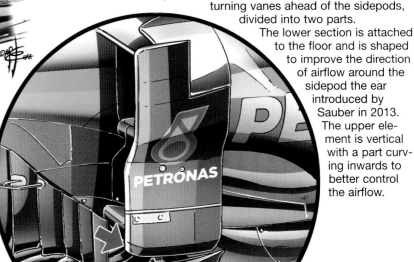

MERCEDES SERRATED WING

A new rear wing was also introduced at the second test, which featured a serrated trailing edge on the main plane deriving from testing at Abu Dhabi where a serrated sticker was placed on the main plane. A similar feature had been introduced at on the front wing (see the Mercedes chapter) Sochi, the experience of which was then transferred to the rear wing. The serrations added to the main plane trailing edge help to re-attach the airflow as the DRS closes, improving stability under braking.

MERCEDES DEBUT

The W07 was a concentrate of new features from its debut, beginning with the front end and the introduction of an S-duct that, thanks to clever interpretation of the rules, permitted the creation of a "ramp" beyond the restriction of 150 mm from the front wheels. At the Brazilian GP, Mercedes created a simulation of the vent in the upper part of the chassis. The nose was also extreme, very short and above all with two fairly closely set vertical supports directing air towards the S-duct intake.

This is a kind of shark's mouth that draws in air somewhat further forwards with respect to what had been seen in the past with Sauber and Red Bull and then McLaren and Force India. Modifications continued to be made at every pre-season session.

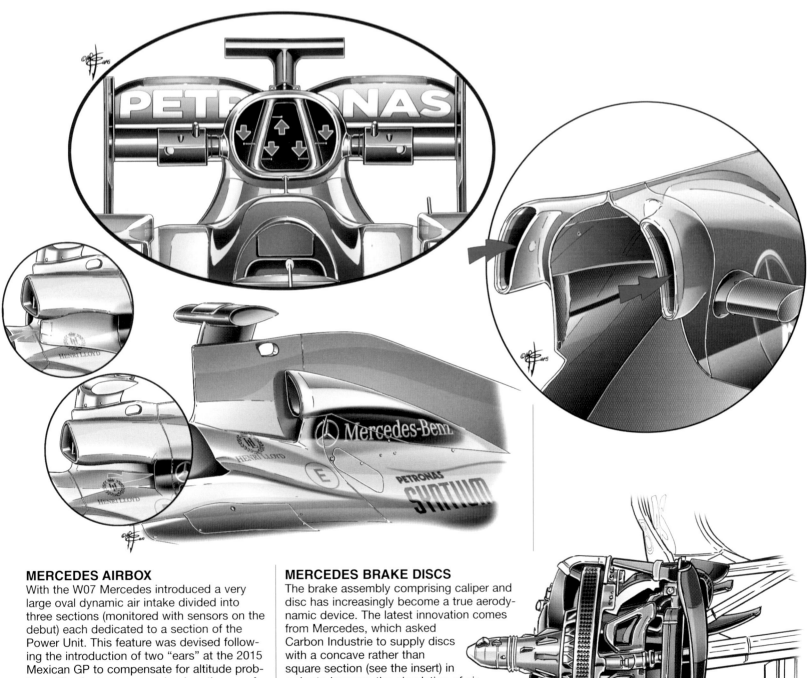

MERCEDES AIRBOX

With the W07 Mercedes introduced a very large oval dynamic air intake divided into three sections (monitored with sensors on the debut) each dedicated to a section of the Power Unit. This feature was devised following the introduction of two "ears" at the 2015 Mexican GP to compensate for altitude problems. The feature was retained on the cars for the following races. It should be noted that in previous seasons Mercedes had already introduced novelties in the area such as a blade-like roll bar equipped with two conspicuous ears to reduce the section as much as possible and improve the flow of air towards the rear wing. This feature was then copied in 2011 by Lotus and Force India before being banned by the FIA.

MERCEDES BRAKE DISCS

The brake assembly comprising caliper and disc has increasingly become a true aerodynamic device. The latest innovation comes from Mercedes, which asked Carbon Industrie to supply discs with a concave rather than square section (see the insert) in order to improve the circulation of air within the closed shrouds. Tested at Barcelona ahead of the Grand Prix, they were raced for the first time at Hockenheim on both cars. In the previous races open shrouds had been used without this feature.

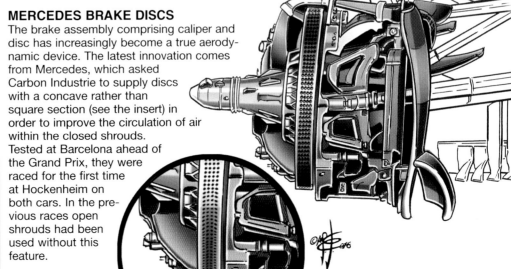

GIORGIO PIOLA

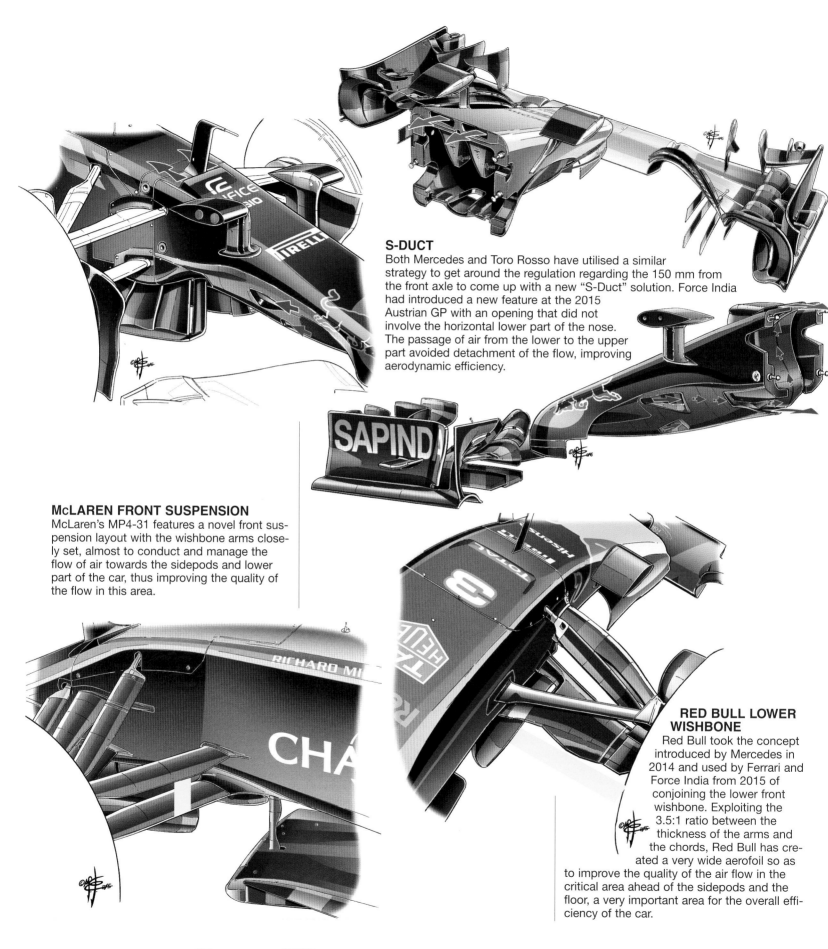

S-DUCT

Both Mercedes and Toro Rosso have utilised a similar strategy to get around the regulation regarding the 150 mm from the front axle to come up with a new "S-Duct" solution. Force India had introduced a new feature at the 2015 Austrian GP with an opening that did not involve the horizontal lower part of the nose. The passage of air from the lower to the upper part avoided detachment of the flow, improving aerodynamic efficiency.

McLAREN FRONT SUSPENSION

McLaren's MP4-31 features a novel front suspension layout with the wishbone arms closely set, almost to conduct and manage the flow of air towards the sidepods and lower part of the car, thus improving the quality of the flow in this area.

RED BULL LOWER WISHBONE

Red Bull took the concept introduced by Mercedes in 2014 and used by Ferrari and Force India from 2015 of conjoining the lower front wishbone. Exploiting the 3.5:1 ratio between the thickness of the arms and the chords, Red Bull has created a very wide aerofoil so as to improve the quality of the air flow in the critical area ahead of the sidepods and the floor, a very important area for the overall efficiency of the car.

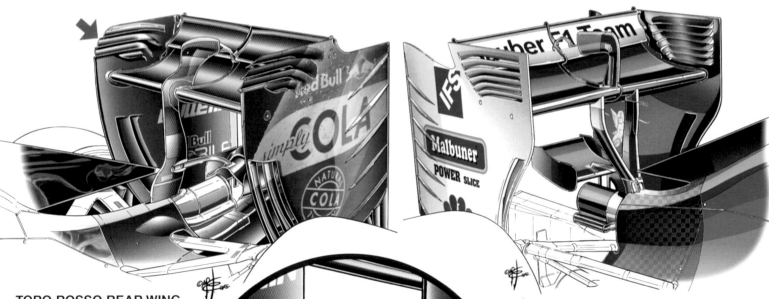

TORO ROSSO REAR WING

The STR11 features a rear wing with revolutionary endplate louvres that, seen from the side, look like as though they are open but are actually joined at the forward most point.

These louvres change how the airflow moves around the rear wing, so as to reduce the vortices that create drag.

TORO ROSSO MONKEY SEAT

The STR11's new monkey seat, like the rear wing, features a radical endplate layout with semi-open slots in the leading edge. Note the small vent of the third saddle-shaped profile and the flaring of the lower part of the endplates.

SAUBER

Sauber's rear wing features a rather unconventional Y shaped centre pylon, in place of the dual support used on 2015. The flow patterns for the leading edge of the main plane were therefore unchanged and the team could take advantage of the Toro Rosso concept from 2015 (copied by several teams) with the mono-pylon passing inside the exhaust.

FERRARI SERRATED FLAP

In the second week of pre-season testing Ferrari tested a flap equipped with a kind of serrated Gurney flap on the trailing edge.
This feature has never been seen at the tracks during the course of the season.

McLAREN TV CAMERAS

McLaren have cleverly interpreted the camera mount regulations in order to gain an aerodynamic advantage by creating a small vent in the mountings to improve airflow quality; a feature then copied by Williams with the new shorter nose.

GIORGIO PIOLA

WILLIAMS

The FW38 is effectively an evolution of the 2014-2015 car. The rear brake duct is a standout feature as it differs from many of the other cars on the grid. The hot air is almost entirely expelled towards the outside while most other cars channel it inside with the external portion closed. The exaggerated seal with the wheel rim led to its failure and the explosion of Felipe Massa's tyre in practice for the Chinese GP.

FERRARI MELBOURNE

At Melbourne Ferrari used this front wing tried in pre-season testing and featuring a small notch in the triangular vane (black arrow) improving the airflow above all at different yaw angles, with a small serrated portion on the leading edge of the first flap (red arrow) helping to control the vortices created at the juncture of the flaps and neutral centre section (50 cm wide) and the blow principal profile.

FORCE INDIA SAKHIR

In Bahrain, Force India introduced a blown front axle already seen in 2016 on the Ferrari, Red Bull, McLaren, Haas and Toro Rosso. This feature vents hot air towards the outside allowing the flow of air to neutralize in part the detrimental turbulence created by the rotating wheels, deviating the flow to the lower part of the car and the diffuser.

McLAREN SAKHIR

In Bahrain, McLaren made several changes to the MP4-31's front wing above all in the delicate peripheral area ahead of the front wheels. The upper flaps are more inclined upwards where they attached to the endplates, improving the extraction of the air towards the outside of the tyres.
The fin within the endplate is also new with a different flap incidence adjustment point.

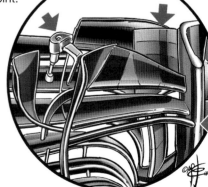

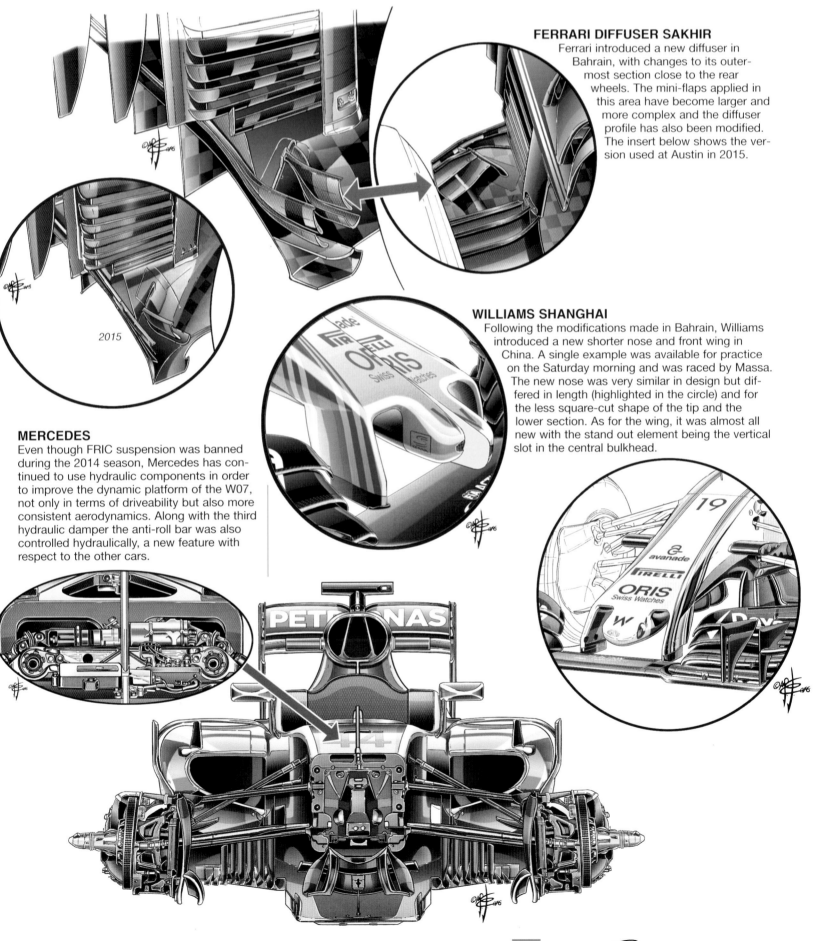

FERRARI DIFFUSER SAKHIR

Ferrari introduced a new diffuser in Bahrain, with changes to its outermost section close to the rear wheels. The mini-flaps applied in this area have become larger and more complex and the diffuser profile has also been modified. The insert below shows the version used at Austin in 2015.

2015

WILLIAMS SHANGHAI

Following the modifications made in Bahrain, Williams introduced a new shorter nose and front wing in China. A single example was available for practice on the Saturday morning and was raced by Massa. The new nose was very similar in design but differed in length (highlighted in the circle) and for the less square-cut shape of the tip and the lower section. As for the wing, it was almost all new with the stand out element being the vertical slot in the central bulkhead.

MERCEDES

Even though FRIC suspension was banned during the 2014 season, Mercedes has continued to use hydraulic components in order to improve the dynamic platform of the W07, not only in terms of driveability but also more consistent aerodynamics. Along with the third hydraulic damper the anti-roll bar was also controlled hydraulically, a new feature with respect to the other cars.

HAAS SHANGHAI

Haas introduced a new wing in China featuring a horizontal flap (arrowed) mounted to the triangular vane but supported in the centre by another vertical support. The intention of the new flap was to control how the vortices that form on the border of the 50 cm neutral central area.

TORO ROSSO SHANGHAI

In China, Toro Rosso tried a new flap in free practice with a different chord and an undulating trailing edge, in a continual search for the right compromise between downforce and drag for each circuit. For the race however the straight-edged version (in the oval) was used with the addition of a Monkey Seat.

RED BULL SHANGHAI

Red Bull also tried an aerodynamic modification that did not work: a front wing with serrated trailing edge on the penultimate flap, tested on the Friday morning in China and never seen again of the RB11.

TORO ROSSO SOCHI

In Russia, Toro Rosso ran with a medium-low downforce rear wing, featuring the same type of revolutionary louvres as their previous specification, with a single element matching angle of incidence of the wing-flap assembly, thus producing less downforce.

FERRARI SHANGHAI

To guarantee increased downforce, in China Ferrari introduced revised front wing featuring three upper flaps (in the drawing) rather than two (inset).
The greater number of vents permits greater loading without interfering with the central area vortices.

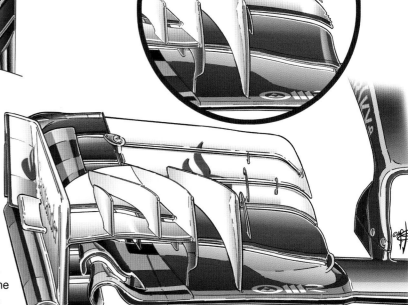

MERCEDES SOCHI

Taken to scrutineering at Sochi but never used on track, this new endplate in equipped with two slots added to better guide the airflow out around the front wheels. This was part of the aerodynamic package devised for the Spanish GP.

McLAREN SOCHI

In Russia, McLaren modified the vertical turning vanes, adding an inverted U-section to link to the upper part of the sidepods already equipped with three vertical fins.

RED BULL MONACO

For Monaco, Red Bull introduced these three upwash strakes to direct the flow upwards and increase downforce. Curiously, Red Bull did not fit a monkey seat for extra downforce as the other teams did. Note the conspicuous vertical slot in the leading edge of the endplates.

MERCEDES MONKEY SEAT

The monkey seat used by Mercedes in Spain was given an additional slot in the upper element. This modified the point of interaction between the exhaust plume and the rear wing.

FORCE INDIA BARCELONA

Force India effectively introduced a "B" version in Spain. The all-new front wing was probably the most easily recognizable element. There main difference was the more pronounced "flare" (1) in the main profile, with a flat area (2) that was wider at the junction with the endplates, much like the design used by Mercedes since last season. In the upper part a fin was added (3) to direct the flow to the outside, together with another two (4) linked directly to the endplate and immediately behind the "upper flaps".

A wing designed expressly to channel the maximum flow to the exterior of the rear wheels.

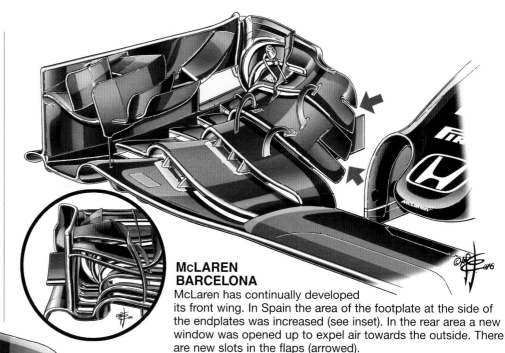

McLAREN BARCELONA

McLaren has continually developed its front wing. In Spain the area of the footplate at the side of the endplates was increased (see inset). In the rear area a new window was opened up to expel air towards the outside. There are new slots in the flaps (arrowed).

McLAREN

After a year McLaren modified the unconventional horizontal U-shaped brake intakes (see insets) in favour of a traditional shroud equipped with a conspicuous ear-like intake, divided into various sectors to cool the individual components of the braking system and send the hot air to the outside via the blowing hub.

FERRARI BARCELONA

Ferrari took specific brake intakes to each circuit, with asymmetric apertures. The one on the right had the window at the top, that on the left only the oval apertures. In Spain the discs with over 1200 holes were not used, the team preferring the version with around 840 drill holes in groups of four aligned horizontally.

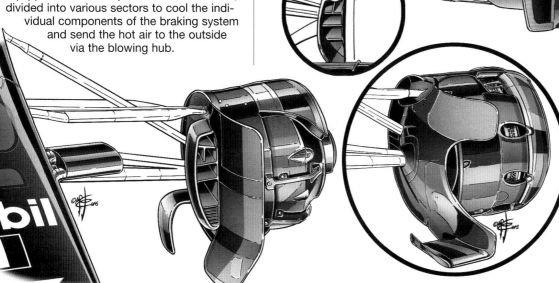

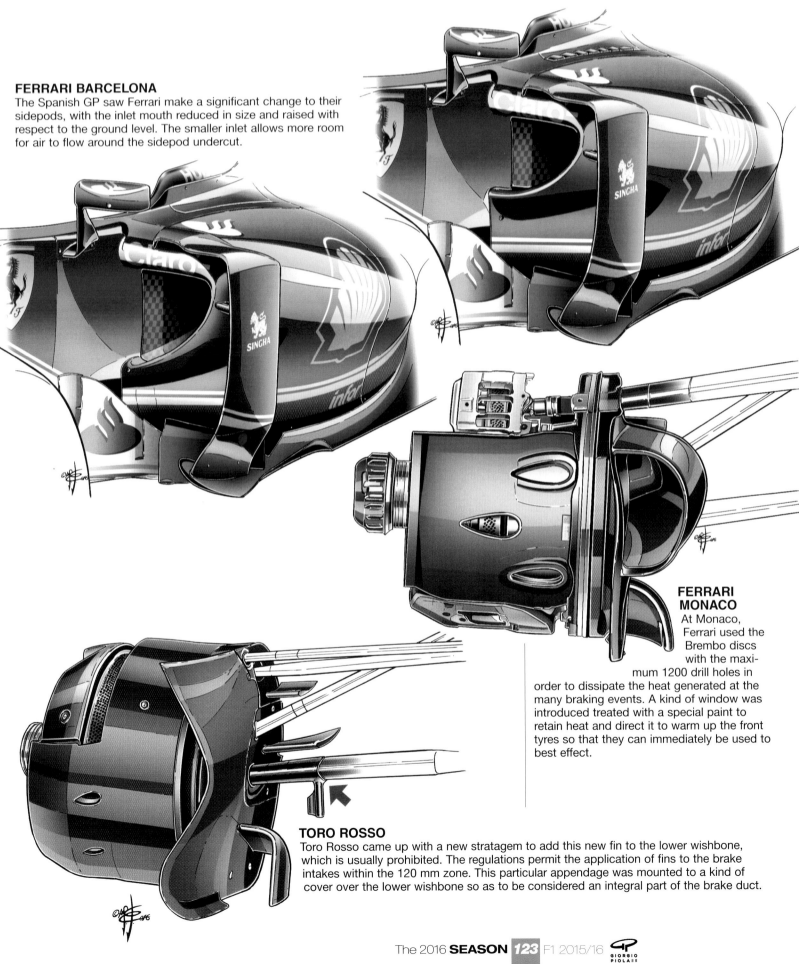

FERRARI BARCELONA

The Spanish GP saw Ferrari make a significant change to their sidepods, with the inlet mouth reduced in size and raised with respect to the ground level. The smaller inlet allows more room for air to flow around the sidepod undercut.

FERRARI MONACO

At Monaco, Ferrari used the Brembo discs with the maximum 1200 drill holes in order to dissipate the heat generated at the many braking events. A kind of window was introduced treated with a special paint to retain heat and direct it to warm up the front tyres so that they can immediately be used to best effect.

TORO ROSSO

Toro Rosso came up with a new stratagem to add this new fin to the lower wishbone, which is usually prohibited. The regulations permit the application of fins to the brake intakes within the 120 mm zone. This particular appendage was mounted to a kind of cover over the lower wishbone so as to be considered an integral part of the brake duct.

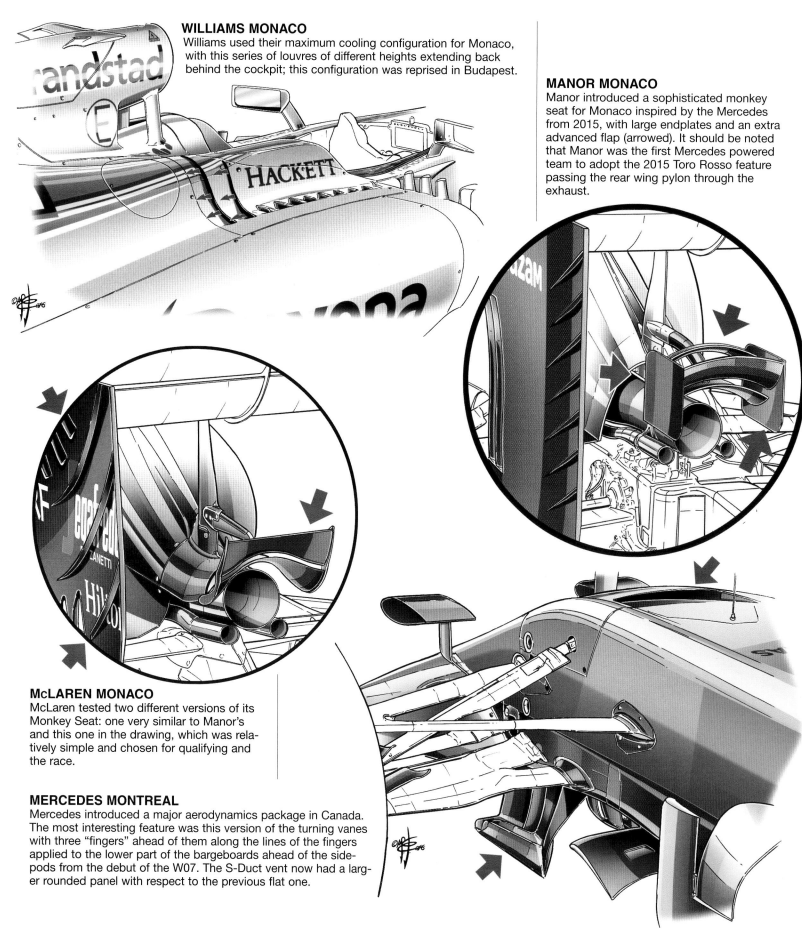

WILLIAMS MONACO

Williams used their maximum cooling configuration for Monaco, with this series of louvres of different heights extending back behind the cockpit; this configuration was reprised in Budapest.

MANOR MONACO

Manor introduced a sophisticated monkey seat for Monaco inspired by the Mercedes from 2015, with large endplates and an extra advanced flap (arrowed). It should be noted that Manor was the first Mercedes powered team to adopt the 2015 Toro Rosso feature passing the rear wing pylon through the exhaust.

McLAREN MONACO

McLaren tested two different versions of its Monkey Seat: one very similar to Manor's and this one in the drawing, which was relatively simple and chosen for qualifying and the race.

MERCEDES MONTREAL

Mercedes introduced a major aerodynamics package in Canada. The most interesting feature was this version of the turning vanes with three "fingers" ahead of them along the lines of the fingers applied to the lower part of the bargeboards ahead of the sidepods from the debut of the W07. The S-Duct vent now had a larger rounded panel with respect to the previous flat one.

MERCEDES FLAP

These strakes set towards to the outside appeared on the top flap of
the W07s in Canada.
Together with the serra-
tions applied to the
trailing edge of the
second flap, they
increased the effi-
ciency of the
wing's yaw perfor-
mance.

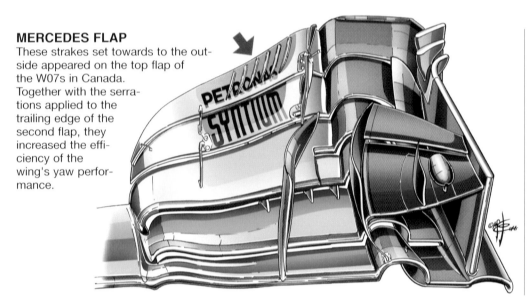

FERRARI MONTREAL

Fast circuit bodywork for the end part of the
SF16H's sidepods in Canada. In practice, the
upper part was cut away, revealing the internal fairing of the hot air vent. In comparison,
on the left the bodywork used through to
Monaco with the upper part aligned with the
upper wishbone of the suspension.

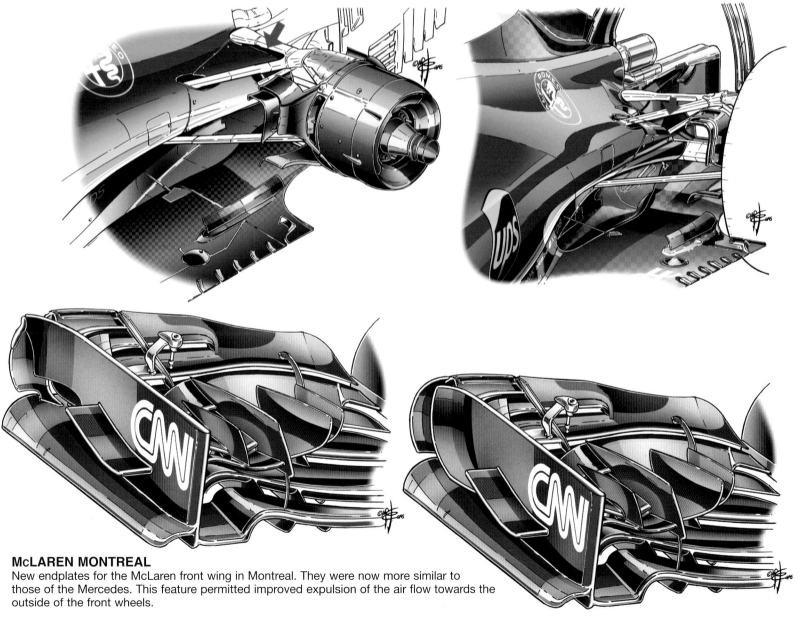

McLAREN MONTREAL

New endplates for the McLaren front wing in Montreal. They were now more similar to
those of the Mercedes. This feature permitted improved expulsion of the air flow towards the
outside of the front wheels.

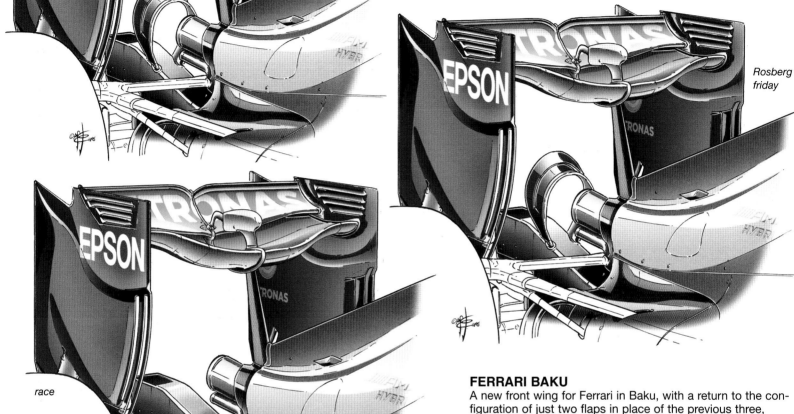

Montreal race

Rosberg friday

race

MERCEDES MONTREAL

A new Monkey Seat in Canada for the Mercedes with an unusual new oval shape in order to modify the interaction between the exhaust plume and the air flow from the diffuser and the rear wing.

FERRARI BAKU

A new front wing for Ferrari in Baku, with a return to the configuration of just two flaps in place of the previous three, therefore with a different chord and shape: the arrow highlights that the maximum available chord was not used. The leading edge of the flaps was also different. This new wing was then discarded by both drivers who preferred the previous wing that guaranteed better front-end performance.

MERCEDES ROSBERG AT BAKU

On the Friday Nico Rosberg tested a dished rear wing, then reserved for the Baku track alone. The new Monkey Seat fitted in practice at Montreal was not used in the Baku configuration. The dished shape was nothing new, but it offered the possibility of diversifying the downforce between the central section and the lateral areas that create less drag.

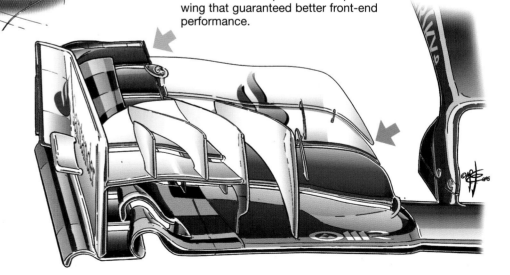

GIORGIO PIOLA

FERRARI BAKU

The rear wing was also new in Baku. The endplates had just two slots in the upper part to fit profiles with a smaller angle of incidence in order to privilege maximum speed. The previous version was then chosen for the race.

HAAS ZELTWEG

Like the Ferraris, Red Bulls, McLarens and Force Indias, the Haas cars had blowing front hubs, but at Zeltweg they did not exploit the feature with the hubs being practically closed.

McLAREN
ALONSO AT ZELTWEG

Only Alonso trialled these new and extreme endplates with tall vertical slots. The feature was almost immediately discarded as it created uncontrollable downforce variations.

WILLIAMS ZELTWEG

New endplates for the Williams too modified in the area of the vertical "fringes" in the lower section near the wheels.

GIORGIO PIOLA

FERRARI SILVERSTONE

Ferrari introduced these inverted V fins in the lower part of the chassis to better control the flow of air passing under the lower part of the car.

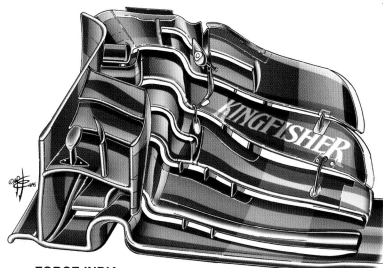

FORCE INDIA

In practice the modification to the front wing introduced by Force India in Spain ahead of the Zeltweg race consisted of a slight reduction in width of the last two flaps, highlighted in yellow.

test

FERRARI
MONTREAL AND SILVERSTONE

It was only noticed at Silverstone, but this curved fin applied to the internal part of the front brake intakes had already been introduced in Canada. In the classic front view it resembled another flat fin.

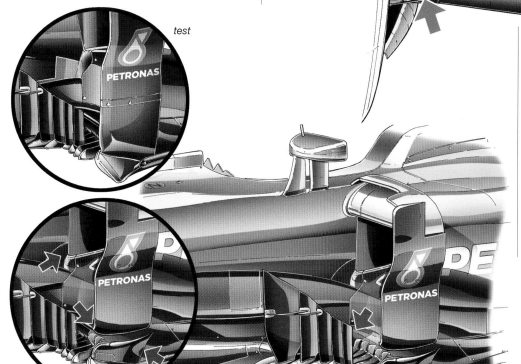

MERCEDES BARGE BOARDS

A further evolution of the bargeboards in front of the sidepods of the W07. In the insert, the debut version, below the one for Melbourne and, in the drawing, the one introduced at Silverstone with two fewer vertical elements and with the horizontal "teeth" thus more evident.

Barcelona

Silverstone

MERCEDES SILVERSTONE

Toro Rosso set a trend with its open slots (with just a narrow seal between them) at the top of the leading edge of the endplates, a feature that was even copied by the leading team, Mercedes.
In the insert, a detail of the endplate of the STR11, used from its debut.

Toro Rosso

W07 Silverstone

SAUBER BUDAPEST

Sauber also copied the Toro Rosso, testing firstly at Silverstone on the Friday morning this new rear wing then introduced at Budapest. The endplates are wholly different, not only in the area copied from the STR11.

WILLIAMS SILVERSTONE

A comparison between the new front wing (introduced at Zeltweg) and the old version.
A new curved vertical vane (1) with a conspicuous vertical vent.
A small fin (2) was added closed to the endplate, along with a vent (3) in the second, straight vane.
The fin outside the endplate (4) was sharply flared. Tested on the Friday, but never raced, the new nose equipped with more square-cut lateral supports (in the circle).

Silverstone Bottas

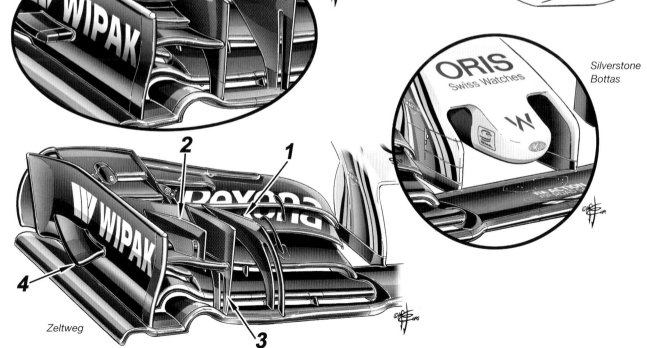

Zeltweg

GIORGIO PIOLA

FERRARI SILVERSTONE

A new endplate for Ferrari at Silverstone, modified above all in the final part that was curved and very similar to that of the Mercedes, as can be seen in the comparison between the two elements.

new

old

MERCEDES BUDAPEST

New slots either side of the cockpit of the W07 to cope with the heat of the Budapest circuit; the shape of the raised fairing enclosing it was also different.

FERRARI DIFFUSER BUDAPEST

There was a further modification to the area of the diffuser between the rear wheels.
As well as the usual miniflaps (introduced at Austin in 2015) a conspicuous triangular fin was added to direct the flow and increase downforce in this area.

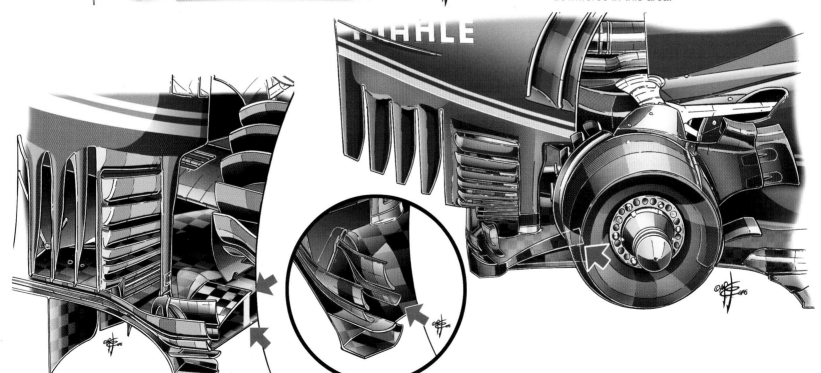

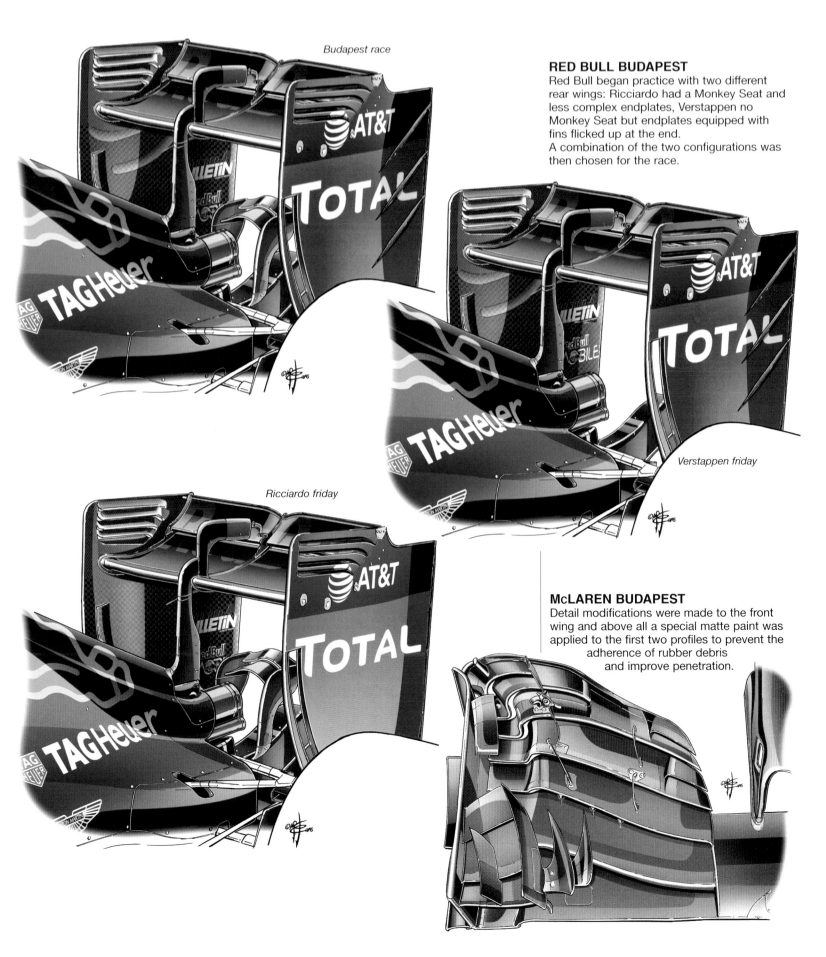

Budapest race

RED BULL BUDAPEST

Red Bull began practice with two different rear wings: Ricciardo had a Monkey Seat and less complex endplates, Verstappen no Monkey Seat but endplates equipped with fins flicked up at the end.
A combination of the two configurations was then chosen for the race.

Verstappen friday

Ricciardo friday

McLAREN BUDAPEST

Detail modifications were made to the front wing and above all a special matte paint was applied to the first two profiles to prevent the adherence of rubber debris and improve penetration.

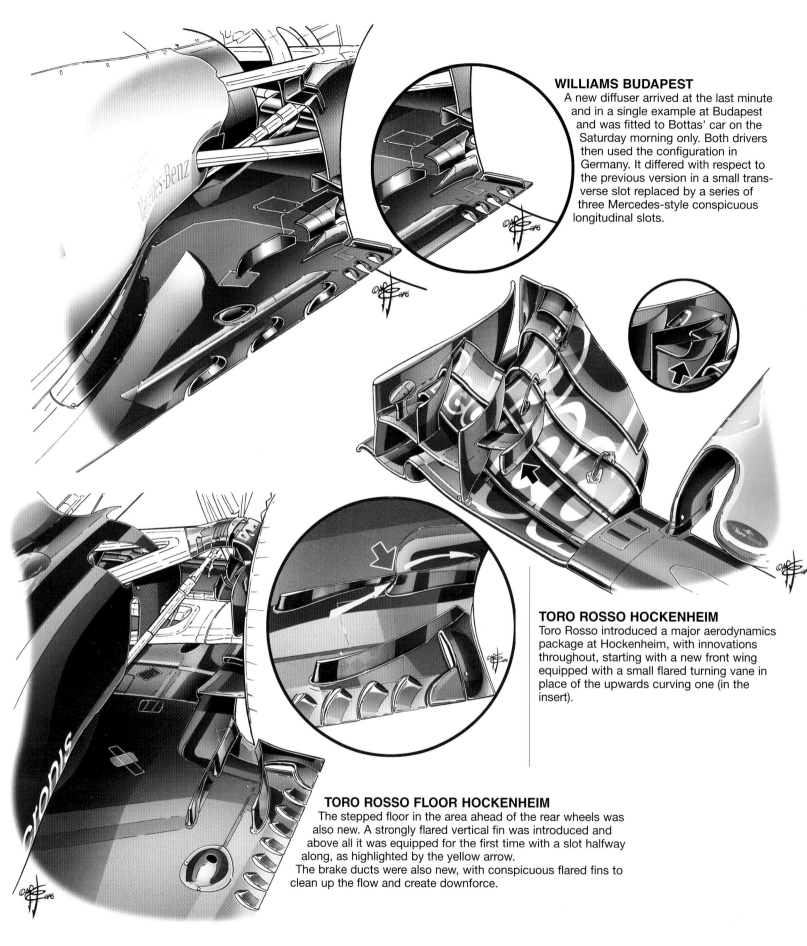

WILLIAMS BUDAPEST

A new diffuser arrived at the last minute and in a single example at Budapest and was fitted to Bottas' car on the Saturday morning only. Both drivers then used the configuration in Germany. It differed with respect to the previous version in a small transverse slot replaced by a series of three Mercedes-style conspicuous longitudinal slots.

TORO ROSSO HOCKENHEIM

Toro Rosso introduced a major aerodynamics package at Hockenheim, with innovations throughout, starting with a new front wing equipped with a small flared turning vane in place of the upwards curving one (in the insert).

TORO ROSSO FLOOR HOCKENHEIM

The stepped floor in the area ahead of the rear wheels was also new. A strongly flared vertical fin was introduced and above all it was equipped for the first time with a slot halfway along, as highlighted by the yellow arrow.
The brake ducts were also new, with conspicuous flared fins to clean up the flow and create downforce.

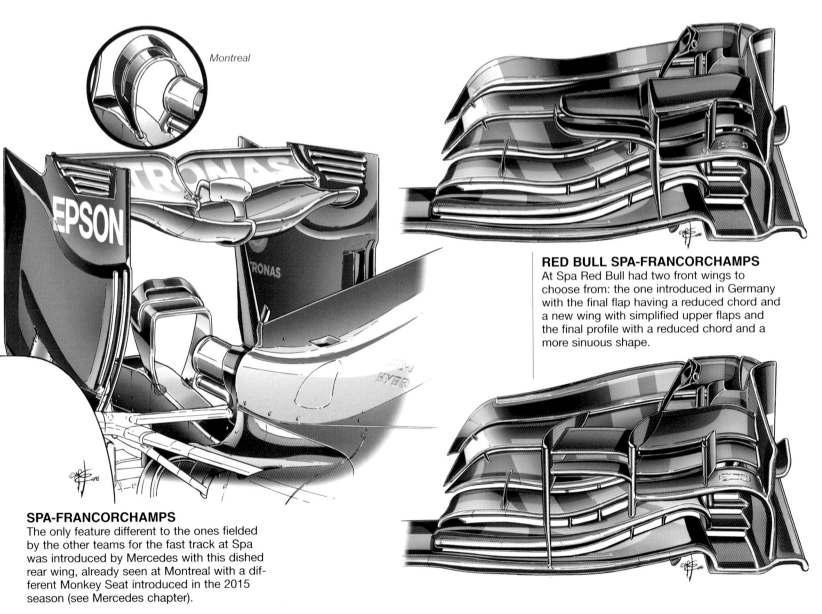

Montreal

RED BULL SPA-FRANCORCHAMPS

At Spa Red Bull had two front wings to choose from: the one introduced in Germany with the final flap having a reduced chord and a new wing with simplified upper flaps and the final profile with a reduced chord and a more sinuous shape.

SPA-FRANCORCHAMPS

The only feature different to the ones fielded by the other teams for the fast track at Spa was introduced by Mercedes with this dished rear wing, already seen at Montreal with a different Monkey Seat introduced in the 2015 season (see Mercedes chapter).

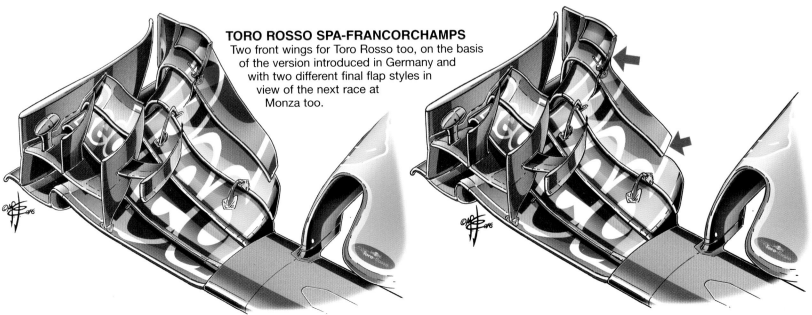

TORO ROSSO SPA-FRANCORCHAMPS

Two front wings for Toro Rosso too, on the basis of the version introduced in Germany and with two different final flap styles in view of the next race at Monza too.

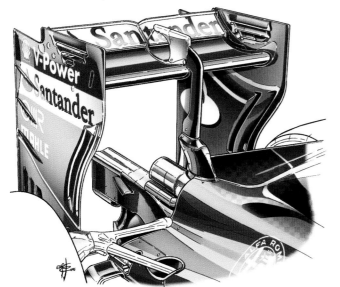

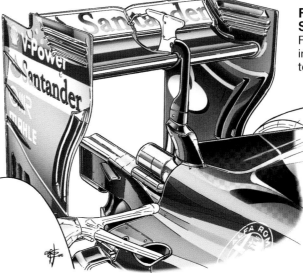

FERRARI SPA-FRANCORCHAMPS

Ferrari conducted experiments in view of Monza at the rear too. The team took a low downforce wing to Belgium (with just three slots and profiles with a lower angle of incidence) that was tested on the Friday before being replaced in qualifying and the race with one with more downforce with endplates with four slots and steeper profiles; note also the different DRS control.

RED BULL SPA-FRANCORCHAMPS

Red Bull was the team that tackled the Spa track with least downforce, starting with the wing used in Sochi with lighter profiles and endplates that retained the long horizontal slot. However, this version had a slot less at the top and walls that were smoother without the oblique mini-fins on the trailing edge.

Sochi

RED BULL MONZA

The rear wing that Red Bull fielded at Monza was a revised and improved version of the one adopted in 2015, both in terms of the profiles and the endplates with no slots. The wing support pylon and the DRS control were different to those used in Belgium.

Monza 2014

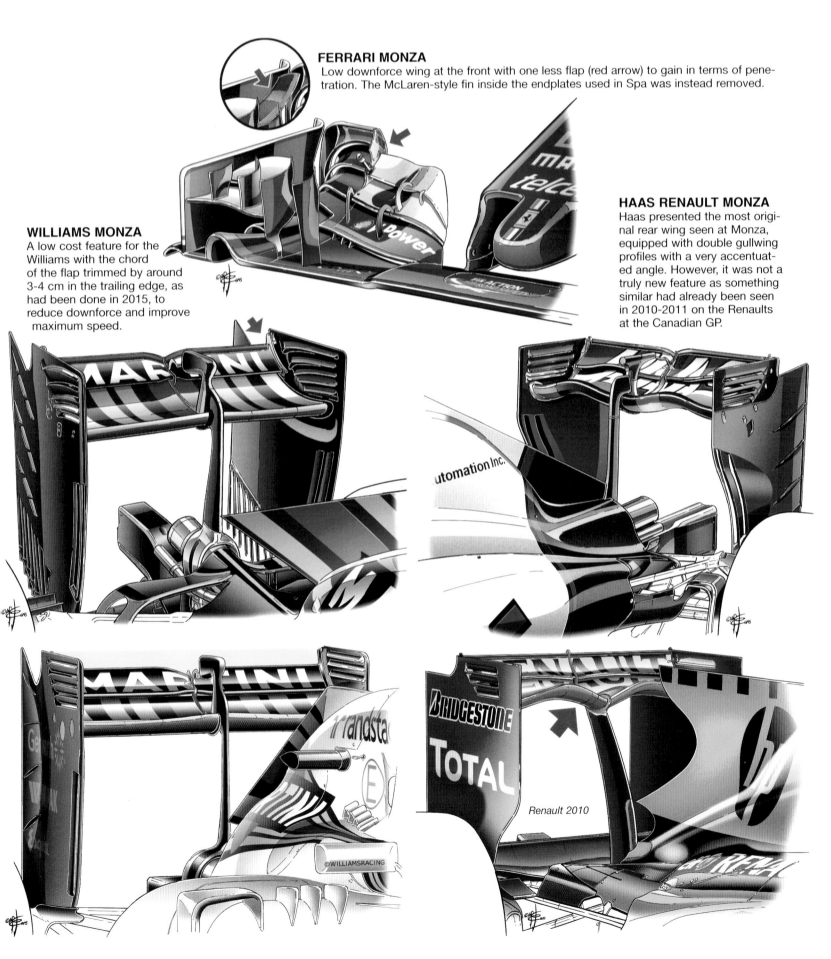

FERRARI MONZA
Low downforce wing at the front with one less flap (red arrow) to gain in terms of penetration. The McLaren-style fin inside the endplates used in Spa was instead removed.

WILLIAMS MONZA
A low cost feature for the Williams with the chord of the flap trimmed by around 3-4 cm in the trailing edge, as had been done in 2015, to reduce downforce and improve maximum speed.

HAAS RENAULT MONZA
Haas presented the most original rear wing seen at Monza, equipped with double gullwing profiles with a very accentuated angle. However, it was not a truly new feature as something similar had already been seen in 2010-2011 on the Renaults at the Canadian GP.

Renault 2010

GIORGIO PIOLA

RENAULT MONZA

On the Friday Palmer tested the evolved version of the Renault in view of its use in Singapore before returning to the base version for qualifying and the race. New lower sidepods, new engine cover and diffuser; the megaphone vent in the end part of the sidepods was an extreme feature.

FERRARI

Ferrari also adopted a kind of vanity panel, but of much reduced dimensions

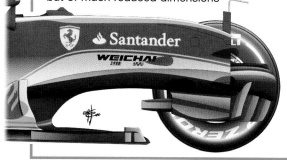

FERRARI SINGAPORE

On the Friday morning both Ferraris were fitted with a new front wing characterised by a serrated trailing edge on the penultimate flap, as seen on the Mercedes from the 2015 Russian GP.

MERCEDES FRONT SUSPENSION

The Mercedes front suspension was at the centre of attention from its debut in experimental form at the 2015 Brazilian GP. What aroused curiosity above all was the generously sized transverse hydraulic element that controlled the ride height and roll, a feature jealously concealed with a kind of rudimentary fairing.

RED BULL

A middle way was represented by the Red Bull design, with a vanity panel larger than that of Ferrari's but with the chassis structure respecting the spirit of the regulations too. The third transverse element was exposed and permitted easy adjustment, but the shape of the aperture in the chassis fully respects the dimensions of the B-B and A-A sections.

and equipped with apertures for accessing the suspension elements inside the monocoque.

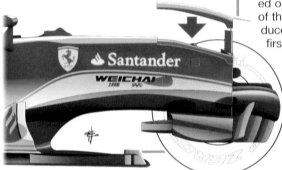

MERCEDES

The engineers not only have to interpret the regulations to the letter but also intuit by reading between the lines what might eventually be permitted. In the 2014 season the FIA had drastically lowered the height of the monocoques at the point of section A-A from 625 to 525 mm, leaving unaltered the regulation that provided for apertures in the structure for accessing the suspension. Almost all the teams worked on this aspect to created a kind of cover. At Mercedes they took advantage of the lack of dimensional restrictions on any apertures so as to create an area in which they could work on the suspension "in the open air", using the Vanity Panel to meet the regulations. This feature might be seen as going against the spirit of the regulations but was irreproachable from a practical point of view as it even respected the safety regulations after having passed the crash test even without the voluminous Vanity Panel.

SEPANG
McLAREN REAR WING
Following Sauber and Mercedes, McLaren too adopted open slots for the upper part of the endplates, a feature introduced by Toro Rosso from the first laps of winter testing.

WILLIAMS
SERRATED FLAP
At Sepang, Williams introduced a small serrated section to the flap, As shown in yellow in the drawing.

TORO ROSSO REAR WING
A new feature introduced by Toro Rosso at Sepang, with the mail plane curving upwards while the trailing edge and the flap retained the straight configuration.
The endplates instead retained the so-called "open" slot configuration.

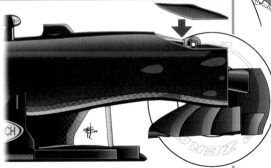

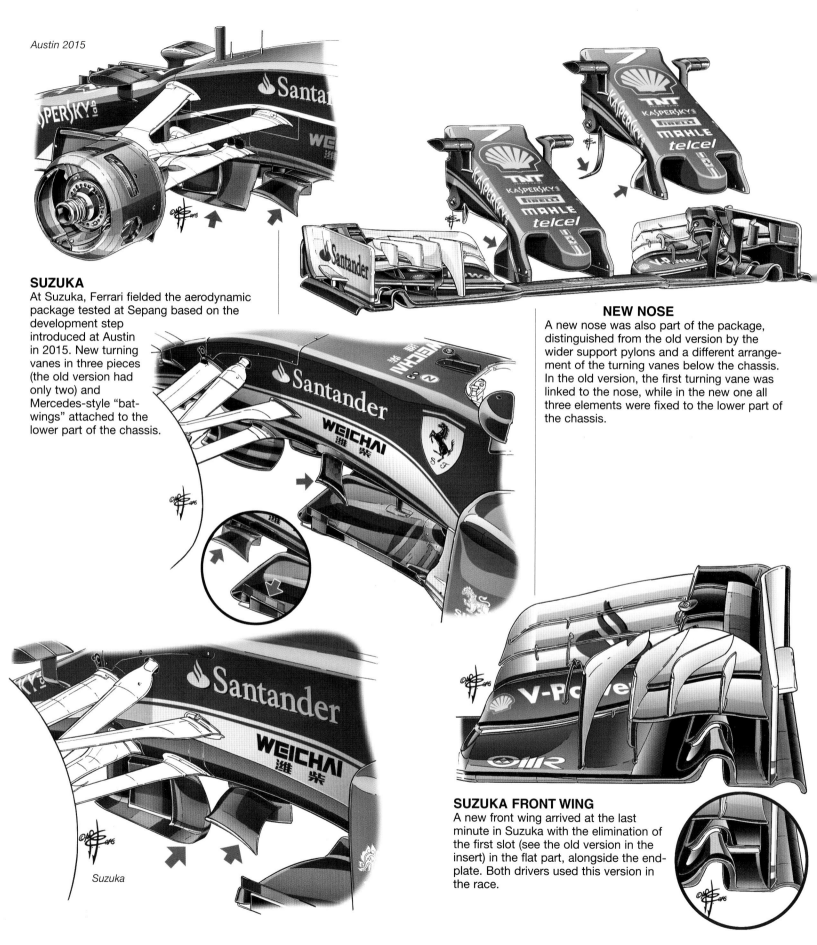

Austin 2015

SUZUKA

At Suzuka, Ferrari fielded the aerodynamic package tested at Sepang based on the development step introduced at Austin in 2015. New turning vanes in three pieces (the old version had only two) and Mercedes-style "bat-wings" attached to the lower part of the chassis.

NEW NOSE

A new nose was also part of the package, distinguished from the old version by the wider support pylons and a different arrangement of the turning vanes below the chassis. In the old version, the first turning vane was linked to the nose, while in the new one all three elements were fixed to the lower part of the chassis.

Suzuka

SUZUKA FRONT WING

A new front wing arrived at the last minute in Suzuka with the elimination of the first slot (see the old version in the insert) in the flat part, alongside the end-plate. Both drivers used this version in the race.

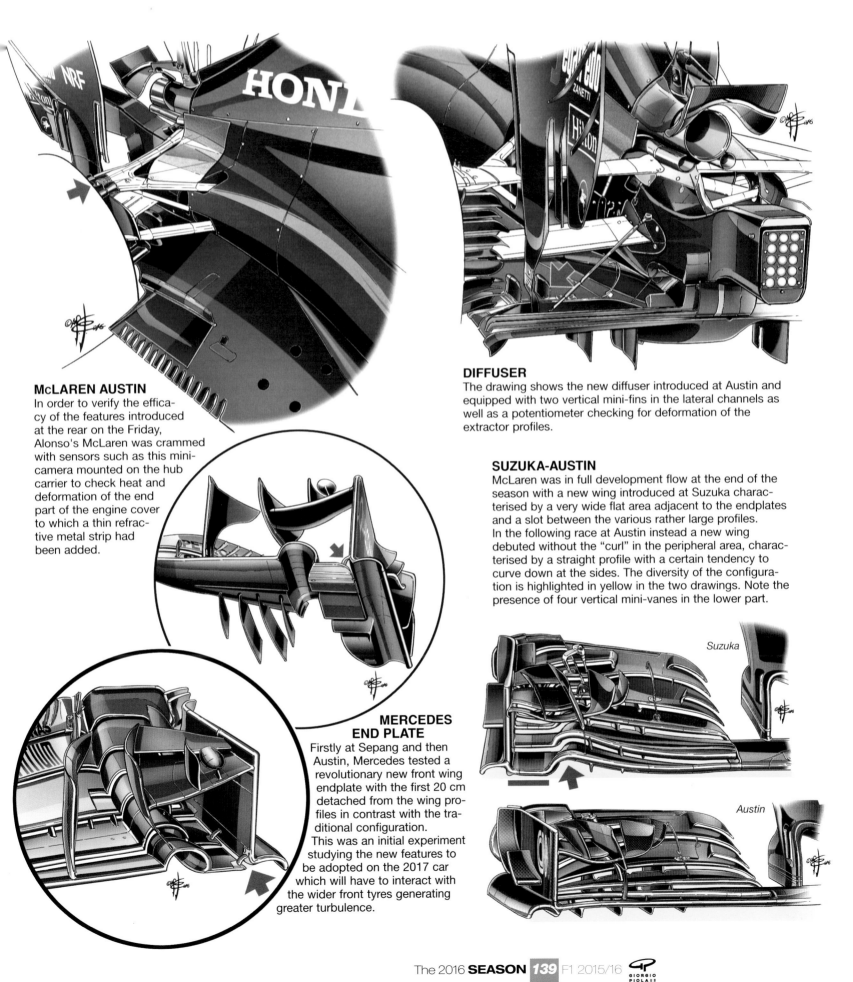

McLAREN AUSTIN

In order to verify the efficacy of the features introduced at the rear on the Friday, Alonso's McLaren was crammed with sensors such as this mini-camera mounted on the hub carrier to check heat and deformation of the end part of the engine cover to which a thin refractive metal strip had been added.

DIFFUSER

The drawing shows the new diffuser introduced at Austin and equipped with two vertical mini-fins in the lateral channels as well as a potentiometer checking for deformation of the extractor profiles.

SUZUKA-AUSTIN

McLaren was in full development flow at the end of the season with a new wing introduced at Suzuka characterised by a very wide flat area adjacent to the endplates and a slot between the various rather large profiles.
In the following race at Austin instead a new wing debuted without the "curl" in the peripheral area, characterised by a straight profile with a certain tendency to curve down at the sides. The diversity of the configuration is highlighted in yellow in the two drawings. Note the presence of four vertical mini-vanes in the lower part.

Suzuka

Austin

MERCEDES END PLATE

Firstly at Sepang and then Austin, Mercedes tested a revolutionary new front wing endplate with the first 20 cm detached from the wing profiles in contrast with the traditional configuration.
This was an initial experiment studying the new features to be adopted on the 2017 car which will have to interact with the wider front tyres generating greater turbulence.

Formula 1 is turning over a new page in 2017. With the new technical regulations intended to improve the performance of the cars by five seconds per lap with respect to the times obtained at the start of the 2015 season, the wide Pirelli tyres will play an important role in lowering times and it is easy to predict that every lap record will be beaten. This is the first time in modern Formula 1 that changes have actually been made to the regulations to increase performance rather than, as in the past, to restrict the constant increase in performance so as to avoid breaching certain safety thresholds.

The 2017 regulations instead open up wholly new scenarios that will lead to the creation of cars capable of generating previously unseen levels of downforce, values that it is said will represent a 30% increase with respect to 2016.

Taking as an example the Barcelona circuit that has been chosen by the teams for simulations, it has apparently emerged that at the end of the start line straight the cars will be reaching the same maximum speeds seen in 2016 (Felipe Massa reached 346.3 kph with the Williams FW38 when slipstreaming with the mobile wing open), because the development work in the wind tunnel has compensated the greater drag caused by the wider tyres, while a huge increase in cornering speeds will be seen.

There is talk of 35/40 kph higher speeds through the fearsome Turn 3 on the Catalan circuit, while similar predictions can be made for Copse at Silverstone. Kinks that are now tackled at half-throttle will be taken flat. This means that the drivers will be driving at full throttle for much longer on each lap.

To gain an idea of the forces acting on the tyres, just think that an additional 50 kg will be bearing on the driver's helmet.

This will oblige the drivers to strengthen their neck muscles to resist the kind of enduring stress to which they are no longer accustomed.

The Pirelli engineers began development work on the wide tyres on 1 August 2016, when Sebastian Vettel took to the track in a Ferrari SF15-T fitted with rain tyres (full wets and intermediates) that prefigured those that will feature next season.

A debut that took place on an artificially drenched Fiorano circuit.

As well as Ferrari, the testing programme also involved Mercedes, which modified the W06 Hybrid, and Red Bull, which used the RB11. Each of the top teams conducted seven days of testing that will be followed by the three of the group test at Abu Dhabi immediately after the end of the 2016 season.

The tyres chosen fro the 2017 season have a 10 mm larger circumference with respect to those used in the tests, while their width has been increased by 25% with respect to 2016, the fronts measuring 305/670/13 and mounted on 12.7x13" rims and the rears 405/670/13 on 16.9x13" rims.

The new dimensions have determined an increase in the weight of the tyres of 1 kg for the fronts and 1.5 for the rears, with the covers therefore accounting for an increase of 5 kg in the mass of the cars.

Through to the end of November, the tests were conducted on aluminium rims and only in the group phase will they be replaced with lighter forged magnesium versions.

The FIA and the teams have asked for different characteristics for the wide tyres with the aim of having covers that decay less rapidly than in 2016, aiming for a product less sub-

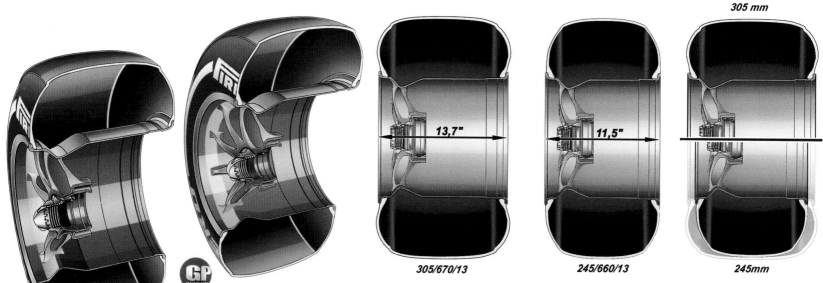

305 mm

13,7"   **11,5"**

305/670/13   **245/660/13**   **245mm**

PIRELLI TYRES 2017

The tyres chosen for the 2017 championship have a circumference 10 mm greater than those used in testing, while the width has been increased by 25% with respect to 2016. The front tyres measure 305/670/13 and are fitted to 13.7x13" while the rears are 405/670/13 on 16.9x13" rims.

The new dimensions guarantee notable mechanical grip but naturally also entail an increase in weight: 1 kg each for the fronts and 1.5 kg for the rears, hence the tyres account for an increase in the unsprung weight of the car and have led to a higher minimum weight.

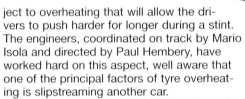

The perspective drawing shows a simplified preview of the 2017 car, while in reality there will be numerous surprises and differences from one car to the next.

ject to overheating that will allow the drivers to push harder for longer during a stint. The engineers, coordinated on track by Mario Isola and directed by Paul Hembery, have worked hard on this aspect, well aware that one of the principal factors of tyre overheating is slipstreaming another car.

In this situation there is a significant loss of aerodynamic downforce which leads to increased wheelspin.

The Bicocca team have designed compounds less sensitive to this phenomenon so that the effect is reversible, in other words the tyre can cool down once the driver regains downforce after leaving the slipstream.

The tyre will retain stable performance through to the point at which it will degrade to facilitate different race strategies.

The 2017 range will again comprise five compounds: Ultrasoft, Supersoft, Soft, Medium and Hard with three being used at every race. The compounds have been formulated in relation to a grand prix in which the Hard and the Medium will be asked to cover the race distance with a single stop, while there will two or three stops when using the softer compounds.

A difference of a second per lap is predicted between one compound and the next, while deterioration should increase from the hardest through to the softest.

Not having achieved with the 2015 "laboratory" cars the aerodynamic loading seen in the simulations, Pirelli has reserved the right to make updates to the tyres after the first winter test session with the new 2017 cars.

In order to prevent the top teams from drawing concrete advantages from the development of the tyres, the FIA ordered that the modifications allowed that concerned sideskirts and large wings did not correspond with those permitted by the new regulations.

However, with these restrictions it was difficult to achieve the degree of downforce that the designers are

counting on for the 2017 cars.

The simulations that every team has delivered to the FIA have been passed on to Pirelli in anonymous form.

The individual teams, having received the mathematical model of the wide tyre produced by the Milan-based firm and the scaled-down covers for wind tunnel development, have developed their simulations by hypothesizing grip and lap times at the beginning and the end of the championship.

The initial observations revealed widely differing data, while as development proceeded

the numbers drew closer although there was still a significant difference with respect to those from the first track tests. Pirelli is read to satisfy the expectations of the teams, although the Bicocca firm is still counting on opportunities for testing during the course of the 2017 season in order to fine tune the tyres in relation to the real world performance displayed by the cars on the track.

The challenge has therefore only just begun…

Franco Nugnes

SLICK COMPOUNDS

In 2017 Pirelli will continue to supply the F1 teams with five types of slick wide tyres and two rain versions, characterising each compound with an easily identifiable colour on the shoulder of the tyre. The P Zero Hard is orange, while the Medium is white and the Soft yellow. The Supersoft is red and the Ultrasoft is purple. The two wet weather tyres are the Cinturato blue for the full wets and green for the Intermediates. The FIA verifies, with the tyre off the car, that the minimum inflation pressure is in line with the indications provided by the single supplier on a race by race basis, as with the camber values, while the temperature on emerging from the heat blankets may not exceed 110°. From 2016, the Milan company has also indicated the maximum suggested duration, expressed in laps, for each tyre in relation to the data collected during free practice in order to avoid safety issues with extremely worn tyres during the race.

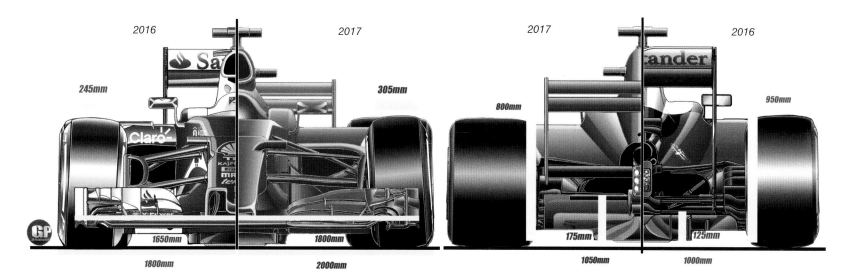

2016 — 245mm — 2017 — 305mm

2017 — 800mm — 2016 — 950mm

1650mm — 1800mm

175mm — 125mm

1800mm — 2000mm

1050mm — 1000mm

2016/2017 CARS

At the start of the summer the FIA ratified the regulations that will come into force in 2017 through to 2020, effectively providing greater support for the McLaren project that with respect to the configuration of the 2016 cars, provides for a 25% increase in downforce.

The Red Bull proposal was shelved as it was felt to be too extreme with an even greater increase in downforce. With respect to the final Red Bull version there were a number of differences that had already emerged in the one realised in the final race weekend at Abu Dhabi. In these drawings we have highlighted only those details that have been modified with respect to the preceding proposals illustrated in the chapter 2015 Regulations.

1) A greater distance between the front wheel and the front wing endplates,

2) the maximum width of the bodywork and therefore the floor set at 1,600 mm with no obligatory cuts or indents.

3) The extractor profile ramp has been restricted in length to 175 mm (against 330 mm), therefore reducing the capacity to create downforce felt to be excessive in the Red Bull version (in the circle).

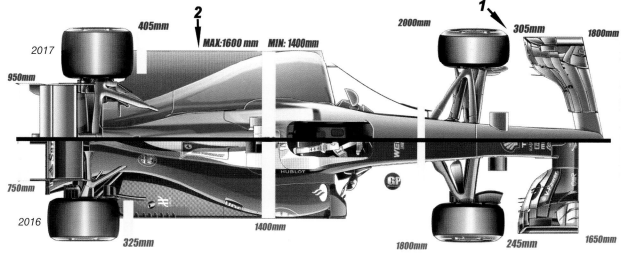

405mm — 2017 — 950mm — 750mm — 2016 — 325mm — 1400mm

MAX:1600 mm — **MIN: 1400 mm**

2000mm — 305mm — 1800mm — 1800mm — 245mm — 1650mm

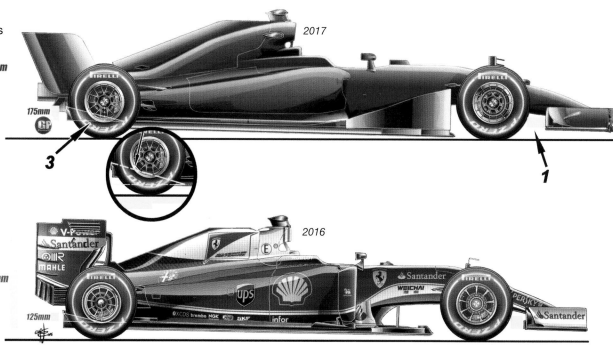

800mm — 175mm — 2017

950mm — 125mm — 2016